One life – a
little gleam of time
between two Eternities.

Thomas Carlyle, 1795-1881

SAUL

Between Two Eternities

Rosemary Kay

Inkhorn Press

First published in Great Britain in 2000 Headline Book Publishing, under the title *Between Two Eternities*.

First published in 2001 in paperback by Headline Book Publishing, under the title *Between Two Eternities*.

First published in USA in 2000 by St Martin's Press, and in Canada by Random House, under the title *Saul*.

Published in 2013 by Inkhorn Press under the title *Saul: Between Two Eternities*.

Design & Layout by Lighthouse24
Cover Photograph by Tim Lambert

ISBN 978-0-9575252-1-4

INKHORN PRESS.
www.inkhornpress.co.uk

"Like no other book you will ever read, moving but also uplifting." The Scotsman.

"The most amazing celebration of life ....what makes this book so remarkable is that the first person narrator is Saul himself. So convincingly has Kay caught the imagined voice of a tiny creature, unsure as to whether the battle to live is worth the trauma, that you suspend disbelief, never doubting the authenticity of the brave cry in the dark." The Times

"This imaginative account captures the sensual world of eyes and ears that are new to life, and fear and distress as well. In registering the parents' feelings through the buffering filter of Saul's perception, Kay renders the story deeply affecting." Publishers Weekly

"One of those rare books that make you perceive your world anew. It kept me reading through the night. In the early hours of the morning, when I finally turned the last page, exhausted, rung out, and yet strangely uplifted, I knew that I would never be the same again." New York Reviewer

"Written from Saul's perspective we see the adult world through his eyes, interwoven with a deep stream of consciousness which links him to the history of earlier generations of his family. This is a remarkable and original insight into the tragedy of losing a baby, written with immense courage. Far from bleak or morbid, it is a moving celebration of life. Between Two Eternities *marks the stunning debut of a hugely talented writer."* BerkelouW Books.

"Any parent - anyone at all – will find Saul's story wrenching, although it is also an adventure story and a tale of courage." GoodReads

Part One

Dancing in the Aisles

Sometimes, no most of the time, I thought it was all about to end. It was only because of the voice in my head going - that's it, it's not time to give up yet, just a little more - that I got through it at all.

It's funny looking back now, because you forget the hurting. But you can remember all the nice things, like my Perfect Red Sea and the spinning wheels and falling over headstands, or when she sang and he went Tiddly Pom Tiddly Pom, or learning to float with Lami and sneaking down to the milk kitchen to spy on the nurses.

There are so many stories to tell, aren't there? Mine is a good one, so I'm going to remember it all, the good bits, the funny bits and the bits I want to stay buried. Because I did it, didn't I? The hardest bit I did all on my own.

And here I am now, not hurting, not fighting, but dancing....

Dancing in the aisles must be naughty because people are turning around to frown at me. I'm making the dust dance too. It swirls in the tube of sunlight. We swirl together to the music. Jolly jingly music. You *have* to dance. I don't know how they can all just sit there, hunched, silent.

It's cool and dark in the church. I'd rather be outside. So I skip into the sunshine. I'm going to visit one of my favourite places.

There are gravestones all around the church, tall and thin and leaning over in lots of different ways. If you wanted to be tidy you would have to straighten them all up, but they'd only start lolling backwards and forwards all over again. Maybe they'd rather be lying down, because they are very, very old. This is the old part of the churchyard.

The new churchyard is up the hill, through the black gates, along a grassy path. You don't know it's a churchyard until you get to the two great trees with branches that meet over your head. Then you see all the gravestones, with their backs to you, forever looking down the valley. Some of the stones are squat and black, but the one I want is tall, brown, rounded with a pointy top.

They put Grandpa in the ground a long time ago. It was only his body though, he went somewhere else. Of course, he comes back here sometimes, because it's the sort of place that makes you want to come back.

Past Grandpa's grave, the grass is really long and full of flowers. If you pull the grass aside, you can look down at the ants marching in a line around the grass stems. They're working really hard, as if it really matters. There's no time to waste, hurry, hurry. They pick up seeds and broken leaves to carry them home. Tidying up.

It's quiet here, except for the cows tearing at the grass on the other side of the prickle hedge, or the crows going *graaw graaw* in the great oak tree, or the stream which is going *gurgle-plollop* at the bottom of the field. It *is* quiet really, because all the noises are soft. I like soft noises.

The prickle hedge goes right the way round the new churchyard, hiding us from the fields. If you peep through the hedge you can see the stream down below gushing into Wild Granny's garden. You can just see the roof of her house, and the little wooden bridge Grandpa made, and sometimes you can hear her singing loudly to herself. Not today though. Today there are people gathering outside her front gates.

The first time I came here with Mummy, it was a really angry day. The wind was twisting everything round and round, pulling at her hair and clothes. The grass was wet and Daddy held her arm tightly. Black clouds rushed across the sky, throwing handfuls of rain at us. The rain bit into her face and made her glasses smeary.

She tried to arrange flowers in a pot. The wind snatched at the flowers and broke some of the stems.

"Just bog off!" She shouted at the wind. The wind just laughed and whipped the words out of her mouth.

"Tim, shield me from the wind can't you. Bloody hell, why didn't we bring the oasis?" She was angry like the sky.

"Never mind, sweets. This'll do."

He put the pot in the special hole made in the headstone. Then he piled up little stones around the pot to keep it steady in the wind.

She pulled her hair out of her face and mouth. "Not that they'll last five minutes in this."

"It's the thought that counts."

"You never did like flowers anyway, did you Dad? Still...."

Raindrops battered the flowers as we hurried away.

Today there is no wind. Today the sun is so hot even the grass looks tired. In the distance the air shimmers. Far away down the valley, the Hanging Stone wobbles against the green hills. And after that are the Roaches, black and jagged against the blue sky. And after that, ah Grandpa, tell us what you see after that....

Day 1: Wednesday 17 April

When you float up here on the ceiling, you can look down and see everything. Down there in the grey corridor are four people and a plastic box on wheels. They move quickly. The wheels of the box go *eek eek eek* as a woman in a blue tunic and trousers pushes it round a corner. A man with floppy hair hurries ahead and holds the double doors open. When they all get to the lifts, he's already pushed the buttons.

"Porter's lift is stuck again. Have to use the patients'."

"Bloody hell." The other man has tired eyes. "Can't stand the stupid voice in there: *Doors Openin'*. Drives you mad."

Floppy Hair grins. "Yeah, you'd think they'd have recorded someone with a sexy voice or something, instead of a Salford slapper who thinks she's the Duchess of York."

The other woman laughs. She has a sunny smile. She puts her long fingers on the top of the plastic box. "Have we still got him?"

The woman in blue is checking the flashing lights and tubes and wires. Then she peers through the plastic lid. "Doing alright in there poppit? Oh, look at his little nose!"

They all peer in and smile. Except Tired Eyes who is jabbing at the lift buttons.

"Come *on*."

The lift goes *ping!* and you can hear a muffled voice inside. "Sixth floor. Doors Openin'."

They all laugh and echo together: "Doors Openin'" Except Tired Eyes. He doesn't laugh. He puts a thumb and finger up to the top of his nose and rubs the inside of his eye sockets.

The lift doors open. Floppy Hair turns. "I'll take the stairs. See you up there."

The others squash into the lift with the plastic box.

"Doors Closin' Goin' down."

The walls inside the lift are covered with colourful pictures of the sea and there's a smiling sun painted on the doors. No one looks at it. The woman in blue is looking at the other woman.

"That's a gorgeous dress, Mel."

"Oh thanks. Got it in London."

Tired Eyes glances at them. "How'd you afford that then? They paying you more than me?"

"Ah, no family commitments. One of the perks of being a single woman."

Tired Eyes scowls.

The woman in blue checks the flashing lights again. "Did anyone see *Friends* last Friday?"

Tired Eyes is trying to stretch but there isn't enough room. "Never watch it."

"Oh you should. Look like you could do with a laugh."

He yawns. "Better things to do."

"Yeah, like what?"

"Sleeping."

The lift slows. "Fifth floor."

The women grin. "Here she goes again: *Doors Openin'*"

The lift stops. "Doors Openin'"

They all laugh. Even Tired Eyes.

Floppy Hair is waiting for them. They walk quickly, not quite running, down more corridors. The walls are full of colour now. Other people in blue make way for them. At last they come to a room. It's noisy and bustling and bright and very, very big.

"Okay folks, new addition to the family. Where'd you want him?"

"Only space we've got left. By the x-ray screen."

From up here, you can see everything. The whole room spreads out below me, stretching away to the double doors at both ends. There's a long window along one wall with piles of yellow blankets and white sheets on the windowsill.

People in blue swim calmly up and down. Some sit writing at the long narrow desk which runs down the middle of the room. It's covered with files and papers and cups of coffee and bottles of water, and a half eaten cake on a plate. A woman in blue stops writing, takes a lump of cake and eats it. She licks her fingers.

High up on the pillar at the end of the desk, is a small black cupboard. It buzzes and when you look at the front of it, you see fuzzy grey pictures of people standing in a corridor. The woman licking her fingers looks up to the grey pictures. "Anstey family are here, Jen."

"Okay, let them in."

She reaches up and pushes a button. "Come in."

Down at the other end of the room, next to the double doors is another smaller door. A woman in blue comes out. "Who's got the keys to the drugs cupboard?"

Some people in blue swim towards her. "If you're doing drugs I'll join you. Got a tricky steroid to work out."

"And I need a shot of Phenobarb."

They go into the little room and shut the door.

At first that's all you see: people in blue, doors, bright lights. And then you look again, along the walls, at the important things in here: the Boxes. Along every wall, squeezed in, no space to waste, right down to the walls at the bottom and back again, are rows of plastic boxes. Bigger than the little box they wheeled along the corridor. See-through boxes, so see-through that you don't even see them straight away. But you can see the tangle of wires and tubes snaking out of the end of every box. They twist up to the bank of machines that are piled up to the ceiling. The machines blink and bleep against the walls. Some boxes have machines at the other end as well which hum and spit into the room.

In every space there is a box and in every box, a baby. Small babies, fat babies, pink or grey or yellow babies. They all lie on white sheets and they all have tubes and wires coming out of them somewhere, out of mouths, noses, arms, legs, chests, bellies. Some of the babies look up at me on the ceiling and screw up their eyes against the bright lights.

There is only one empty box in the room. It is down by the double doors where we came in. Behind the doors is a big metal bin which clanks open and shut. Next to the bin, in the corner is a sink and on the wall is a white screen spilling blue-white light onto the floor. It lights up the black and grey pictures pinned to it. And next to the screen is a tall bank of machines with wires and tubes dangling. And in front of the machines is the see-through box, open, empty, waiting.

Floppy Hair and the others are scrubbing their hands at the sink. They do it quickly but carefully, squeezing brown sticky stuff between their fingers. The bin clanks open and shut when they throw their paper towels away. The woman in blue is handing round a little bottle. They sprinkle something on their hands and rub it in.

"Right come on, let's get him to bed."

The woman in blue takes the lid off the little box on wheels. Inside all you can see is a white blanket. She peels it open. Hidden inside is something red and wrinkled. A frog baby. She slides a hand underneath it and lifts. Its eyes are squeezed shut and its chest goes in out, in out, very quickly. Another woman in blue is helping her, holding the tubes and wires already coming out of the baby. Together they lay everything inside the bigger see-through box.

"Temp's falling." Tired Eyes is suddenly awake. "I'll close up this side. Turn the incubator up to maximum temp and humidity for now." He lifts the whole wall of the box into place and snaps it shut. Then he opens two little windows in the side, making holes just big enough for his hands to fit through.

"Right let's get these sites in quickly. Stephen – arterial in his ankle. I'll do the long-line in his arm. Mel – umbilicus. Nurse, give him a boost of oxygen till we're finished and keep an eye on his BP...."

Suddenly there is a jolt. Everything begins to swirl and fizz. The pictures fade. It's all gone black. Now it is only voices, noises, and the nasty feel of fingers prodding. The frog baby must be breathing hard. Suckpush. Suckpush Suckpush.

The frog baby is me.

Day 1: The First Few Minutes

Hands are funny aren't they? There are lots of hands, cold hands, hot hands, sweaty hands, all harder and drier than anything you've touched before. They do things to you and you have to let them. You can smell hands, and this is a funny thing, they all smell the same! All the hands are rubbed in something that makes your head spin when you breathe it in, makes your tummy lurch. But you have to get used to it, or else your head would go whizzydizzy all day. Because, you see, the hands never really leave you alone.

The hands began to stab me. First the fingers rubbed my arms and legs, searching along my body, pulling my skin tight.

"That vein looks promising...."

And then they stabbed me with something fat and blunt.

"Is this the smallest catheter there is? Jesus...Just can't...come *on*...this one just isn't going to...how about that one on his ankle...?"

Then someone pushed at my belly, and pulled, and pushed again, until it was raw.

I could feel my skin. It was warm where I was lying on it and cold against the air. I could feel them breathing, their breath freezing wind on my face. It was dry skin now, so thin the stabbing slipped deep inside.

My ankle stung where they left something in and my arm throbbed and my belly button burnt and all the feelings got sucked up into the rest of me.

"Right, umbilical line's secure... arterial one in his ankle... and how's the long-line in his arm...?"

They think I'm asleep, but I'm just lying still, feeling it all, learning about living.

One thing I learnt is that you have to keep going suckpush or else you die. You have to suck in the air and push it all out again, see like this, really fast, over and over, never stopping even though it hurts, even though the air here is tough and dry. Suck push suck push, it's the only thing that matters.

And I learnt about my Hot House. I didn't know I was in a house straight away, I had to work it out. I can't see, of course, my eyes are stuck, shut up. But you can feel you're in a sort of house because all the noises bounce and echo. You feel closed in with all the smells. You can hear noises outside, but the air in here is still. So it must be a sort of house. And it's lovely and hot, that's the best thing about it. Because the air outside, all that Big Air, where people in blue must still be swimming, is a really cold place isn't it?

Day 1: The First Hour

There's a cluster of voices above me.

"...doing better than I expected... Normal head scan...."

"...Sites... Not easy...."

"...Makes him one pound four ounces...."

"...Blood gases... on five then, and see how he.... Resp drive good.... Oxgen's he in? ...Air, is he really...?"

"...White blood count...maternal infect...general antibio..."

"...Well done little...not getting the parents excited...long way to...critical...tell in the next few hours whether..."

And the voices fade away.

They pushed a Tube deep into my chest, just after I was born. It's still there, see how it fills up my whole mouth. I can taste it and push it with my tongue, but it doesn't move. It's stuck tight inside me. Sometimes it goes *clunk thud whoosh!* and bursts fat needles of air into my chest. But the rest of the time it's me doing the breathing.

"X-ray! Coming through!"

More people, more things to learn. And that's how it is. The hands and voices just keep coming. And I know it will never be like before again. A bit of me is sad and another bit of me is excited. They keep coming and doing things to me. And I let them.

"Oh no. I've just got him warmed up. Might have known you'd turn up now!"

And I think they're laughing.

"Sorry. Needs must. Orders is orders and all that."

"Hope you're not going to make him cry."

"Come on. Put your armour on and shut up. My job to make babies cry. Terrible way to make a living, I know, but someone's got to do it. Anyway, you'll be picking him up, so he'll blame you. I just point and press."

And then there's more laughter. When they open up my house the laughing rolls in. Cold fingers slide under me again. . "Okay poppit, here we go." It's a flying game. I'm lifted up and my arms and legs fly free, except I'm still tied down by the wires and things.

"God, he's a tiny little thing isn't he?"

"He is. He's a little cutey."

Then the fingers lay me on something colder. It makes me want to cry but I've no time for crying. Got to keep going suck-push, haven't I?

"X-RAY!"

They lift me again and this time put me back in my warm bed.

"Isn't he a good boy? I love these tinies. Is he going to be here long, do you reckon?"

"You never can tell. He's a little fighter though."

"Isn't he just. Look at those little chest muscles go. Well, keep it up baby. I expect to see you still here tomorrow."

"Well, you never know..."

I just keep going suckpush suckpush suckpush.

Day 1: The Second Hour

I've done a whole hour, and I didn't give up once. That's very good, isn't it?

Click clack ack ack.

And I've worked it out. That *click clack ack ack* is when they open up the doors of my Hot House. It makes your ears tingle. It means there will be fingers, like the cold ones that smell of clean flowers. They've been there from the beginning. But that noise - *click clack ack ack* - lets the cold air roll in and the Big Air noises come surging round my ears. Like now. "Just checking your sites, poppit." Clean Flower Fingers. She touches my arms and my legs, picks them up softly, turns them, presses them, pushes my belly, checks my bottom. She is sure, firm, quick. Knows what to do. "All over." And the hands are gone. *Clack click ick ick.* And the air begins to warm again.

And somewhere someone is sobbing. I know the sound of sobbing. I can remember. It was before I started to do This Living, when I was in my Perfect Red Sea. Everything went soft and slow back then and I was always warm and glowing.

Oh my Perfect Red Sea. I loved the way I could stretch up my arms and legs and push my bubble into the soft squashy bits. And I loved the way I could bounce off the walls and tumble and dance. Oh, the spinning wheels and falling over headstands! With one great double kick I could make waves that would crash back at me and roll me feet over head. And I loved the sound of her Voice: "Are you planning to do the rumba in there all night? Mmm?"

But I can also remember the time when she sat on the stairs and it was cold on her buttocks but she didn't care, she just leant her head against the wall and her whole body shook, and so did my Perfect Red Sea. That was the sound of sobbing. I lay still and listened to her chugging breath and let myself roll with the waves of sadness.

And I thought just now that I heard sobbing again. But now it's lost in all the other noises.

It's like all the noises get into my house and are trapped and then they echo round and round. There's that *uuuummmmm*, a deep grumble that never stops. And you can hear a *bleep bleep bleep!* - that's a high one, sort of urgent. There's always a *Bleep* coming from somewhere. Or a *Pling pling pling!* - they're slower ringing ones. And of course my *clunk thud whoosh*! And underneath everything you can probably hear that *sssshhhhhhh*. Oh and further away: *peeeeeeeeeeeek!* and "My vent!" And remember, just a moment ago that loud and terrible *eeeeeeeech!* that made everything jump, and it's still bouncing around in here. And then sliding in through all that, are the voices. Shadowy voices, "Baby Anstey's mum's here, Paula, shall I...." Calling voices, "Has anyone got the keys to the...." Oh, it all slaps backwards and forwards, doesn't it? And somewhere deep inside all this noise, if you listen ever so carefully, squeeze to hear it: babies crying.

I don't cry. I lie quietly, going suckpush suckpush, listening to my new world.

Because you see, I *know* that Someone is watching. There's a little space of silence out there. And voices. You have to listen all the time to work out which voice, of all the voices, is important....

At least I know Clean Flowers is there. "Try to see beyond the wires. He's doing ever so well, you know, really."

"..........."

Someone is definitely watching, out there in the middle of all the noise and smelliness.

"It must be ever so frightening, when you first come in here...."

"..........."

"Did you get the photos we took?"

"Yes.... Thank you. Here...." So there *is* a Someone!

"Look, I put a biro in when we took them, to give you an idea how.... See, there's the biro. Later, you'll forget."

"......."

"Have you thought of a name for him yet?"

"Saul." And there's *another* Someone. I like this guessing game.

"We were going to call him after his Granddad...if it was a boy.... Doesn't seem right now...."

"Saul's better anyway."

"Saul's a lovely name. Sounds very grown up. He'll have to grow into it."

"..........."

"Would you like to touch him?"

"......!"

"It's perfectly safe."

"Won't it...?"

"It won't harm him"

"No, I don't want to."

"He might like it, you know. Go on. Put some of this on first, rub it over your palm and fingers, that's it, kills all known bugs...."

Click Clack ack ack. Hot fingers touch my arm and try to stroke me. But they rub too hard. The hand pulls away. *Clack Click ick ick.*

Now the Someone is crying.

"He's doing ever so well, you know, honestly. He's only on five breaths a minute. That means he's doing most of the breathing himself. Some babies are on fifty breaths. So, that's ever so good. And he's in air...."

"........."

And the smell left behind melts into all the other smells. I thought I remembered it from somewhere, but no, it's gone, and I can't seem to....

"Were you going to breast feed?"

".....?"

"Because, when he starts to feed, breast milk is better than formula."

"Oh. Well, I was... I don't know now."

"Well, if you wanted to, we advise Mums to express milk, if they can. Then when baby, when Saul's ready, he can have your milk, tube-fed, of course."

"Oh...well...Will he...when?"

"He might be ready in a week or two, it depends. But you have to start now. The sooner the better. We can freeze it until he's ready."

"Oh well I'll do that then."

"Even if it's only for the first few weeks, it'll help him.

"Right...good. How?"

"Ask a nurse on the maternity ward for a pump. She'll show you how to use it."

"Right. I'll do that."

"Yes, we'll do that. We'll do...whatever..."

"Why don't you wheel her back to the ward. You've got to keep your strength up, it's probably going to be a long haul...."

And I know that what's happening now is linked somehow to before. I have to keep remembering to make sense of it all. I like to ramble backwards anyway, back to my Perfect Red Sea, to the time when it all went *thurump thurump thurump* all the time. And sometimes it went *gurgle gurgle.* It was a soft and muffled rumble-drumble of noises. And far away, smothered in layers of something, the voice went: "Whatever are you up to in there?" Her voice. And I giggled and gripped my toes, really excited, because I knew she was talking to me!

And when I listened carefully, I could hear another voice too. His voice, a very deep rumble that made you smile inside. And after a while I came to love them and it was easy.

Sometimes I heard her even without her voice. Sometimes it was just her thoughts that seeped right into me. I didn't even have to listen, I just knew what she meant. *Thurump thurump thurump...we will be strong together and not let go...thurump thurump....*

So when the Someone comes again I'm going to listen really hard and work it all out. It all makes me tingle because I know it's important and I can't wait for the next clues to make it all fit.

I don't have to wait long. The Someone and that Someone Else are here again. I can smell them, mixed in with the smell of Clean Flowers.

"But he's only on minimal ventilation, you know...." (That's the voice of Clean Flowers.) "...the machine is on the lowest setting at the moment. Any lower and we'd take him off the ventilator altogether. He's doing all the other breaths himself. See, his little chest going up and down ten to the dozen."

"And how does the machine know what he...?"

"We check his blood gases every few hours. Then the doctors can work out how much help he needs. And I can adjust the amount of oxygen he's getting here look, if he needs a quick boost. He's in air, which is brilliant...look at this dial."

"But it says he's in twenty-one percent oxygen..."

"Air *is* twenty-one percent oxygen."

"Oh, yes, course, you told us that already. Sorry."

"It doesn't matter. Ask me as many times as you like. Whatever you want."

"Oh, right, thanks, so er, ...what... why... er..."

"But you don't have to ask questions. There are no rules."

"Oh we do.... We need to keep.... Tell us again about his incubator and these wires here and...bout.... Tell us about this monitor.... Tell us about....... Doesn't it hurt?"

"What, the monitor?"

"No. Everything. What you're doing to him."

And I knew then that it was all out there, waiting for me, the voices, the smells and those great, strong waves of sadness, emptiness, despair and of course, the sound of sobbing. And I bundled it all away to piece together later.

Day 2

The next day I waited for the Someone to arrive. All the noise and smells and hurting were mixed up, all in a big mess and me in the middle of it. The only sure thing I had to grasp onto was that the Someone would come back.

I waited and waited. Hands came and went. Voices loomed and burst above me. I drifted on the noises sloshing inside my Hot House. It was scary, exciting, confusing. I knew that I needed the Someone, if only the Someone....

And suddenly it was there. The voice I wanted to hear was seeping out of the sea of noise. "Well the nurses told us that just getting through the first day was a miracle. You're a miracle baby Saul..."

"Well, indeed. What I say to parents in your situation is: the first few hours are the *Most* Critical, and the first day is still *Extremely* Critical and the second day is still *Very, Very* Critical and the first week is still *Very* Critical, and the weeks after that, well they're just Critical. So you see, I won't lie to you, it's not going to be easy...." This was a Calm voice, a Make You Feel Safe voice. I'd only heard it once before but I knew it was important.

"...We have had babies as premature as Saul, though not many.... There have been a number of babies born at twenty three weeks who've survived intact, that's to say, they've grown into healthy children with no obvious problems, if you see what I mean.... But I suppose you've already been told the chances of survival...."

"Thirty percent." I wished the Someone would make more noise. So I could work it out.

"Yes well, it's fairer to put it between twenty and thirty percent..."

"Not very high is it?"

"No, it's not very high. I'm sorry. We have to be ...."

"It's just that....Sorry."

"No....Go ahead."

"Well it's just that.... We don't believe in...I mean, if the quality of his life is obviously going to be...awful...then we don't want you to....We don't want him to suffer unnecessarily...and we want you to know that before...it's too late to...you know."

"...Well, let me tell you, I'm not the sort of consultant who rides rough shod over patients, over parents' wishes. Saul's quality of life is obviously paramount, of...."

"It's just that...we've seen programmes...about this sort of...where doctors, where medicine prolongs life...prolongs suffering...just because...because you *can*...even if it isn't right."

"I know....." It was a soothing voice. Made me go floppy. Made the Someone out there go quiet. "And I'm not saying that doesn't happen, where a patient's needs are....But it's never happened in this unit, I can assure you. It's not about trying to make the unit look good. I promise you, whatever decisions we take, and we'll always discuss all difficult decisions with you, whatever decisions are made, Saul's needs will be uppermost in our minds."

It was a Know What to Do voice. It *made* you listen.

"But I must say, it's not a case of poor quality of life, as things stand at the moment. Yes, he's got a long way to go, but his head scan is normal, which is a very good sign, if we're talking about quality of life.... So please, be hopeful...." (It felt like being stroked by that voice sometimes. It was lovely) "I'm a great believer in being positive. We wouldn't even attempt to treat him unless we believed there was a good reason to hope. He's certainly a little fighter. But what I always say to parents is: hope for the best. Prepare for the worst, if you see what I mean...."

And when I lay very still and didn't try too hard, just listened, it was easy to remember my Perfect Red Sea, and her patting my roof and her voice going "When you're older, we'll bring you here so you can see how fabulous it is for yourself..." And I remembered how all the voices back then were soft and far away. They just wafted into my Red Sea and into me. Not like now. Now it was all jagged. Voices were spiky sounds that pushed into my thinkings....

"I suppose we're lucky really. If it'd happened any earlier...."

"Well even a couple of days earlier and it wouldn't really have been possible.... He really is on the borderline...."

"It could've happened up a mountain in Scotland, easily.... At least you've given him a fighting chance. Thank you."

"Well, he's in the best place...well not in the...the best place is inside you, but failing that...."

"See Saul, you're in good hands. You're very lucky really."

And suddenly it was really clear. It was the same voice as before. Except before was soft and muffled and this was sharper, louder. But it was *her* voice.

And then I knew she'd been there all along, waiting for me. I knew she would be. Of course she wouldn't run away. She said *we will be strong together and not let go*. It was a sort of promise. I knew she wouldn't let me down.

Wednesday 17 April: Before

I loved smells, the way they all swirled together, the soft ones hiding in the strong ones, making your insides scrunch or your nose tickle. Hot plastic, clean sheets, warm rain, sweaty hat, dried blood, smell of wee. Best of all though – the smell of *me*.

Me smelt of all the hands that touched me and all the things they touched me with and something else. I had to wiggle about to make it waft. So I wiggled and sniffed and wiggled and sniffed until...Yes that's it, I remember, I smelt of *her*! *She* was on my skin!

And then I felt a hurting in my chest, not needles of air sort of hurting, but a sadness. When I smelt that old smell and thought of her, when I realised that I was in here, just me, and she wasn't, and I didn't know where she was, and only her smell was left behind, then I felt something lurch in my tummy. I was on my own wasn't I? And all I had left of her, really, was re-memberings...

I remember how she turned into an angry giant that day. Squeezed me out. And what day was that? (Because every day made a difference.) It was a Wednesday. My birthday, two whole days ago.

We did our best that day. Me and her. We tried to be strong together and not let go. Oh, she seemed to do that bellowing for a long time. You see we had to keep fighting. We would have kept going for weeks and weeks if we could. But it wasn't our fault. And in the end, when we had to let go, then all the fight drained out of her.

"What's the point? That doctor said it was going to die any-way. Oh God, what's the bloody, bloody...." And she bellowed. And I suppose it was then that I lost her.

"I don't care what you do...just...give me something, now. Stop arsing around asking stupid fucking questions and tell him to give me a bloody epidur...." Another bellow....

She was angry and vicious now, like the walls. Where did the real one go? The one who used to laugh and tell me about the mountains and the snow and the sunshine and sing little songs to me?

She screamed and I was slithering. Sliding downwards. I couldn't stop it. There was nothing to cling onto.

"Not yet! Wait till the intensive team gets here. You can hold it for a few minutes more!"

"I can't!"

"Yes you can sweets. You can do this....."

Somebody caught me when I shot into the world. "Like a little cork from a champagne bottle!"

But there were no celebrations. Just hushed whispers.

"You've had a little boy."

They were silent.

The air was bright and dry, so icy sharp it made you gasp. And everything was so *loud*! But I could hear someone in my head going, That's it, you show them, don't give up just because it's hard. That's what I think you said, Grandpa, Show them the fight you've got in you....

I pulled at the hard cold world with my chest. Suckpush. Suckpush. To show them I could do it. I forgot to be frightened, I think I quite liked to feel my chest going up and down. Really hard. Really fast. Like new. And I kicked their hands to show I was strong. They wafted me with sweet air. I was good at it, even though it was hard. See me! I can do it! Watch me doing it. I can. I can!

"Okay. Let's go for it. Intubate."

Kind hands slipped something warm on my head. Hard hands pressed my chin down. Gentle hands held my head back. Rough hands pushed the Tube into my mouth, sharp, it hurt my throat. For a moment I had to stop going suckpush. They forced it deep down, inside and then...

"How about pressures..... sixteen over four to start with...?"

A hurting burst of air inside me... *clunk thud whoooo-oooshhhhhh*.... And I was up on the ceiling.

"Would you like to see him before we take him up?"

Down below was a woman lying on her back. A man stood frozen, staring at the bundle of white blanket. Somewhere lost in the folds of blanket was a little red nose.

The woman looked, then turned her head away.

Clunk thud whoooooooosh!

Day 3

Suckpush suckpush.

Today I discovered someone else. It happened when I was discovering the Ooze. (I felt sort of full, and when I let myself go floppy, I oozed. Mmm. It was warm and wet, trickling somewhere, it made me forget to work out the noises just for a moment....)

"Oh, Rose, you've forgotten to give the nurse the milk."

"Oh...sorry... It's not much. Here...."

"Oh, it is. I'm impressed. Look, Saul, some lovely milk for when you're feeling more...."

"Bit of a funny colour...."

"No, that's normal. Colostrum's supposed to be like that. Means it's full of goodies. Yum, yum, Saul's thinking. Much better than having a drip going into my arm. Can't wait, Saul says...."

Oooooooze. It was getting even warmer and even wetter and I oozed until there was no more oozing left and it felt lovely.

"It's not enough though, is it?"

"It's plenty to start with. You'll have filled up the freezers before he's ready at that rate."

"No, I meant, mothers are supposed to look after their babies a bit better, aren't they?"

"You mustn't worry, try not to....."

"Not much of a mother am I Saul? Teaspoonful of milk. That's your lot and I've left the rest to you. That's pretty rubbish, isn't it?"

"Everyone's tried to tell her it's not her fault...."

The lovely warm was getting colder. So now I was cool and wet. And then cold and wet and then wet and...clammy....

"Do you want to touch him? Dad, do you want to try? It'll be alright. No need to worry or anything. So he can know you're here."

"He won't be able to tell though, will he?"

"Oh he will, probably. He'll recognise your smell, well Mum's smell at least, well yours probably too, and probably your voices."

"I don't know...."

I'd already worked out that she was never alone. There was always the smell of.... Someone Else. I worked out that every time I heard her voice, there was the deep rumble as well. And I wondered about it for a long time....

Click clack ack ack. It was like splinters of fear coming from his fingers. The finger was a tree trunk. A great rough, strong, gnarly tree trunk. I pushed my hand against him and closed my fingers. "He's gripping my fingertip! He can squeeze my finger!

"And look at his little fingernails, he's...so perfect." (Her voice was full of wonder like when she told me about the mountains.) "He's perfect isn't he?"

"Of course. What did you expect?"

"I don't know, I just thought, at first, he'd be, you know, when he was first born, I imagined, there'd be something wrong, you know, legs in the wrong place, or something...But he's perfect."

"Lots of Mums worry about that. That they'll be monsters or something."

"But he's not. He's just a miniature version. Skinny, like a fledgling bird."

"Well, one pound four ounces is one of the smallest we've ever had. But he's perfectly formed, everything's in the right place, right proportions. So you don't need to worry..."

I gripped the finger. Warm finger.

"Oh look, he's got your feet, Tim!"

"My feet wouldn't even fit in there."

"They are. Look, long big toe."

"Poor Saul, lumbered with Daddy's feet. Well if that's all you get of mine, you've got off lightly. Got Mummy's nose, which is a blessing. Born with a hooter like your daddy's, now that *would* be unlucky!"

And I thought, that smell and that rumble together, they belong to me. I heard the rumble and I heard her and it matched and I remembered. It was *Him!*

I gripped his finger and the cold gripped me. Not him, he was warm, he smelt safe. But the cold was creeping right through me, down to my toes, they were the coldest, and up to my head.

"Actually, do you mind leaving him a minute. We'd better shut the portholes. His temperature's getting a bit low."

He sucked his finger away. I tried to grip on. Come back smell, nice smell!

Clack click ick ick.

"It's hot in there though."

"It has to be... I'll just check... There we are. That's why, it's because he's weed. They lose body heat quickly. Yes, monkey, you're a very good weer. Yes, you are. I'll just change... Getting too cold is one of the most treacherous things, so we have to be careful. That and infections...."

The hands stroked me with something rough and dry, took away the wet, made it warm again.

All day I listened to her and I listened to him and it made me sing inside with excitement. It made me want to touch them, to reach out and play with them. Somehow, I str-e-e-etched my legs, heavy legs, stre-e-tched them up to the sky. It wasn't like in my Perfect Red Sea, when I could go tumbling over and over. But it felt good. I wiggled my legs around.

"Wow! Look! He's dancing. Saul, you're dancing!"

I was dancing! I couldn't spinning-wheel, or tumble, any more. But I could still *dance.*

Day 4

Suckpushsuckpush got to keep going suckpush....

"Has anyone got the keys to the drugs cupboard?"

Suckpushsuckpushsuckpushsuckpush...

"Are you having one of these chockies, Ginny, a thank you pressie from the whatisnames?"

"You're joking. At a thousand calories a throw?"

Never give up suckpush....

It was all still mixed up of course. It *was* only my fourth day of This Living so I couldn't quite fit all the pieces together yet, not properly, but I had learnt about some Important Whos. Most important was he and she of course. And then there was the Calm One. And then there was Clean Flowers. I liked her fingers and I liked the sound of her clean flower voice....

"...And this red flashing light is the saturation monitor. Measures the oxygen in his blood. It's flashing high at the moment, ninety eight, that's very good. Flashing high means he's doing fine. I'll just turn the oxygen back down to air. He needed a bit before I sucked his tubes out. I gave you a jolly good hoovering didn't I? Yes, I did, gorgeous."

"Why did you have to...."

"Well, bit of a catch twenty two really. The tube in his chest causes secretions to build up, which make it harder to breathe. So we have to suck out his tubes every now and then. The sooner you get off this machine the better, poppit... There we are. See he's at ninety three, now. Perfect."

"It's all so... I never realised...."

"I know. Bit technological, bit scary at first. You'll get used to it...."

And I'd learnt how to make Clean Flowers go *Click clack*. First I oooozed. And at the same time I stretched my back and pushed my belly, so I didn't just ooze, I *squirt*ed. I made it rain....

Pling pling. "What's up with your temperature, Saul... Oh Saul! Thinks he's weeing for England, this one...."

So, *that*'s the way to make Clean Flowers wrap me up all soft and cuddly. She stroked my forehead. "Not looking quite so wrinkled are you today? And your skin's getting better. Not so much like cling-film any more, is it, eh poppit?"

And she cared for me with her soft, cold fingers and always she smelt of Clean Flowers. My Nurse Clean Flowers.

Another Important Who was the Chirpy Bird. She came whenever Clean Flowers went away. "You know what, Sauly boy, Huggies is a stupid name for these nappies. Swampies, more like... Designed to tickle naughty little boys under the armpits, eh?" It was a chirpy voice. "Look at him. I've folded them over three times and they're still up to his chin...And we can't have that, can we? We need to see your little chest... Yes, we do, we do...." Her fingers felt light and warm. They hardly touched me at all. They just hopped around my body really quickly, like a tiny bird. "And that hat's far too big, isn't it? Hmmmm, you're thinking, aren't you, I look a right wally in this, I'll have to grow into it, yes...."

"Ginny, have you started wearing make-up?"

"Might have. Why not?"

"Oh and who's this for?"

"No one. I can wear make-up just for myself."

"It couldn't be for a certain doctor."

"Don't be daft." Chirpy Bird fingers loosened the strap that held the Tube in my mouth. It had been squeezing my lips into my nose. Suddenly everything felt softer, kinder. "That's *better* isn't it!"

"Ginny, Mr and Mrs Saul are here."

"Oh hi! I'm looking after Saul again tonight. And you're not to worry...you just come whenever you want, you don't have to...just don't worry... Great name by the way...."

And I worked out that Nurse Chirpy and Nurse Clean Flowers did the same things over and over, like a dance. First they went *click clack ack ack,* to open up the air and let their hands come into my Hot House, "Just checking your sites, poppit." And then they picked up my arms and legs one by one and pressed my belly. It was fun because I was used to it now and I could guess which bit of me they were going to touch next.

And sometimes, instead of the Leg-and-Belly-Checking-Dance, they did Hisser Snake. I had to stop doing the suckpush when Hisser got going, and it always came when my chest was getting too tight to suck.

First they put something round and cold on your skin and listened. "Sounds like you need a bit of suction, poppit." Then there'd be clicks and hisses and they brought the snake into my house. It went *hissssssssssss* and they fed it into my Tube. It blocked me up so I couldn't breathe. I was choking and frightened. I thrashed my arms to fight it away, but it was too strong going *Zzzzzzzuuuuoooooouuuuooog* and I didn't know what to do. Grandpa, tell it to stop! It would suck at your insides, searching for stuff in your chest and then it would slide out again.

"That's better isn't it?"

But that wouldn't be the end of it, oh no. Hisser Snake would go down a few times, and then it would be in your mouth, sucking around the Tube...*zzuuuug*...and into your cheeks and the back of your throat (more choking) and then it went up your nose! As if it didn't care *where* it went, it could go where it wanted and make you want to cry and you couldn't do anything about it!

"There that wasn't so bad was it?"

Hisser Snake would hiss out and away.

"Good boy"

And I suppose, you shouldn't mind really because when it was all over, it was always easier to breathe afterwards and you'd be full of air.

So easy! Suckpushsuckpush. I can do it. Watch me, Clean Flowers, Chirpy Bird! See me do This Living!

Day 5

There were times when voices huddled around my Hot House and talked across me. A magic voice was one of them, another Important Who, mingled in with all the others, and I knew it needed matching up with something from before.

"Right then, so which one of you young things is going to take us through Ward Round, this morning, mmmm?"

"Er, well, er I'll do it...."

"Again, Janet? And there was me thinking it should be Stephen. Well I can't be right all the time, can I?"

"Er, well...."

"Word of advice, Janet. Don't attempt to cover up for your colleagues. I've been at this game long enough to recognise an absent S.H.O. when I see one. Right. Well, let's make a start, shall we? Janet."

"Okay. This is Saul. Fifth of life...."

Then there was a loud bang and some thuds and someone rushing in. "Not missed anything, have I?" It was the magic voice.

"Nice to grace us with your presence, Stephen. Not encroaching on your playtime, I trust?"

"Sorry, Prof. Had to nip out to move the car. Gets harder every day to find a place to park the old Lamborghini."

"Very funny. You can take over now. You've been on the overnight, haven't you?"

"For my sins.... So, Saul, as you can see.... Just starting his fifth day of life. Born at twenty three weeks and three days.... Weighed in at five-sixty grams. Just compatible with life. Actually he's done really well since then. On minimal ventilation since he was born. In air mostly...sorry...lifts broken...had to run up five flights...."

"Won't do you any harm."

"Erm... Normal head scan. Good respiratory drive... CPR and white blood count are normal...."

That wasn't the first time I heard the magic voice. There was yesterday....

"Well, if you look at his x-ray, Prof...."

"Hmmm. One of the advantages of this phosphorescent lighting. Shows up the creases in your shirt, my boy. When was the last time you saw an iron?"

"The last time I saw a bath and a decent meal."

"Oh, the hardships of being a junior doctor."

"Thought I was looking rather smart today, considering. I'm waiting for some enlightened designer to create a fashion that celebrates the un-ironed look. Creases are Cool. That sort of thing. Anyway, Saul's chest...."

And the day I was born, he was there too. *"How about pressures.... sixteen over four to start with...?"*

But I have to go further back than that to remember the very *first* time I heard Dr Magic's voice.

It was when we were thinking strong thoughts together. That Tuesday, the day before my birthday. She was trying to eat sandwiches, she knew I would be hungry, but she wasn't doing very well. He and she were both thinking hard, but saying nothing. She was holding his hand. I was trying to lie very still and quiet. I couldn't move much anyway because I was all dried up, but I didn't dare to try even, because I knew that every little bit of these moments really mattered.

And then....

"Hello. I'm, sorry were you eating? Carry on, I can...."

"Are you the paediatrician?"

"I am, I'm from the neonatal intensive care unit. Apparently, you wanted someone to explain about Maternal Steroids."

"We don't want it to suffer. Whatever happens."

"Of course, of course. That's perfectly reasonab...."

"We just thought that, if it *is* born...soon, the doctor downstairs told us it couldn't survive, so won't giving steroids just make it live and suffer for longer without...?"

"Maybe if I try to explain...." You couldn't help liking the voice. It was slow and gentle but you knew it could be full of laughter and tears. "....Is it okay if I sit on the end here... Don't move, the first thing you learn as a doctor is how to perch on the end of a bed... Well. As you know, there is a very strong possibility that your baby will be born sooner, rather than later... If your baby...."

"Sorry..." She was trying to be strong, but the tears fell anyway.

"Please don't apologise. It's alright. They usually have a box of tissues somewhere...."

"Go on, you were saying...."

"If your baby is born in the next few days, it...almost certainly won't survive, without maternal steroids. If, however, you are injected with steroids now and they reach the baby before it's born, then it will have a chance of survival."

"But what sort of chance?"

"Well you're twenty three weeks aren't you? In this hospital we have a policy of resuscitating babies if they show that they are capable of responding to treatment. So the chances of survival.... with the steroids, *if* we decide to resuscitate...maybe thirty percent."

"So there's a seventy percent chance it could die anyway. But the steroids would make it live longer and so suffer longer."

"Well not exactly. Steroids only...."

".............."

"...I'm so sorry...."

Just heartbeats. And tears.

"Go on."

"Steroids won't cause suffering, but they'll make a very big difference in terms of survival. Steroids mature the lungs of unborn babies very quickly and since the lungs are the last thing to develop, steroids are the single most important factor in saving the lives of extremely premature babies.... I would strongly advise you to have them, especially...."

"Do they suffer?"

"Er, you mean....?"

"In Intensive Care. Do babies suffer?"

"Well, it's not the ideal place. But if the ideal...isn't possible... Do they suffer? Well, I won't go as far as saying that babies have *never* suffered in Intensive Care...."(Ah. Remember the magic? They trusted him now) "...but this is one of the best units in the country, and we like to think that we do everything we can to avoid any suffering...."

How she hung onto those words, and the feeling she was trying to bury, melted just a little. Just enough. He told them the truth but he made it disappear. And then he told them what they wanted to hear. *But this is one of the best units in the country, and we like to think that we do everything we can to avoid any suffering.*

I lay all soft and soothed by his magic. He said he would rescue me, didn't he? He promised to pick us all up in his arms and carry us to safety, didn't he? Didn't he say that? Not in words but I *felt* him say it. I'm sure that's what he meant....

"Well if you think it's the right thing to do...."

"I do. I'll organise the injections then. Immediately. You need at least two and it'll take eighteen hours to reach the baby. So whatever happens, try to hang on for at least eighteen hours."

"Oh, we're staying put for at least five more weeks, aren't we Baby?"

"That's what I like to hear."

And he made us smile. Oh Dr Magic with your voice to make us melt. And I said, when I grow up I'm going to be a doctor, a magic doctor like you.

Day 6

And so another day done, that's *very* good, isn't it? Because every day makes a difference.

At first day and night meant nothing. There was no difference that I could tell, same noises, same smells, same suckpushsuckpush. I didn't really know that days, hours, seconds really mattered. I just let time roll around me.

But by the time I was six days old, I'd worked out that when Nurse Clean Flowers came again, a whole day had rolled by. Clean Flowers was day and Chirpy Bird was night. The Leg-and-Belly-Checking-Dance was lots of times a day. Hisser Snake was a few times a day. The Huddle of Voices was twice a day and "X-ray!" was only once a day. And between all these things were little pockets of time. Little pockets I had to fill with fighting.

Never give up, someone was saying.

No, I'll never, *ever* give up.

But today was full of long, hard moments. Moments are very long when breathing is hard. Days are even longer.

The best thing I discovered that day, my sixth day of living, was that there was another important Who. My Nurse Scurry. It was a busy day, packed full of details that I've forgotten, but in the end, it was a bad day.

Nurse Scurry wasn't there at the beginning. It wasn't Nurse Clean Flowers or Nurse Chirpy either that day. It was someone else. Someone Always Talking...

"...Took them to Alton Towers in the finish. But I warned them, you're not getting me in one of those contraptions. And that wall of death! Still you're only young twice!"

I was suddenly too tired to listen any more. If I could just do one more day....

"...And the cost of it... He looks a bit dry... Still it's worth it. They loved every minute of it. Slept like logs on the way back. So did I… How old is this one, again, six days? Won't give him any moisturizer yet then. How do you turn the humidity up in these things?"

The air was getting too tough. Now, I had to suck with everything. I scrunched up my tummy, my arms, my feet with every breath….

"*Raunchy!* Oh no, I don't think he'd be *raunchy*, especially not between the sheets. Too much of a gentleman. I can remember when he first arrived – very shy and mannerly. Probably scared stiff of the likes of you. Anyway his wife is very beautiful and intelligent, so you've no chance. Raunchy? Nah. Mind you, when you think about it…."

Oh, but a whole day of this! It wasn't suckpush any more, it was drag squeeze, drag squeeze. Every moment was a great effort, and seemed such a long time, thinking I might not get through the next moments, and the long day stretching out in front of me. Nurse Talking still talked, I still breathed, but only just. Drag squeeeeze, my chest was tight now. Draag squeeeze, like breathing against a rock. I sucked harder, the air just wouldn't come. Harder! Now my insides were solid. I sucked, really *sucked*, nothing happened, sucked and sucked, still nothing. Pulled in hard, pulled with every bit of me, Pullpushpullpush! Nothing. Nurse Talking still talked. *Bleepleepleep, plingplingpling!* Suck harder! Squeezed my eyes, tore at the air, I'm not breathing any more, Grandpa! Everything was singing and I was straining and stretching and scratching at the air. *Bleepleepleep, plingplingpling.* High above, someone called. "This baby needs…. It's Sat's are down to sixty and dropping fast. Alright blossom, let's take a look at you…."

Click clack ack ack. They were tiny fingers, it wasn't Nurse Always Talking, these were different fingers, hurry-skurry fingers. "All right, blossom. Just hang on, while I have a listen…." She touched me with cold steel, so quick, so sure.

"Sounds like his tube is blocked."

Hisser Snake slid in. *Zzzzzzzzzuuuuuooouuuuuug.* Even Hisser Snake couldn't suck.

"Can I have some help here please. And quickly. Can someone get a doctor? I think this baby needs a new tube...."

Flurry, scurry. *Click clack ack ack.* Four cold hands, whizzy-dizzy smells, jumbled sounds, my head went whizz and whizz and everything began to sing and tingle and spin red-orange-purply-spangly and I was going whizz and whizz and slide and twirl, just floating...floating...floating.....

And here I am back up on the ceiling, looking down. There is a plastic box. It has four plastic doors, little portholes, and they are wide open so that arms can reach inside. And around the box is a circle of bowed heads. Busy people playing with tubes and machines and alarms and red flashing lights.

"Yep. The tube's completely blocked. Right. Re-intubate."

In the box is a little blue doll, only as big as one of their hands. Its arms and legs are as thin as their fingers. They pull a tube out of its mouth.

"Dear oh dear, look at that!"

"Bloody hell, he's dropping fast. Sat's down to thirty."

"Bag and mask him, someone."

The face of the doll is covered with a mask, with tubes running into a black bag. The bag fills with air. A hand squeezes it empty. Bag full, bag empty. The bony little chest goes up and down.

Busy people, doll's head back, light down the throat, rip the tube out of the wrapping and into the mouth. Alarms. Flashing lights. Six bowed heads, very busy people. A doll, the colour of night before dawn.

"Mum and Dad have arrived!"

"Shit."

"Put them in the Parents' room."

But Mum and Dad have seen the alarms and flashing lights and the colour of night before dawn.

"He's fine. He's just having a tube change."

It was Nurse Scurry who ushered them away....

That was just a little slither backwards. I woke up and knew straightaway I was still doing This Living.

Clunk thud whoosh. In, out. *Clunk thud whoosh.* In, out. *Clunk thud whoosh.* But it wasn't me breathing. Now it was that machine going *clunk thud whoosh.* I could lie and do nothing. No need to go suckpush, I couldn't anyway, I was too tired. *Clunk thud whoosh clunk thud whoosh....*

"Seems to have stabilised a bit. Leave him on forty five breaths. I'll do a gas later. And order an X-Ray. And he probably needs a head scan as well...."

Nurse Scurry stroked my chest with velvet fingers. Tiny fingers. "All right then, blossom. All done now. Feeling better now?"

I felt safe and easy. Thank you Nurse Scurry, for letting me breathe again.

Day 6: Later

After that the day was short and minutes were easy. Someone came and put jelly on my head and slimed around. They were nice hands, full of sadness. And I could hear someone crying I think it was her and Nurse Scurry's voice sounded kind. And I think there was Dr Sun in the Garden, the woman who had been there at the beginning, being kind too.

"I know, you've had a rough day...and it's not fair but sometimes that's how it is, one step forward, one step back... but you know lots of babies have bleeds, and it's only into the ventricles, it hasn't damaged the brain tissue yet and some bleeds resolve without damage, most do...."

And later, when he was there too, I could smell despair. They were out there watching, like the first day, and they were listening to another voice.

"I think you're worrying about the wrong thing, personally. To be honest, whether the bleed resolves with or without damage, it won't make a blind bit of difference if...we're not out of the woods yet, I'm afraid. It's still extremely critical, you know. You should prepare yourselves for profound changes from hour to hour and don't worry yourselves about what may or may not happen in six months, just think about this evening....."

".........."

"Look, there's no point thrashing yourselves. You've been here solidly every day, you must be exhausted. Why don't you go home and have a bottle of wine or something."

"No. We'd rather stay... If time's going to be so short...."

And so, on my sixth day, I just lay there. I was still fighting. But the machine was going *clunk thud whooosh.* No need to breathe. I just lay there and explored sore bits. Scratched throat. Solid chest. Swollen jaw. Groin pumped full of air. Head. Oh my head was full of screaming. *Clunk thud whooosh.* Never mind. Let it go *clunk thud whooosh.* I'll just lie here and let Nurse Scurry stroke the hurting away. ...Or maybe, for the first time, maybe, do you think I dare, Grandpa? Maybe I'll just go to sleep. *Clunk thud whoosh clunk thud whoosh clunk thud whoooooooooo-ooooooooooooooo......*

Part Two

Mountains and Music

All I can do today is lie here and drift. It's not that I've given up, it's just that I need to forget about This Living for a while. I need to remember what I used to know, to ramble away to my Perfect Red Sea again. I loved it there. I wish it could be more than a remembering, that I could go back and stay there forever. Ah, but you can't go backwards, can you? That's the thing about This Living, there's no going back.

They all think I'm asleep but I'm not. I'm remembering…

We were in the car, on holiday. "Perfect. Just right to go with the scenery. You've got to guess what it is. I'll give you a clue. It's one of your favourites. Discounting all the rubbish music you like, which cuts out Dylan, Elvis and Burly Shassey."

"You're just cruising, aren't you?"

And it seeped into my Perfect Red Sea. The tiniest sighs at first. Tunes, notes. I know about Music. Everyone knows. Even if you pretend you don't. Even if you're locked inside This Living and your world is full of hard edges and loud thick noises which hide all the knowings you used to have. Even if you build a wall to keep the knowings out, bits of music will drift into your soul and you won't even realise.

And in those days, there were no hard edges, no loud thick noises to get in the way. The music didn't have to seep, it flooded and crashed and rolled me over. It was soft at first, just whispers and flowing and sweet gliding songs, and you just had to dance. It made you smile inside yourself.

"Look. What are you up to in there! Going to be a timpani player are you? Give over!"

It made you go tippy-toe with it. Tiptoeing through her feelings. And the beats of the music tippy-tapped with the beats of her heart. And she told me about the beauty of the heather and the grandeur of the mountains. She told me all about it. Not in words, in *feelings*. All about the blue sky and the April sun sharpening up the snow, still on the mountain tops. She sang to me in time with the music and the music lit up my Perfect Red Sea.

"Don't you recognise it yet?"

"I'm not very good with...alright. Beethoven."

"Nooo! Later. Different nationality. Actually some people think he was mad as a hatter. Might be why you like him."

"You're getting a bit too cheeky for your own good... Ravel."

"Come on. You *know*. You're favourite bit of all time is coming up. I've timed it so we'll hear it just as we get the first sight of the Three Sisters...."

Swooooolyla lyla lyla laa lalaaa..... Swirly, curly, turning sounds. Like rollers on the seashore. Roller after roller and it's stirring up my sea. And the roller rollers faster, rollers higher, rollers louder. Till it shatters and it splashes into droplets all cascading and a million million notes all flutter down into the water. And my sea is just a ripple where the music flows away....

"Rachmaninov?"

"No."

Sweeping tunes, swell through your blood and rumble judder whisper. Sweeping tunes that thunder-thud, then sail away to mutter....

"Brahms?"

"No! Come on. How can you not know?

"Give me a clue."

"It's your favourite. That's a pretty big clue."

"How can it be my favourite, if I don't recognise it?"

"Because you're being stupid. Alright, this bit isn't your favourite. It's the opening of the fourth movement that you like."

To make you ache and want to cry. To make your fingers clench and then uncurl. To make your toes stretch to the roof. To make your whole inside go wobbly and your heart turn upside down. To make you want to sing the whole sound on your own, and then with everyone. This is sound that *knows*. All about your feelings, about your fears and all your longings. And in there somewhere are the answers. In the notes that jingle past us. Something true and there forever....

"Look, thickie, we'll be at the best bit soon. What's your favourite instrument?"

"Haven't got one. Alright, cello."

"That's not your favourite."

"It is."

"Alright. What's *my* favourite instrument. And I'm not talking musical, here."

"What? Oh, I know. Organ....Concerto. Saint-Saens. Brilliant! That *is* my favourite piece of music. Brilliant...."

"God, you're thick sometimes..."

With a *ching ching ching* to tell us to be wary. Then *duddle doo duddle duddle doo duddle duddle dooooo. Duddle doo duddle duddle doo duddle duddle dooooo*. Always running on, will not let me stop, will not let me go, make my head go hot, make me twist and turn, make my heart flip-flop, make my tummy burn.....

"Ready? Here it comes. It's coming...up...now! And look, Tim *there they are*!"

Music stops and then

CHOOOOOOOOOO!

All the noises in the world all at once.

CHOOOOOOOOOO!

Dunk! Dunk! Dunk! Duunk! Dunk! Dunk! Dunk! Du-doooooooo!

CRASH Sha sha sha.

"Wow! Tim. Just look. Stop the car. Look at those!"

CRASH Sha sha sha!

"Wow! That's even better than last time."

CHCHOOOOOOOOOO!

"Look at the waterfalls!"

Dunk! Dunk! Dunk! Dunk! Dunk! Dunk! Dudu Dunk Dooooooo!

"It's just....stunning"

Crash sha sha sha

CHOOOOOOOOOO! Dunk! Dunk! Dunk! Dunk! Duunk! Dudu Dunk Dudoooooooo!

"Is this your favourite?"

CRASH Sha sha sha!

"Yep. This is pretty amazing....."

Dunk dunk dunk dunk dunk dudu dunk du doooo.

Thunder and crashes all soaring upwards so your heart lurches.

Duddle duddle doo duddle do de do. Dunkdunkdunk

And her heart seemed to swell with it. With what she was seeing and the music matching. And every sound returning. *Swooooolyla lyla lyla laa lalaaa.....* And her body filled with wonder. And she told me why...*Swooooolyla lyla lyla. Crash sha sha....* It was the greatness of the mountains and the sweeping of the tunes and the clear blue against the snow-line and the silver sparkling of the water... *Crash! Sha sha sha sha shaaaa* and the way that it lifted us outside ourselves.... *Um duddle do um duddle do dunk dunk dunk dunk dunk dunk. Um duddle do um duddle do dunk dunk dunk dunk dunk dunk.* Like climbing mountains with your soul. *Dunk dunk dunk dunk dunk dunk.* And more and even more *Dunk dunk dunk dunk dunk dunk! And faster. Kchooo, choo choo choo choo choo choo.* And every note that ever was and every tune and every sound and every feeling you ever felt all piled on top until there's nothing left to pile and there's nothing more to bear. *Until Kchoo thump thump thump. Kchoo thump thump thump. KchoooooooooooooooooooooooooooooooooooOOO!*

The end.

Day 8

I love mountains. There's always a mountains to be climbed somewhere. I chose a hard one, didn't I?

Every moment of living was packed full of details, important details at the time. Now, looking back from the top of the mountain, they all merge together. All those little moments of hurting and being scared and slithering backwards that seemed to go on forever, are lost in the big moments....

"Ten, nine, eight, seven, six, five, four, three, two, one... Thirty-six minutes past twelve, Saul. You've done it! You're one whole week old! What a little superhero!"

He and she were smiling. I could hear it in their voices.

"You've done the hardest bit of all, the Most Critical."

"And the Very Critical. You've only got to get through the Just Critical now."

"Oh, Just Critical, eh? Easy!" Nurse Chirpy Bird was laughing.

"You're amazing Saul. And so are you lot. I can't believe how you've.... We've done a week. I never thought.... You're just amazing....."

This morning I thought I could see the top of the mountain, that I was nearly there. I felt full of bounce and happiness. *Um duddle do um duddle do dunk dunk dunk dunk dunk*! I like This Living!

"Don't get too excited though. He's still very, very poorly. He's still only the equivalent of twenty four weeks."

"Twenty four weeks.... You're supposed to be blooming at five months according to all the magazines. I read all the books, you know. Nobody warned me. Miriam bloody Stoppard never mentioned all this. Just makes me feel so inadequate, like I'm the only person in the world this happens to."

"Well you're not. I suppose they don't want to frighten people. But this place is always full. And then there's all the miscarriages and abortions going on downstairs."

"Hey isn't it still legal to abort a baby at twenty four weeks?"

"Yeah, and technically you didn't give birth at all, you miscarried...."

"And the magazines call it nine magical months...."

And this afternoon, (you see how quickly things change,) I am bone-weary, my body aches right through with the effort of it all.

"The next big hurdle really, is to get him off the ventilator. You've been told that he's showing signs of chronic lung disease?"

"Somebody mentioned...."

"It's the ventilation that causes it, ironically. Fragile things, lungs, especially with prem babies. So we want him breathing on his own as soon as possible, then the lungs can recover. Lungs grow back at this age you know, so don't worry. Anyway, that's what we're working towards now. We can't really relax until then...."

And yet, when I drifted awake again, I felt a bit better. And I thought, today *will* be a good day, no matter what happens. Because today for the first time, I'm going to open my eyes.

I'd been seeing shadows, shadows that floated and grew and shrank. I could see Light, which was red and Dark which was black, both mixed together to make patterns. All with my eyes shut.

But today, when I stretched my forehead, I could feel my eyelids pulling apart. Just a bit, just enough to make a slit for the world to seep in, so bright, so white, only for a moment. And then I was stuck together again.

"It won't be long now, you can see he's been trying to open the left one. Look."

Shadows loomed and hid the light, shadows that smelt of Clean Flowers, of her, of him.

"I don't know whether I'll like it... He might...give me an accusing stare."

"He won't."

"He'll look at me and say, this is your fault, how could you do this to me?"

"It isn't your fault, Rose...."

I waited until they were ready. Until I knew they were watching me and then DaDaaaa!

"Rose, look! He's opening them, look!"

"He's looking at the sheets...Did you see that?"

"He heard your voice then, I'm sure he did."

Click clack ack ack. "Saul. This is my hand. Can you see Daddy's hand?"

It was a mountain. Ridges and furrows and dried up river beds. I opened my eyes wider. I looked at their voices. There was a see-through wall. I knew it had been there. I could hear it bouncing back the sounds. Their faces wibbled on the other side. Wet faces. Smiling faces. The Big Air was watery and round. He put his fingertip against my palm. I looked at it and squeezed.

I always knew they were there. Smelt them, heard them, sensed them. And now, I could see. They looked strange. Do they belong to me? Do I belong to them? With their wobbly faces, red eyes, wrinkled skin. His face was clearer than hers, more black and white. I thought it would be different. I thought I would be able to see the clouds of smelliness, that I would *see* the sounds. But I could see shapes that were nothing to do with smells or sounds. I looked at their voices and saw *faces.* I stared. Seeing made my eyes ache.

"You are so clever. What can you see Saul?"

I couldn't move my head, but I could roll my eyes from side to side. It was all blurry but I could see the white sheets, and bits of my body, my chest, huge lumpy nappy, my leg, my foot, more white sheet and wires and tubes trailing away to the end of my house. And on the other side of the see-through wall at the bottom. I could see machines with shaking lights. When I rolled my eyes to the top of my head I could see the tube which was curling out of my mouth, and above that a bit of blue hat on my forehead. And at the side was a bit of ribbon tied to a bit more of blue hat. And then my hand, clutching his finger. What a big finger, what a tiny hand. One day that tiny hand will grow as big as his hand. Perhaps... The thought of all that growing made me droop. I closed my eyes.

"Sing to him"

"People might hear."

"So. Just quietly. See if he hears."

And she began. Quietly, nervously.

Hushaby my baby, hushaby...

I opened my eyes to watch. Her mouth opened just a little. When she sang she almost whispered it, *Hushshshshshsh*. It made me want to sleep. Like last night, when I slept, deep and sweaty, and the machine did all the work. And I let it.

So, I closed my eyes again. Seeing the world like that was very...it was all too.... I'll just listen and maybe let her hush me to....

You are mama's angel boy,
You are papa's pride and joy,
And we'll watch over you,
So hushaby.

Day 9

"Can someone put another Arterial Line in Saul today? Then we can get the Umbilical line out. Time he started feeding. I think he might just tolerate it, don't you?"

I was good at Screaming. It was Doctor Shaky Hands who started it. She didn't mean to hurt me. But she did and I screamed as loud as I could. I screwed up my face and opened my mouth wide. But there was no noise.

"Come on Saul, give me a break."

I pulled my arm away from her. She was gripping it tight, making it throb. I twisted my head and screamed for help.

Then I heard another voice, her voice and I was so glad. She would stop Dr Shaky wouldn't she?

"Is he crying?"

"Er, maybe."

"He's screwing up his face and...oh my God, he *is*. He's screaming. Why can't we hear him?" She was rubbing the whizzy-dizzy stuff on her hands.

"It's the ventilation tube...goes through his vocal chords. It doesn't damage them.... You'll hear him when he finally gets it out.... If he gets that far.... You'll wish you couldn't hear him then...." Dr Shaky Hands was digging with the needle till my arm stung in lots of little places...."

"Oh, Saul. I'm so sorry...so, so sorry...oh darling...." *Click clack.* Her hands came into my house. She tried to stroke my forehead. Dr Shaky Hands gripped so tight it pinched. I squeezed my face up tighter, squeezed the hurting away.

"Oh, Saul.... What can I do to help him?"

"You're probably better getting a cup of tea or something. Getting an arterial in can be tricky."

When I first felt Dr Shaky's fingers, I knew she was scared. Her fingers said: *Just keep calm, it's only a baby....*

I was scared too, my life was in her shaky hands.

Yesterday Dr Shaky had made them sizzle.

"Maybe she doesn't realise that we're waiting for her?"

"Course she does. She's just bloody ignoring us."

"Well maybe what she's doing is important..."

"She's chatting him up. Look at her body language.

"No. She's just.... No, you're right, actually."

"Oh, God.... We'll wait a few more minutes and then I've *got* to go and express some milk."

"She'll come now. Now that he's...oh no, now where's she going....?"

And when Dr Shaky came over at last, I could smell the clouds of trembling that they were breathing out....

"The nurse said you wanted something...?"

"Er, well, Saul's consultant is on holiday and no one's....Saul's had another x-ray today, we noticed, and we just wondered, if it told you anything....and how he's doing sort of thing...."

"Well he's doing what you'd expect really."

"So, is the x-ray alright then?"

"This one? Well it's what you'd expect really."

"Which is what?"

"Well his lungs are very immature and not very well formed."

"Is that grey bit good or bad then?"

"It's all a bit unclear, bit grey and fuzzy, which is normal for a baby of this gestation. A healthy baby with healthy lungs would be more, well clear. Okay?"

"Yes. Thanks."

And Dr Shaky was gone...

"Well, that was instructive."

"Little madam, if she was one of my students...."

"How old do you think she is?"

"Dunno. Too young for this."

"Yeah, sign we're getting old, when the doctors and policemen are getting younger."

"God it's scary. She must only just have qualified, and imagine being in charge of all these critical babies."

"Suppose they've got to learn somehow."

"Yeah, rather it wasn't on our baby though."

So we were scared of Dr Shaky. I tried to scrunch into a ball to keep safe from her jabbing needle, but her fingers just opened me up and probed into me. She bent my hand backwards over her fingers, stretched my skin, open and raw, rubbed my veins, tried to poke the needle in again.

"The trouble is, it gets harder as they grow up. When he was first born, his skin was so transparent, the veins were easier to see, now they're..."

She squeezed again.

"...Hard to see...."

Fingers getting mad.

"...But not that much bigger. Oh Saul, help me here, can't you?"

She bent my hand back so far it felt ready to snap off. The insides of my arm were burning right up to my shoulder. I screamed again. Squeezed my face into little pieces.

"Oh Saul, I promise, it'll be over soon, oh Saul, Saul. Darling...Squeeze my finger, when it hurts." I squeezed her.

"It'll be much better for you if you go and have a cup of tea....Ginny, is this your baby?"

Nurse Chirpy was here. I screamed for Nurse Chirpy. Maybe *she* would stop the hurting. "Would you like a cup of tea?"

"Thanks, but I'm just... he so... in such distress, is there nothing we can do?"

"Come and have a cup of tea."

"I'd rather stay and comfort him...."

"Don't worry. Just don't worry about it, better not to worry...." Nurse Chirpy put her arms around her and led her away.

They were gone. I was alone with Dr Shaky. "Thank God for that. Now come on. The sooner you stop fighting me...." She gripped me so hard I couldn't feel my hand at all, "....the sooner this'll be done."

There was no one to see me screaming. The fingers were angry with me. I stopped pulling.

"That's better."

She stretched back my hand and dragged her thumb across it. It burnt. I tried to lie still. My face was stuck all screwed up. She gave up on my wrist. She tried on my ankle. Jerked back my foot, stabbed with the needle. I tried not to scream. After a long time of trying, she gave up completely.

"It's no good. Someone will just have to try this evening."

Clack click ick ick. She left me alone. I let myself scream. No one will hear it, no one will know. I scream till I have no screamings left. My arms and legs throb. I can't stop the throbbing. I have to bear it. I am trapped in my Hot House. *Clack click* means the doors are locked tight. I'm not the only baby. I can hear other silent screamers, when I listen properly. Are we all locked in tight? All of us trapped. Even if we pound our fists and feet against the sheets, they won't let us out, will they? I hear them all now, the screamers. I cry with them. No one comes.

But that isn't true, because she's back at last.

"I'm so sorry Saul, I'm so, so sorry. But it's done now. It's all over."

"Actually..."

Nurse Chirpy goes *Click clack ack ack* and strokes my screwed up face.

"...She's obviously not managed to do it yet."

"You mean he's got to go through that again? Oh Saul. Why does he need another line in anyway?"

"I know it looks distressing but he does need arterial lines. They need to take the umbilical line out, and that's got his glucose drip in at the moment."

"Why? Why can't they leave the umbilical one in?"

Nurse Chirpy is soothing. I unscrew my face.

"It goes right up to his heart. It's been in over a week and it's a source of infection. It's safer to take it out. And they don't like to start the milk with an umbilical line in. It'll be good when he can have your milk, won't it?"

"........"

"After you worked so hard to produce it. Yes, Mr Sauly boy, that'll be nice. Yum, yum, where's my dinner, he says. Upset your Mummy with all that screaming. That's better. That's better."

And somehow she soothes all the screaming away.

Day 10

I knew that today I couldn't be naughty, because today, relatives were coming. I had lots of relatives. They came to see her and him really. And they went "Oooh" and "Aaah".

Auntie Ruth was the best Ooer.

"Aaah. Look at his little hands and his little hat. Aaah! Inni lovely, he is though. Ooh! Inni though."

Uncle Marcos made Daddy sniff.

"So he's doing alright then? So he's a little fighter then? So he's not doing too bad then? He's a real credit to you, mate."

That's when Daddy sniffed.

And Uncle Andy made Nurse Chirpy grin and Daddy cry.

"He's a wonderful little fella, isn't he? I think you can be proud of him brother." That's when a tear dripped off Daddy's nose.

"And you nurses are pretty marvelous too, you know." That's when Nurse Chirpy grinned. And all the time after that, whilst Uncle Andy put his arm round Daddy's shoulders, Nurse Chirpy grinned and looked at Uncle Andy out of the corner of her eye.

Relatives often came, more aunties and uncles, Granddad Bernie, important friends. But today, was special because Wild

Granny was going to visit. You see, I knew that if I was going to be doing This Living for a long time, (and I *did* want to do it for a long time), I knew that I had to make friends with the important people.

The first day she came – I can hardly remember it – I'd only just learnt about voices and I was very busy making sure that I didn't forget to breathe.

"I know it's a bit frightening at first but if you try to ignore the wires and just look at him, Mum, he's not...there's nothing wrong with him except he's so tiny, if you look, Mum, he's just a perfect tiny little man.... Mum?"

I wiggled my legs for her.

"Oh wow, look at his legs, Mum." That was another auntie.

"Mmm."

"Well, The Royal Ballet are interested in him already, but we said No, we're responsible parents, so we're sticking out for something more classy like the Bolshoi." Even back then when I was only a few days old, Daddy was trying to make us all laugh.

Granny wasn't laughing. "Well, I did warn you that children would ruin your life. I suppose you wish you'd never bothered now."

"..........."

Time seemed to stop. He and she just hung there, saying nothing. At last an auntie – perhaps it was Auntie Isobel, I'm sure it must have been her – tried to get time started again. "He's just *amazing*, Ros, I can't believe how perfect he is, and *I* think he's prettier than all those other fatty, chubby babies, he looks like a miniature athlete...."

Granny sniffed "So what's wrong with that baby over there?"

"......"

"That one, seems perfectly normal to me. What's supposed to be wrong with it?"

"We don't ask. You're not supposed to look at other babies."

"Why not?"

"Confidentiality."

"Hummph!"

"Well, I wouldn't want the families of fourteen babies staring in at Saul."

"Well, who's been staring in at him? That's the trouble with hospitals. People are awful. Is that a doctor or a nurse?"

"...A nurse. The nurses are the ones in blue pajamas."

"Not very flattering. And what do the doctors wear?"

"Nothing. Just ordinary clothes."

"Well that's no good, they could at least wear white coats or something. How can you tell if they're doctors or not? Is it for cutbacks or is it a silly fad thing?"

It wasn't hard to work out, was it? Granny was really angry. So every time she came after that, I tried to be a very good boy. No making it rain when people weren't watching, no silent screaming, no rambling away to Important Places. I had to be the perfect baby for Wild Granny.

Today, as soon as she glanced in, I tried to look into her eyes. She looked away quickly.

"New baby next door I see. What happened to the other one? Did it die?"

"I don't know, Mum."

"So how old is this new one then? Doesn't look very well. Is it as poorly as yours was? Well, yours is much better now, isn't he? Won't be long now and he'll be a normal baby."

Granny sneaked another look at me. I made my eyes as wide and deep as I could.

"Getting very fat in the face."

"That's the steroids. He needs them to...."

Granny's eyes drifted away. Mummy looked at me and we smiled.

"That woman over there, in the short skirt, I met her in the lift. Her baby was thirty two weeks. That's nothing is it? Anyone can survive thirty two nowadays, can't they? I told her about yours, and how well he's done just to get this far. Takes after his grandfather. He was always very tough. Poor little thing...." And she sneaked another look. I stared deep into her eyes. She was surprised. Just enough to make her nearly smile.

"Anyway, I'll leave you two to do...whatever it is you find to do all day in here. I did warn you, wasting your life away, babies, such a burden...Don't walk me to the lifts, I can find my own way...."

Mummy looked at me and smiled. "You're *never* a burden, Saul." And we smiled. Because we both knew that Granny was softening.

Wild Granny

I remember Granny from before. I remember the day we were all walking up to the new churchyard, Granny and her and me in my Perfect Red Sea. She felt drained, as if her blood was too thin. She wished the hill wasn't so steep, that the watering can wasn't so heavy, the roses she was carrying so thorny, that Granny wasn't so angry.

"I don't know what I've done to deserve you children. Ungrateful sods the lot of you."

I could feel her shrinking inside her coat. She felt mean.

"It's just a holiday really and we'll visit Tim's family whilst we're up there, get married and come home. It's no big deal."

"It is to me." As she had expected, Granny was upset.

"But I asked you a few weeks ago if you'd mind and you said No."

"I didn't. You didn't ask."

"I said, what would you think if we went to Scotland and got married whilst we were there, and you said, you couldn't care less as long as we got on with it after all these years. That's exactly what you said."

"Yes but I didn't think you meant it."

"That's why I asked, to see if you minded not being there."

"Well I do mind."

Her heart fluttered and her tummy churned. "Oh, Mum. It's only a few I Do's in a poky little registry office. I don't know what all the fuss is about."

"Why can't you have it here in the village. Then everyone can see what you're wearing."

She groaned loudly inside, it thundered into my Perfect Red Sea.

"I hate all that pomp and circumstance. It's a shameless waste of money."

"No it's not, and I'll pay anyway."

"You can't afford to waste money. And anyway, we want it quiet."

"It would be quiet."

They reached Grandpa's grave. She began to arrange flowers. Granny looked on, silent for a moment. Then her voice rang out clearly in the still air.

"Well I think you're being very selfish. You've been to all your cousins' weddings and I was looking forward to inviting them to yours."

"Oh God. I'm definitely not having a wedding with extended family arriving in coachloads. Can you imagine if Tim invites all his distant relatives? We'd have to hold the reception at Old Trafford. That's why I've never wanted to get married before. I knew there'd be a big fuss and people getting upset."

"I'm not getting upset. I just think you're being mean. I'm your mother and you don't want me at your wedding."

"It's not that we don't want you. Oh Mum, I want it to be quiet and simple. Look why don't you come to Scotland with us...."

"What do I want to go there for? Horrible cold place. You can get married here and stop being so immature."

For a moment there was a flicker of a smile in her heart. Then she sighed deeply again. "I think we'll just not bother."

She worried about it all the way home. Her mind raced. She felt sick. She drove badly, angry at other people in cars, angry at herself, building up to be angry at him.

It made my Perfect Red Sea judder and turn jangly.

"Didn't go well then?" He was there as soon as we came through the door.

"She's really upset."

"She'll come round...."

"She won't. She'll never forgive us. She's always wanted to be Mother of the Bride..."

"Well, let's stick with the big wedding idea then...."

"Oh Tim, I can't...."

She sank down into the sofa, breathed deep, breathed the tears away.

"I don't...I can't do a big wedding as well as everything else. I'll be desperate for a break at Easter, I don't want my holiday turning into a mammoth family celebration. I should be taking it easy, not...oh let's call the whole thing off...."

"Well tell her you're pregnant then, and that's why you want to quieten down the wedding preparations."

"I don't want to tell her yet, I'd rather not discuss it with her till it's definite, if I could just get past three months. To be quite honest I can't handle the aggro there's bound to be, and if it all goes wrong again... God, I'd really rather she didn't know...."

"You'll have to tell her sometime."

"Are you sure? Can't I keep it a secret and then when it's thirteen and has been briefed to be *extremely* well behaved, just present her with a perfect grandchild?"

"Yeah, and hide it under the piano every weekend when we go to visit?"

"Or. We could pretend it's a rather bald cat and then she'll love it to bits...."

They laughed but it didn't stop her worrying....

A week later we were at Wild Granny's again. We were eating tea and cakes. You had tea and cakes at Granny's. They were trying to tell her something important. About me. She was nervous, I could feel a heavy lump turning over in her tummy.

But Granny was talking.

"...and, oh, guess who I bumped into? Mrs Oakley from the old post office. I told *her* about the boiler and *she* thought it was a lot of money too. I haven't seen her for, oh...how old are you?"

"Thirty one."

"Well, for nearly thirty years then. Because she had a daughter, same age as you. And guess what, she's got three children, the daughter has, and another on the way!"

She took a quick breath and – But Granny got there first.

"Poor fool. Some people! She was never as clever as you of course. But that's her life over with. I said to Mrs Oakley, has she never heard of contraception? Anyway it's your birthday soon, any ideas for presents?"

This was it. Her heart lurched.

"Some Mothercare Vouchers?"

"What?"

"We'll be needing a few things from Mothercare soon. In about five months."

"Oh no!"

She pretended to laugh. "You're supposed to say Congratulations or something."

"I thought you had more sense."

I felt the heavy lump press into my Perfect Red Sea.

"You make it sound like we were caught round the back of the bike sheds."

"Well I hope you know what you're letting yourself in for."

She couldn't think of anything to say. He came to the rescue. "We've been trying for a long time, actually."

"And what about your career?"

She sighed. "What career?"

"It'll ruin your life. You've no idea what bloody back breaking work they are. You won't have a minute's peace. But I suppose you young people have got to make your own mistakes..."

She pushed the sadness down like a blanket, pressing me into the old, old feelings, years old, that bubbled below.

"Anyway, don't tell Gran, we want to tell her ourselves."

"She's already guessed. She's waiting for you to tell her. Been whittling on about it all week. I kept telling her you wouldn't do anything so silly. Seems I was wrong...."

And the sadness and anger sneaked away to a hidden place, but ready to burst out later....

"Bloody career! I don't care about a bloody career. What's a career anyway? It's just bloody hard work, killing yourself so that someone else can take the credit, pay you peanuts and guilt trip you into a nervous breakdown.... I'll be bloody glad to be shut of it...."

"Forget about it sweets, we've told her now."

And she pretended to forget about it and she sent it down to the dirty pool where all the other forgotten things bubbled.

Day 11

Suckpush suckpush! I dance with my legs today and wave my arms about to the music I'm making up in my head. I go *Duddle doo duddle duddle doo duddle duddle doooo,* full of bounce this morning.

"And what's Indomethecin?"

"It's to try and close the arterial duct in his heart. And this drip up here is TPF: Total Parental Fluid, sort of glucose solution that's fed into his long line until he can take milk...."

I loved the velvet fingers of Nurse Scurry.

"...He's also having some bicarb, to try to correct a persistent acidosis. And he's just been prescribed some plasma, to replace the blood we keep taking out of him, poor blossom, and he hasn't got much blood in him to start with...Theophylline, that's to stimulate his respiratory drive, which is very good actually at the moment. Look he's doing about thirty breaths a minute himself, see those spikes on the monitor. Some hospitals use caffeine instead. And there are some days when I wouldn't mind a shot of it myself. In fact there are some days, when it gets really busy, and I think, oh just put me on a ventilator someone, I could do with a bit of life support right now!"

I screamed with Nurse Scurry today. I didn't need to, but it was the shock of it....

"Anyone free to help me weigh Saul?"

Nurse Scurry took off my nappy. I didn't scream when she peeled the sticky things off my belly, even though it hurt. And I didn't scream when she opened up one whole side of my Hot House and let the big cold air flush in over me. And I didn't even scream when she flew me up and into the Big Air. It was when she plunged me into a great freezing steel dish. Then I screamed. The cold air clamped onto me. I was frozen heavy. And frightened. The air out there was so *big*. If I fell I would fall for ever. And so loud, and so near and so far and so much of it. The wires and the tubes were yanking at my legs and arms and belly button and the Tube in my mouth jerked and twitched down to my throat. I thought I could be pulled inside out by all those wires.

So I screamed, and thrashed my arms and legs to escape. Maybe I could swim out of the dish to somewhere safe. But then Nurse Scurry scooped me up and flew me back to my warm house.

"All done, blossom."

The sheets were new and crisp, and I was cold, right deep-down cold. Nurse Scurry wrapped me up in a prickly blanket. Heavy blanket.

And as I felt Nurse Scurry's velvet fingers, I thought, she wouldn't have let me fall, I should just let myself melt into her and do what she wants. That's the way to say thank you. You have to let people do things to you in This Living, Grandpa told me. You have to Trust. Learning to trust is a nice thing, said Grandpa. And just thinking that made me feel warmer. I don't need to be frightened. Not in Nurse Scurry's hands.

"Saul's actually put on weight! I've just worked out he's five hundred and ninety grams, which is....one pound, five ounces, which is one ounce more than when he was born."

"No! Are you sure you've calculated right."

"I know. But I've taken everything into account – hat, ventilation tube and mask, long line, line in his ankle, line in his arm, splints, two-way adapter. Heart monitors, temp monitors, saturation collar and nappy I'd already taken off...so that's everything, isn't it. Putting on weight Saul! After barely a week. That's unheard of!"

"You pile on those pounds Saul. It's better to be a miniature Sumo wrestler than be in here with us, eh?"

Day 12

Today I learnt about the opposite of screaming, when you feel something and you like it and it makes you smile inside and you want it to happen all over again.

Today, I was twelve days old. I was a bit fed up of all the hurting by now. You can bear it for so long and then you get sick of it. This was another day of trying with the needle.

"Sorry Saul, but if we don't get this arterial in, you can't grow up big and strong."

They all tried lots of times. And when it was Dr Shaky's turn, I kicked at her hands and tried to hide under the sheets.

"Bit unco-operative your son, isn't he?"

By now, I'd learnt to smell whoever was coming, even when I was pretending to be asleep. If I smelt Nurse Chirpy, or Clean Flowers or Scurry, then I would be able to smile inside, but if it was a doctor coming to steal blood or try with the needle, then I would hold my breath and pull in my arms and legs ready to push them away.

So today, when Nurse Clean Flowers went *Click clack ack ack,* I went floppy and smiled inside, ready for something nice like the Leg-and-Belly-Checking-Dance. But instead she took my nappy off and put something over my eyes. It was cold without my nappy. And then suddenly it was bright hot all over my body. There was a box of happy light above me. I could feel the heat shining on my skin. And it was lovely. I stretched out in the sun and soaked up the warmth.

"It's perfectly normal for babies to get jaundice, even healthy babies. The phototherapy lamp will clear it up. Look, quite a few babies have a lamp.

"Oh look, you've put sunglasses on him. Oh he's so lovely, he looks as if he's on a Miami beach or something."

"He loves it, doesn't he? Wish I could get in there with you, poppit. Could do with a bit of sunshine therapy myself. I made the sunglasses out of cardboard, couldn't get any small enough. He needs them to protect his retinas. Fragile things retinas."

"Oh, how clever, you're brilliant. Saul-size sunglasses. What a clever nurse you've got Saul. What a lucky boy."

Ah, this was better than screaming. Thank you, Nurse Clean Flowers, I said and I stretched my back and wiggled into a comfy position. I liked it best with my arms above my head. It was warm. It was like when we were on a beach, he, she and me....

She was lying in the sand and I was wading around in her thinkings.....*Lossiemouth. Lovely name, mouth of the River Lossie, that'll be the river bed, tide's out....*

And I could tell she loved it. It made her melt and all the knots around me began to unfurl. The sun warmed her skin and flowed into me. But the air had chilly sea breeze in it.

Well it is only April.

She breathed deep and filled me with sea fresh smells. It was a long way away, but if I strained, I could hear the sound of the sea. It was grinding the grit, this way and back again. And above it a lonely seagull cried.

There are some things you know about. The sea is one of those things.

I knew so much back then. I knew things from just moments ago. (Very fresh and clear.) From two months ago. (Clear, but sometimes they didn't make sense.) And then I knew things that, well things that Just Are. They're not now or then, near or far, clear or fuzzy. They make sense but you can't explain. Now when I sit still and try to think about what I used to know, I can feel the knowing just sailing away. When I began, I knew everything. But even now, with only a little time gone by, the knowing has started to melt and the not-knowing is growling in the background.

You never lose the knowings about the sea, though. The way it crashes bad and angry and the way it ripples all calm and pretending to be safe, the way it stretches all the way into the sky, to other worlds, the way it disappears into itself, deep where no one can ever go. The sea is in everybody's heart, somewhere. It's in her heart and in her memories.

She had lots of memories, of seasides, of churchyards and of Grandpa. We played inside them as we lay on the beach. She remembered climbing the yew tree outside the church, when she was very small and I pretended to be doing it with her. We looked down on all the hats going into the church and we giggled. And then there's the remembering of Grandpa in the sailing boat and falling in the water.

Her memories were such fun. And I could rummage through the hidden pools of her mind and pick up remembered bits and pieces which weren't even hers. They were her mother's or her mother's mother's. Or even further back than that. She had picked them up when she was as small as I am now, wandering round the sleeping mind of her mother. And Granny's memories were borrowed from Great-granny. Back and back. It was all there, just waiting for me to climb inside and explore.

"...Tide's coming in." That was a deep rumble, to remind me that he was there.

She breathed deeply. "Mmm".

"Are you bored?"

We were still half asleep, exploring memories. "No. Are you?"

"No."

We woke up properly. "Yes you are."

"No, I'm alright."

"You must be, otherwise you wouldn't have asked."

"Thought you might be bored."

"I was asleep."

"Oh sorry."

"Don't you like it here?" We knew the real answer. He never did like beaches much.

"It's beautiful, yes."

She sat up and stretched. Her feet were getting cold. "What do you want to do then?"

"I'm fine here. If you are."

We smiled to ourselves. This is a game we played often. "What shall we do then? Back to Nairn? To a teashop? Further up the coast? Where do you want to go?"

"Well, wherever you want. There's a malt whisky factory down the road. Glenfiddich."

She laughed. "I knew it. How far down the road?"

"Half an hour. But you don't want to go, so let's stay here."

"Look if you want to go, let's go."

"The tour's free, and you get a free shot of whisky."

"Great. Although I'll pass on the free whisky. In my condition"

"Oh you're right. Stupid idea. We'll stay here."

"You're going to get such a slap in a minute," she said. "It's getting chilly anyway. Get your shoes on and come *on*."

The sun had gone in and there was a cold wind blowing from the sea.

"Thank God, thought we were never going to manage that."

"Looking a bit on the chilly side, aren't we?"

While I was dreaming of beaches, Dr Magic had been in. He'd put something in my arm and taken something out of my belly button.

"Thank God, thought we were never going to manage that." He pushed his floppy hair out of his eyes.

The hot light had gone. I was feeling cold. "Looking a bit on the chilly side, aren't we?" Nurse Clean Flowers was fiddling with my new wires.

"Sorry, but it was such a tricky one, easier to do it without this great brute in the way.... Let me put it back.... Now, young Saul, don't go thrashing about too much, pretending to score the winning goal. We don't want that arterial coming out after all the trouble we've had getting it in."

"You should get yourself down to the milk kitchen, Stephen. Apparently you can hear the cheers coming from the stadium. If you lean out of the window and the wind's in the right direction."

"I'm not that sad...here." He wheeled the box of light back into place. The bright heat snapped back on.

Nurse Clean Flowers was laughing. "I think you are."

"Look, how often is it that Britain hosts the cup? Anyway, I seem to remember you think Shearer's a bit of all right."

"Is he the one with nice legs?"

"That second goal! He was definitely Man of the Match. OBE material if you ask me."

"Hey, have you got blood on my little boy's nice clean sheets. Oh honestly, Stephen. Doctors! Use a tissue can't you?"

"Saul! Save me from bossy nurses. You don't mind red and white sheets do you Saul?"

"He does. He's not going to grow up a slob."

"You grow up in whatever way you want. Don't let her browbeat you. Just as long as you support Liverpool...."

"Get out of it... Now, I'm just going to put a tube down to your tummy, poppit. Time to try a bit of Mummy's milk."

Nurse Clean Flowers put another tube in my mouth, a tiny one, and pushed it down.

"Fancy having your first feed so early. You're very good aren't you? Just checking that it's in the right place. Don't want it in your lungs, do we? ...Right. You're first meal, poppit." Something warm spread into my tummy. "You can only have half a mil, just to see how you like it."

At first I think my tummy is going to scrunch up and send it back. But then it makes me feel warm and happy. My tummy likes it. I remember that I've had a sort of hollow feeling there for days now, a sort of hole getting more and more sore, and now the hole isn't empty. I don't feel so hungry any more.

"If you're very good and don't throw it back up, you can have a bit more each day. And then you'll be a very clever little boy."

Dr Magic was smiling at me. "What do you think of that then, Saul, my man?"

The Important Story

I'm a good learner. That's what I'm here for. I want to learn everything. Not just about tubes and Big Air noises and whizydizzy smells. I know there's more to This Living, My Living, than all that. There are Reasons and Answers somewhere out there and I'm going to find them out.

I have an inkling, a knowing deep inside me that there's an Important Place for me, with an Important Story that I need to discover. I don't know where this Important Story is. Maybe it's buried under all the little details of This Living, or maybe it's hidden deep in all the rememberings I took from her when I was in my Perfect Red Sea.

So, when they think I'm sleeping, really I'm searching for the Important Place, sifting through all the rememberings I borrowed from her, matching my story with all the others, looking for clues.

Day 13

Sometimes it's hard to be strong. Like yesterday, when I felt bad. And the day before that, when I felt worse. And I slept and didn't move and no one woke me. You never know what you're going to feel like. It goes bad, good, bad, worse, bad again.... It changes from hour to hour. Nobody knows which way it will change, not even Grandpa.

Today they were washing me.

They had been learning to do Cares for days now. Important jobs. They weren't very good at it. They had been even worse the first time....

"But how do you...oh you put your right arm through this porthole and your left...it's so...awkward...and...what, you have to hold all that with one hand? ...But I can't.... How do they do it? I'll hurt him.... Tim, go in through the other side and hold his legs and then...."

"Careful! You've pulled off one of those monitor thingies...."

"Bugger.... does it just stick back on.... I can't...oh no, the wires, where are the wires...?"

"They're trapped in his old nappy, hold on...."

"I'm sorry, sweetheart, poor little Saul...let's put his legs down and start again...."

They tried to be gentle and I laid still, to make it easier. I let them pick up my legs and put them down. Pick them up, down again. Up, down. Everything was clumsy and slow. Hands in the wrong place. Fingers fumbling. Starting all over again.

"Look, you hold his legs while I thread the nappy through the wires...."

Peeeeeeeeeeeeek!

"...What's that alarm? Have you knocked something?"

"I don't know. Where's the nurse? Nina! Something's alarming."

Nurse Clean Flowers was already there.

"My vent! Now, poppit. Are you making a noise over here? Has Mummy knocked your ventilator tube."

"Oh my God. Saul, I'm so sorry. I didn't mean... Did I nearly kill him? Is he alright?"

"Course he is. Don't think you even noticed, did you poppit? He's doing plenty of breathing for himself, today. There we are, tube back in place. Look, he's enjoying every minute of it. Aren't Mummy and Daddy brave doing all your Cares today?"

"We can't do it. We're hopeless. I can't even change my own baby's nappy.... I think it'd be better if you...."

"You're doing ever so well, you know. You're doing fine. Try cleaning his mouth. He likes that. He won't let me have the cotton bud back when I do it. Sucking reflex already. That's a good sign. Go on, put the bud in the water, no, in this water, this is for his mouth, you've got to keep everything really sterile...now take the cotton bud into the...."

"Oh bugger. Sorry, dropped it...."

"No, don't pick it up.... Try with another one...that's it."

I liked the cold wet stick in my mouth when Nurse Clean Flowers did it, when it rolled around smooth and firm, cold and fresh. But when they tried, the first time anyway, it was sore. They couldn't find a way past the strap across my lips. They poked and rubbed.

"You can push it in further than that. Give his gums a good clean, get right inside and to the back."

"I don't want to hurt him.... What about the tube? ...He might choke.... I might kill him.... Can you finish it, sorry, I can't...."

They had got better. I even started to enjoy it. Sometimes, I would be naughty and kick the nappy away. And sometimes, I would wiggle and arch my back so they couldn't hold me. And when they tried to put the new nappy under me, I pummeled their hands and made them laugh. They let me be naughty. "Well all right, if you want the nappy off for a while...But if you wee, you're in Big Trouble."

"Get some cotton wool ready then, otherwise he'll need new sheets as well.... Quickly...oh no! ...I told you he'd wee everywhere...."

It was the cold water. It made everything inside me scrunch up and I couldn't help it. And since I had to Ooze, I thought I might as well Squirt as well. Because that's how you make people laugh, isn't it? When it rains they always laugh.

"I caught some of it, anyway...what do we do with it...?"

"I think they put it in this specimen jar.... Better call a nurse to help change his sheets. You're so naughty Saul, these nurses are busy enough...."

"You lift him, Tim. He likes it with you..."

And I never screamed when he lifted me. I just wiggled and soaked up all the warmth in his great sweaty hands.

So today, when I was thirteen days old, when they made me clean, I tried to be a good boy. I wanted today to be really nice for them. So I helped him and lifted my legs up ready. He didn't know it, but he was going to find something new, because today,

I wasn't just wet, today I was *really sticky*. He was slow and careful. I jiggled my legs to tell him to hurry up. He unpeeled the nappy ever so slowly, opened it up ever so slowly, pulled it down...

"Oh my God! It's *green*! Call a nurse! Ginny, he's got something...it's like tar."

Nurse Chirpy started laughing.

"Sauly boy! What filthy knicks. We like to see filthy knicks like that, don't we? Means you know what to do with all that milk, eh?"

"Is that...normal?"

"It's *very* healthy. Isn't everybody's poo like that, Saul's saying. Mind you, I wouldn't go near it myself without a cap and gown. And a pair of wellies and gardening gloves. In fact, poo like that has caused major industrial action, before now. It's higher rates of pay for poo on that scale!"

Laughter. Lots of it. Real, loud, happy laughing.

"I'm glad you waited for your Mummy and Daddy to be here, Saul. That poo is definitely their responsibility. So. Which one of you is *going in*? And do you want a snorkel?"

"Well my fingers have started to react to the stuff we have to wash in, so Tim's doing the Cares, today."

"Oh, well done. She's played a blinder there, Tim!"

"It's *true*. Didn't I say this morning, Tim, my fingers are really cracked and sore so I'd better lay off the Betadine?"

"I think Saul tipped her off, didn't you Saul?"

It was so sticky he had to rub quite hard. But he got every bit off. I tried to be good for him. I didn't wriggle or cry or squirt. I lifted my back off the sheets when he slid a dry nappy in through the wires. The nappy came up to my shoulder blades. He folded it round my legs and over and over at the front. He was very careful and neat. He did everything as if it really mattered. And then he breathed deep. And tickled my feet.

Days 15-18

You've got to expect to fall once in a while. That's what happens if you're poorly. I fell a lot, over the next few days. Slipping back further than I had just climbed. And always round every corner The Big Fall was waiting.

It wasn't anybody's fault. You couldn't blame Nurse Columbine. She did everything she could. I was two weeks old when I first met her.

He and She were singing.

Happy Birthday dear Sa-aul, Happy birthday to you!

"Two whole weeks Saul. That's just marvelous. You're a miracle baby...."

They leant over the top of my Hot House to look at my face. I was lying on my back. The glue in my chest had got so heavy that I couldn't breathe on my side. So I lay flat, staring at the world on the ceiling. It wasn't very exciting, it was hidden by dazzly lights. I tried to see behind the lights but they made my eyes sting. I had to screw up my eyes to bear it. I couldn't twist my head away because of the tubes.

I wished I could lie on my side. On your side you could see the Big Air and all the things in it. The Big Air wobbled all the time. At the far end of the Big Air there was The Light and The Dark, swapping over from night to day and back again. Along the walls were the see-through boxes, shut tight, with machines clicking and spitting. And the shadows at the far end swam up and down and when they swam up to me they were blue nurses with bright white shoes. The floor was grey and if you twisted your eyes, you could see all the things they'd dropped, cotton wool, paper wrappings for the Hisser Snake tubes, gloves all-inside out and rolled up into thin rubbery sausages, white tissues dotted with blood. The woman with the big round floor polisher cleaned the floor, and then it went from dry to shiny wet and back to dry again.

And if you looked hard enough you could make out all the different Sad People, with the red raw eyes, who hardly moved. They stood and stared into their boxes, leaning on them heavily, because really they wanted to sit down but there weren't any chairs.

So there was always plenty to watch when you lay on your side. On your back wasn't half as good.

But that's how it had to be when I was two weeks old, when I first saw Nurse Columbine. She leaned over and looked me straight in the eyes. There had always been lots of other eyes and faces to get to know. There was Nurse Black Hair and Nurse Watery and Nurse Loud Voice and Nurse Scrubbed Arms and Nurse Smiley and Nurse Rough Skin and Dr Keen and Dr Slow but Sure and Dr Too Tired and Dr Sun in the Garden and all the Floor Polishers – oh, lots and lots – too many to tell you about. I got tired of new faces sometimes and they were always gone before I had worked them out. No, there were only a few people who really mattered. And Nurse Columbine was one of them.

"You're gorgeous, aren't you? Yes you are. Yes you are."

She was soft and thin and delicate and pink. But her eyes smiled grey and sort of steely.

"That hat's a bit small for you, sweet pea. You've been growing into it. Shall we sort you out and make you more comfy?"

I liked Nurse Columbine straight away. She found ways to make me feel better. She fiddled for ages with the ribbons at the side of my face. I watched out of the corners of my eyes, and I knew that whatever she was doing, it would be something nice in the end. She made the tube in my mouth wobble. I gripped it.

"Oh I see. You're helping me are you? Well, hold tight then, while I...."

She peeled the ribbons away from my cheeks. They had been cutting into my face and when she pulled them away.... Aaaah! My skin was free.

"You're all chubby cheeked aren't you?"

She loosened the strap which was squashing into my lips and slid the hat off my head. It felt really good, as if my head was ten times bigger, as if it could breathe. And then she washed it and fluffed up my hair. I really loved it when she did that.

"Oh sweet pea, what's this? Has someone left a nasty wee bag on you? And it's full to bursting. Nothing wrong with your waterworks, anyway! Better send it off to the lab, shall we? Poor Saul. It's been cutting into your belly button. Poor sweet pea."

And she soothed away the sore bits.

"Yes, you're all awake and lively now, aren't you? Have you been worrying Mummy and Daddy, being so up and down."

"Do the doctors know why he's so unstable?" His chin was very dark today. To match his eyes.

"It's all part of the...being so premature. It's like that sometimes. One step forward, two steps back. Remember, he's still only the equivalent of twenty five weeks; he shouldn't have been born for another fifteen weeks.... Might just be the congestion in his chest. Or the bradycardic attacks. It's normal for babies like Saul to have brady's, but to have so many, and they're very sudden and profound, which is why it's hard.... Or it might be because his pulmonary duct hasn't closed yet.... I don't know. It's difficult.... There's no getting away from it...he is a very fragile little boy at the moment...."

They were difficult days. Up a bit, down a bit, down a bit more. All in one day.

"...Need to put him up to thirty-five breaths per minute...."

"...Well done, little chap, down to twenty breaths now...."

"...Not so good, not really coping, put him up to thirty breaths...."

"...Had a bit of a relapse in the night, so he's on forty breaths just for now...."

That Tube. I was fed up with it. My chest didn't want it. And all the glue, sometimes even Hisser Snake couldn't suck it up. And when it got *really* scary, they had to splash me with the sea:

Bleep bleep bleep!

"There's something really...sticky down there...come on...I just can't...."

Pling pling pling!

"I'll try saline. Might just shift.... Damn, there's no saline left in his locker.... Has anyone got any saline...?"

"In the drug's room."

And she would run away. All I could do was wait, my chest solid and my head starting to spin. And I'd wish really hard she'd come back, because I wasn't sure I could manage much more and I'd start to feel afraid, a black, heavy balloon in my tummy, in case she *never* came back. When she did, long, long moments later, her hands would shake. And she would fumble with the see-through packet and squirt it down my Tube. It looked like water. Her hands would shake so much, lots of it would splash on my cheeks and lips. Like sea spray. I would swim under the sea and breathe like the fishes do.

"I'll just give it a few seconds to do its stuff."

And at last, Hisser Snake would try again. *Zuuuuooorgh.* Snortling up my insides, gnawing at the sticky stuff.

"Got it! ...Look at that!"

"Urgh. That's horrible."

"Isn't it? Pretty green too. Better send it off to be cultured."

Clunk Thud Whoosh. Aah. Sweet air again. And I would taste the sea on my lips.

"You think you're auditioning for *Casualty*, don't you?"

And they would laugh. Well, their mouths were wide and their shoulders shook. It looked like laughing. But Nurse Columbine's face was all dusted with tiredness, paler than the pale blue of her uniform.

And sometimes, if it was really bad, when they had tried everything and still I went whizzydizzy and started to see starry pictures, sometimes they had to pull out the Tube really quickly. Not carefully. All in a rush. And they had to push another tube down. I hated that, it really hurt. Even if it was Dr Magic. Even though he went calm and smooth. And even if I was with Nurse Columbine and knew I was safe, even then, you had to be frightened. Because you never knew if *this* fall would be the last.

Until now, though, they had just been little slithers – dangerous slithers, it's true, scary at the time – but small enough to pick myself up again afterwards. But on my eighteenth day, I knew something was looming. So did Nurse Columbine. When she arrived she already smelt weary.

"It's hard to know what to do really...."

Her fingers slid underneath me.

"...These last few days he's...I don't know... He can't even manage on his back any more. That's why I thought I'd try him on his tum.... Got the tubes? Ready? Okay. Hold tight sweet pea...."

Her fingers gripped me and I began to twirl. It was strange at first, to see the Big Air the other way round. The solid lump lurched around my chest. She lay me down. The sheets pressed bits of me they had never pressed before, my cheek, my shoulders, my toes, my knees. I didn't know how to breathe for a moment.

"Doesn't seem to like it."

"Let's give him a few seconds. Anything's worth a try...."

But bit by bit, I sunk into the sheets. The air cooled my back and Nurse Columbine stroked me. I breathed deep and deep again....

I didn't wake up until I felt Nurse Columbine's fingers turning me over. I didn't want to be turned over.

"Sorry, sweet pea." She was undoing my nappy. "Do you have to do it now? I've just got him stable."

"Best time then, while he can tolerate it. Anyway, the parents aren't here. Quicker and easier all round."

I opened my eyes. Lots of faces. Lots of hands. Nurse Columbine was holding me steady. A great needle hovered above my belly. Fat and steely. Sharp. Glinting.

"Right. Who's going to have a go? ...Jason...just above the pubic bone. That's it...."

The spear pushed into my belly. First it broke my skin. Pop! And then it slid in. I screamed and thrashed. Nurse Columbine just held me tighter. The needle speared the hurting deep and strong.

"Nearly done Sweet pea." Nurse Columbine's hands were strong but her voice trembled. I begged her to let me go. Let it end, let it end, let it end!

The needle sucked at my insides. A tube of hurting, sharp and deep. I tried to squirm my belly away from it. She held me too tight.

"I can't seem to...." The needle twisted around inside. "Is it in the right place?"

"Sometimes it's difficult to get anything up. The bladder might be empty for a start.... Alicia, you have a go."

Another pair of hands. Needle out. Needle in again. Let it end, oh please, let it end. Needle out. Needle in. Searching inside me. Needle out. Needle In.

When it was all over, I cried. I crinkled up my face and looked at Nurse Columbine. "I'm sorry sweet pea. I didn't like that either." She tried to make me comfy again.

"Sometimes there's no urine to collect. We'll just have to try again later. Can you call me, nurse, when he's calmed down a bit? Preferably when Mum and Dad are off the scene."

I had stopped crying by the time he and she arrived.

"He doesn't look very happy."

"I think he's a bit angry with me. The doctors have just tried to get a urine sample out of him."

"Isn't that what the urine bag was for?"

"Well, the results from the bag were inconclusive, which suggests the sample was contaminated. The only way to get a sterile sample is to go straight into the bladder."

"How do they...?"

"With a needle."

Their mouths were open but they didn't speak.

"He seemed to tolerate it well."

They stared but said nothing.

"Anyway, I've given him some suction, so he should tolerate his cares."

I was sorry it happened today. Today she felt brave enough to lift me up when they changed my sheets. It was her first time. She was nervous so I tried to help. But when she slid her hands under me, the glue lurched so heavily that my chest locked solid. Oh no, here we go again! Like breathing against a rock. *Bleep bleep bleep! Pling pling pling.* Nurse Columbine tried all the different things. Sweeter air, Hisser Snake, sea water, more *Clunk Thud Whoosh.*

But nothing worked.

Oh Grandpa.

I knew. Maybe they all knew. This was the Big Fall.

"Can I have some help here please." Voice trembling. "I need some help here. Quickly. Is there a doctor about?" Louder, more urgent. "Please. Anyone!"

Dr Shaky appears. "Got a problem?"

He and she stare. Frozen.

"Sat's down to, bloody hell, that was fast, thirty five, gone off the scale..."

"Bag and mask him then."

Dr Shaky's fingers shiver, saying *Just a body, stay calm, just a baby body...*

Oh Grandpa. I can't help being frightened. I want to feel safe. I want hands that don't shake. Hands that say, *no need to be frightened, I'm here and I'll pick you up and carry you to safety....*

Shaking fingers. *Just a baby....*

Two big frozen bodies back away into the deep Big Air and slide out of the door. He and she are gone. I close my eyes.

"Cardiac resus, someone! ...Not responding too well.... Is Dr Anderson on duty?"

"Oh bloody hell...call him then."

So this was it. I didn't even try to breathe. I didn't fight it any more. Grandpa didn't make me. And the Big Air and the rushing people and all the things I'd learnt about This Living...gently... drifted...away....

Day 18

I'm not alone. Somehow, somewhere, I can't see or hear or smell him, but I know that Grandpa is here. We are high up. We are close. We are scudding across the sky. We are flowing through all the hearts and minds of everyone we know. We are dancing to the music. *Um duddle doo, um duddle doo.* And there's water and sunshine cascading. *Crash sha sha!* We are rushing with the wind and playing in everyone's rememberings. But, Grandpa, I say to him, if we can go wherever we want, I know where I want to go. I want to be with them.

So Grandpa guides me. Down, down. Closer and closer. Till we are floating in the smell of terror, leading us to the place where they have gone.

They are in a little room with dirty walls. Down the corridor, alarm bells ring. They are listening. Her head is tilted back. She stares at the ceiling. Tears run into her ears. He stands by the door, glancing up the corridor.

He is black and white and silent. His knuckles go pale as he grips the door frame. The alarm bells ring.

"How long is it now?"

"Seven minutes."

She wails to herself. *Then he must have died. He can't still be alive can he? Why are the alarms still ringing? Why don't they come and tell us what's happened? Oh God, oh God, oh God. What can we do, what can we do?*

He turns his face to the wall. He turns his face to the ceiling. He turns his face to the door. He can't breathe. He wants to run away but it's in his face, wherever he turns. In his face and down his throat.

These are real feelings. Ugly and raw. I've never seen them before. Not like this. Alive and pulsing. When he and she were by my Hot House, they were calm, even when they were angry. As if they were dead. Red eyed but silent. Except for when they laughed as if they were happy.

Were they hiding the real feelings? Was that what they were doing all that time when they were talking jauntily, trying to make people laugh? Was that all for show? For me? Is this the real bit? This? When they cling to each other and sob? When she wails? When they can't even look each other in the eye?

Maybe all that laughing and singing was all pretend. A way to make us all feel strong: *We will be strong together and not let go. We will, we will....*

Oh let go, Mummy. Daddy, let go. Let the feelings splatter against the dirty walls. I want to feel what you feel. I want to know every burning tear, every choking breath. You are my Mummy and Daddy.

She looks at him.

"Nine minutes."

Her eyes are full of terror. *Not now. We could have borne it at the beginning. But not now...*

"Dr Anderson's just gone in."

"What… why… was he rushing, what was his face like?"

"Couldn't tell."

"That's it then. Oh Saul. Saul, Saul, Saul, Saul."

Oh Mummy, oh Daddy. One day, this will be over. It may be now, or tomorrow, or much, much later, but it Will Be Over. Just a memory. One day it will just be scars. Strong colourful scars, with lots of stories hidden in the pattern. When you escape, when we escape, we will twist and turn and spinning-wheel together. Then you will remember all this differently.

I want them to know I am here. I want them to look up and see me. So they will know I won't fly away and leave them. I said I would fight didn't I?

...Nurse Columbine's voice quivers. "He seems to be rallying."

...No matter how hard it is. I promise I will fight and fight and fight. I don't want to give up Grandpa. Help me to stay, even though it's hard....

...Dr Shaky's fingers sigh with relief. "His Sat's are rising a bit, anyway"

But he and she don't even know I'm here. They can only hear the ringing. And suddenly they are frozen, listening. The alarms have stopped.

Is it now, Grandpa, is this the end? But I haven't finished doing what I wanted to do. What about all the things I've still got to learn? I haven't met everyone there is to meet yet!

But Grandpa just laughs and tells me to hold on. There's no rush. Just wait. You think you've climbed the mountain already? Don't be silly. Such a mountain? The hardest you could find to climb? You think it's over when you've only done the easy bit. You've only just begun.

The door opens. Dr Calm and Nurse Columbine come in.

"It's...all right."

They stare. Pretending. Now I know what Pretending looks like.

"So he's not...he's alive?"

"He's had a tube change and he took a while to recover. But he's alright now...I know it's distressing, but it's just part of the... slow development, I'm afraid. We'll have to expect more of the same before he's finished, if you see what I mean. Anyway, I've put him up to fifty breaths per minute, so he can have a rest."

Should I go back straightaway to the baby body, or can I stay up here floating, looking down at them? But I don't *have* to do anything. If I want to stay here a bit longer, what's the hurry...?

"...But how could he...without oxygen, it was ten minutes at least."

"He wasn't completely starved of oxygen, if that's what you're worried about. He gets oxygen from the bag and mask anyway. It takes quite a few minutes for oxygen deprivation to have a lasting effect, you know. This little episode won't have caused any brain damage, I can assure you."

"It must be so frightening to see us all rush about like that." Nurse Columbine's eye lids are heavy, but she pretends not to be weary.

"No, we want you to rush, it's not the rushing, it's...I know I'm being pathetic."

"You're not being pathetic."

"I'm so useless. I'm used to being the one everyone turns to in a crisis. At work, everyone comes to me to sort out emergencies...."

"It must be very hard to trust us and believe that we're doing our best for him..."

"I thought being a mother would be about caring for him, protecting him, but I'm...nothing. I can't even look after my own baby.... Was it my fault? When I lifted him. I set if off didn't I?"

"No, of course not." There are arms round her and him. Kind people.

Then Dr Shaky pokes her head round the door.

"All right now? He likes to put us all through it. Little horror."

Silence.

They pretend not to be angry, until everyone is gone and then he lets the feelings come in sizzling mutters.

"How dare she! How dare she call him a little... horror, he's a little marvel, he's a bloody fantastic little superhero!" He sizzles really loud.

"Ssh!"

"I don't care."

"It won't do any good. Shouting. Getting angry will only...."

"As if it's his fault.... She should be more...I don't care who hears...."

And yet, back at the Hot House, they're smiling again. Ah yes, now I know about Pretending. They've been pretending all along! How can I work out how to do feelings in This Living if they all go around pretending? I suppose when I *really* think about it, there were some clues. There was always that air of Terror. At first, I thought it was just the normal smell of This Living. Every morning (when all the Sad People had to wait outside to be let in) you could feel the waves of Terror lapping at the doors. And when the doors were opened, all the Sad People came in and the Terror surged in with them. Oh they hid it well, behind all that chatter. "Oh Saul, how wonderful, it's Auntie Anthea again looking after you today, what a lucky boy." But of course the voices if you really listened were too tight, "So how's he been?" And if I'd had a bad night the voices went even tighter. "Forty breaths...he was on twenty when we left."

So all those times I thought we were having fun, really they were wrapping up their feelings, and if I'd been looking properly, I'd have seen, wouldn't I? Oh yes, their faces smiled but their eyes were swollen. And I should have watched their hands, fingers stiff with worry, holding on, holding everything in, putting everything on hold. Hands white at the knuckles, a very big clue. Clenched. And now when I look into their eyes, (they can't hide what's in their eyes), I see their hearts, the same, clenched white. They keep their hearts clenched all day and now I can tell they are heart-weary of it all. It must be tiring walking around, talking, laughing, standing, watching, with a knotted heart, mustn't it?

Why do they do it? Why don't they run away? They're not locked in my box, they don't have wires tying them down. This is my Living and I'm inside it. They have their own living.

Then I think about the ache I feel when I know they're not here. It's like a thread pulling in my belly, very strong but no one can see it. Does it pull in their bellies too? All those times I thought I was hurting on my own, were they hurting with me, feeling every stab, every prick?

And then I feel a thump in my chest because I know I'm right. My living is tied to their living. They *can't* run away (and I don't want them to). They're trapped with me here, like when the doors go *click clack.* And that is why they have to hide their feelings. Because if all the Sad People began to scream when all their babies screamed, then This Living would be a very noisy place, wouldn't it? And it's hard enough to hear sometimes as it is.

I look down on them all. Nurse Columbine is stroking my head. I want to keep holding on to Grandpa, but I want to do This Living too. It looks nice all wrapped up in that blanket. So Grandpa lets me go and I slip down and under Nurse Columbine's fingers. I open my eyes.

"Alright now, sweet pea? Gave me a scare there, Saul. Gave us all a scare. You can't give up yet, you know. We haven't finished yet." Her voice and fingers flutter.

"What will Mummy and Daddy do if you give up now?"

"I thought your shift finished ages ago?"

"Oh it did. But I wanted to stay until Saul was a bit more...."

"But you've just done three fourteen hours shifts on the go.... You must be exhausted. I don't know how you do it."

"I don't know how *you* do it." Nurse Columbine laughs her pink laugh. "At least I get paid for it."

"Well, thanks anyway."

"All part of the service. Just make sure you're still here when I come back next Saturday. Promise me, Saul."

I liked that. Being with Grandpa, slipping away from This Living like that, and then back again. If I could work out how it happened, how to float up there on the ceiling, but still be able to come back down again, that would be a good secret to know, wouldn't it? I want to do it again. I'm going to learn how.

Part Three

Day 20

I am scarred. In lots of different ways. A rainbow pattern that makes me the way I am.

There are scars of the skin. Single blue dots on my belly, from the big needle that makes me scream and thrash, yellow and green splodges on my arms, from when they pump things in. Purple holes in my hands and feet, from when they steal my blood.

Stealing blood from my heel is the easiest. They have to do that lots of times every day. I'm used to it now. It's not so bad, when it's Dr Magic or someone else smooth and soft. I even help, if I'm not too weary, and pull my toes towards my knees. But most times, I push away and say – Oh leave me alone, I'm too tired, not now, not again. They have to grip my foot and prick my heel. They squeeze my toes backwards with their great fingers, until they've squeezed out enough blood to fill a little tube. Before it stops throbbing from the last time, they're back to do it again. Scar on scar.

The Morning Blood takes longer and hurts more. Every morning they have to scrape long and slow at the hole they've made. They make it in the back of my hand, and they scrape to catch the welling blood. Red drops. Sometimes falling on the white sheets. Long, long minutes, twisting my fingers down to make the blood spurt.

Blood is a deep colour. The colour of real life.

Sometimes, if they take too much blood, it makes me feel empty, sort of weak and woozy. Then they have to put the blood back. It waits in a long fat tube to be pumped into my arm. It goes right up inside. Not under the skin, but deep and surging. I can feel it. It's not my blood. I make it mine and it throbs all thick up to my head so my eyelids tingle.

You can have scars inside too. I can feel some of mine. Because *clunk thud whoosh* never stops. Always going *jab jab jab,* like lots of knives inside. Carving out the seconds. I've worked out how to shut out the hurting for little bits at a time. Sometimes I force myself to breathe on my own, even through the hurting. But then Tiredness comes. Tiredness so strong, so full, I can't move or think or even sleep.

It was Grandpa who first told me about scars. It's funny when I hear him. He doesn't have a voice, not like the voices in the Big Air. He doesn't use words or anything, but you know what he's saying. He speaks, and laughs, right inside your head. And he says things like, The hardest things to work out are the best, and the questions that seem to have no answers are the questions that everyone keeps asking. And there *are* answers, it's just that people have lost them, which is why you have to hang onto your Inklings. People are always losing what they used to know....

Ever since the Big Fall, I'd known that Grandpa was hovering. Maybe hiding in the dazzle on the ceiling. Maybe inside the whizzydizzy smell they all put on their hands.

And having him so near makes me feel strong when I am weak, and safe when I am lonely. He knows things I used to know. About Time and how it doesn't count away from This Living, and it's only ever as long or as short as you want it to be. (Which is different from This Living, where every second, every minute must be added up and made to fit, and where things must go in the right order, or else everything gets mixed up.)

And Grandpa knows that you never really forget things, even when you stop doing This Living. Because rememberings don't fold away neatly. Some go so deep they spread into every bit of your soul. These are your scars, the scars of your soul.

Grandpa has rainbow scars, wounds that hurt at the time but now they are pretty and each one tells a story. Like the little blue ones, from when he loved and lost. And the one from many times ago, where he saw a sight so terrible, it left a great red weal, deep and ugly.

You can't see the scars he and she are making at the moment. All you can see is their skin, gone stretched and saggy in the wrong places. Unless you look in their eyes – I learnt that from The Big Fall – to look into the black holes that lead you down to real hurtings. And now I've learnt how to hear it in their voices too.

"But is it safe to give him so many x-rays? He had his fifteenth one this morning."

"Well, we'd rather not. In an ideal world."

"Ironic, really. I hate hospitals, and all that ....intervention. We even worried about having an ultrasound scan, and I was really strict about what I ate when I was pregnant, I wouldn't even have paracetomol, would I Tim, when my pelvis was dislocated? And now look at us. Poor Saul. Up to your eyeballs in drugs and as high tech as they come. I'm so sorry darling."

"It's not your fault, you...."

"Yeah, so everyone keeps saying...it's very kind of you to say so, but I should have..."

"Lots of mothers blame themselves. It's a natural...."

"I dare say, but in my case it's true."

Dr Sun in the Garden had been pressing my head. Her fingers stopped for a moment. "We do try to keep all the procedures and drugs to an absolute minimum, you know. We only use small doses, baby size doses, and without them, well Saul wouldn't be here, and I know it's still touch and go but he's...how old now?"

"Twenty days, three hours and sixteen minutes."

Dr Sun threw her head back and laughed. "You're not bothering to keep track of the seconds then? Honestly Saul. Parents today!"

And then, there are a million tiny scars, from day to day cruel jibes and punishings. Just little pinpricks spread like daisies, a rainbow pattern, so everything you feel and think is there somewhere, recorded, family scrapbooks. From world to world and back again. Nothing is wasted.

Great-Granny

Family scrapbooks. I'm part of it now aren't I? It's good to know about relatives, because then you can work out where you've come from and where you're going.

There's all the great aunts and uncles and Great-grandma, who escaped from This Living long ago. And then there are all the relatives who are still here. And then there's Great-Granny.

I remember Great-Granny. She lived in an old dark house full of spirits and rememberings. They would mostly stay downstairs talking and doing jobs, winding clocks, filling in forms, making food.

But sometimes they had to go upstairs where dust lay in thick layers and the shadows of happy days long ago were waiting to be discovered. And we might have to rifle through her wardrobes where shimmering dresses had hung for years, untouched. They still smelt of music and laughing and dancing. There was a pair of boots with traces of mud stuck to the laces, mud from a mountain probably, maybe from a favourite place. At the back of one wardrobe was a musty fur coat that had stories about distant Christmases and snowy winter days hidden under the collar.

No one hardly ever came into these rooms now. It was just us and the rememberings. Great-granny hadn't been able to get up the stairs for years. I loved it up there. The cold air rippling in the silence.

Downstairs in the little room where Great-granny lived now, it was always stuffy and hot, even though Great-granny shivered. It smelt of old oak coffer, where the cups and saucers rattled, or wind in the chimney.

The last time I saw Great-granny was the day they came to tell her some news. They were excited. They started off with normal things.

"So, how've you been today?"

"I've been tamping mad, that's what. Ever since the breakfast news. I've been writing a letter in my head to that Michael Portillo. Dear Sir, my husband didn't risk his life diffusing Hitler's bombs so that the likes of you could get into power. I decided not to call him a fascist so-and-so up-front, I don't want people dismissing me as a Commie." She coughed. "And I tell you what, aren't you sick to the back teeth with this weather. Gets in your bones and on your chest."

"They think it might ease up a bit next week. And it'll be March soon. Maybe we'll get you out into the sunshine for a bit."

"Maybe. But tell me what you two have been up to."

They both smiled.

"We've got some good news, Gran. Well, *we* think it's good news. You're going to be a great-grandmother."

"Aha! Thought as much. And how long have I got to wait before I can don this title."

"Oh, another five months. Mum said you wouldn't be very pleased about it."

"Oh, I'm pleased as punch! I'm delighted! I'm happy if you're happy."

And she winked at me.

Great-grand Memories

I remember Great-granny in other ways. There are rememberings wherever you go, not just the ones that cling to real things, but also the ones from my Perfect Red Sea.

In my Perfect Red Sea there was always somewhere exciting to play. World after world to explore. All her rememberings, stored away. And not just the ones from her own life, but also, *her* mother's rememberings, discovered when *she* was a baby in her Perfect Red Sea. And when you dipped your hand into one rock pool to pull out an interesting remembering, you disturbed all the other rememberings in the pool and they swirled up to the surface: all the things she'd ever done or seen or felt; all the things Granny had ever done, all the things Great-granny had ever done. And as I played, I made all the rememberings my own.

That was how I got to know Great-granny. I found the day when she first met Great-grandpa and she stuttered and stumbled and didn't dare to look in his eyes, and the day when she danced with him for the first time, and her heart swung round inside her with happiness. And then there was the first time they kissed in the dingy passageway between the houses, where no one could see them. And of course, the day when Great-granny discovered her favourite place.

Great-granny was squealing because the water was like icicles. It felt like lots of tiny needles, tingling right up to her ankles, oh but it was lovely. *Ah! Bliss to get those wretched boots off.* She whirled the water with her feet and watched how it made her legs look bent. *Long, skinny, spindly legs.* She held up her bare arms for the sun. *Skinny, spindly arms too, thin as sticks.*

The sun was hot and her neck felt sweaty. She lifted her hair off her neck and twisted it up against her head. With her spare hand, she reached for twigs and stuck two in her hair. When she took her hands away, her hair stayed up and she grinned. "What do you think of that?" She tipped her head so Great-grandpa could see. He laughed.

"Very Mother Earth".

"I hope not, thank you very much."

She lay back, not bothering about the prickly heather on her shoulders, *bony shoulders,* and her heart swelled. *I think this is the happiest I have ever been.* She looked at the upside-down mountain, The Notched Ridge, a slippery face glinting in the sunshine. *Must have been mad, trying to climb that, but that's what he's like, my man.* And her heart swelled again.

She tilted her head to see the floor of the glen, a long way down, *so green – if you put that in a picture people would think you couldn't paint for toffee,* and the water in the loch like a glassy blue sky.

He came and sat next to her. She watched him untie his boots. *Those fingers, long and delicate, I always was a one for fingers. I think it must have been his hands that made me fall in love with him – oh no, it was his eyes first,* and then he unpeeled his socks, *fine feet too,* carefully because there was blood on his heels, where his boots had rubbed. *And how did I get such a handsome boy to marry me? Gawky, painfully thin, painfully shy, nothing to write home about, little me? And look at me now, lying next to such a man, in such a perfect place,* and he lay back next to her. The hot sun, the empty sky, the empty mountains and just them, *as if the whole of Glencoe belongs to us....*

And she loved it there, at that moment, and so did I. It felt like we'd found the best place, like our souls had found the right body at last, like we were coming home.

I remember Great-granny.

And I remember the day when I was in my Perfect Red Sea and we sat on the stairs by the phone, her body gone stiff and cold, even though her heart thundered through us and she still held the phone in her hand. "I can't believe it.... It was only a chest infection... I thought she was okay.... Oh I knew we should have got the place draught proofed.... I told her...she was always so bloody independent...." Wave after wave of terrible sadness, welled up from somewhere very deep. My Perfect Red Sea throbbed with it. I was frightened. It was as if everything was rocking and I was about to be swamped with something unfathomable....

"At least she didn't suffer, sweets.... Maybe it's for the best, I mean.... She always knew her own mind, didn't she.... Maybe.... Look, we told her she was going to be a Great-grandmother on Saturday, and she dies on Monday.... It just seems that the timing. Maybe she knew it was the right time. Maybe it was what she wanted...."

And I remember how Great-granny had winked at me.

Two days after that, Great-grandpa came to see her in the night and she ran away with him and didn't look back.

Climbing Mountains

Great-granny's remembering made my soul sing because I knew I had stumbled on somewhere important. It was a favourite place for him, and her too, wasn't it? Yes, because I remember when we were on holiday, just a few days before I was born. I remember the sound of Stout Walking Boots. Crunch on the icy puddles. Crunch on the frozen bracken. I could tell the difference between hers and his. Hers went crunch with the bouncing of my bubble and stomp with the swushing of my Perfect Red Sea. It was a good day that. There was water, it gushed and splashed onto rocks. And suddenly, I knew where we were. We were walking below The Notched Ridge. Down in the valley. This was Glencoe.

He was being Safe and Dependable.

"Isn't that the path, over there?"

But we knew a better way. We knew that he'd follow us to stop us from slipping or doing something stupid.

"You be careful." We wobbled on a boulder. She made a face at him, but really we loved it when he worried about us. He would be there to catch us if we fell. That's what Safe and Dependable means.

I loved all the tipping and juggling, the rush of all that freezing air. We stood on a jut of rock and breathed deep – waves of fresh air to make my blood tingle.

"It's rubbish here, isn't it?"

"Yeah, shall we go back home?"

"Find something decent to look at."

"Like the Arndale."

"Or the M60 flyover."

"Or Strangeways."

She put her hand on her belly. "When you're big enough, we'll bring you back here to see it for yourself."

"On its first birthday."

"First! You'll have to carry it. Anyway, August is no good, too many midges."

"I won't mind carrying it. Alright, Spring then."

And in my Perfect Red Sea, I thought, that's funny, because they think I know nothing, and that if they talk and tell me things then I will know more. But that's not how it is. If they could only listen, I could whisper to them: I know this place. I know The Three Sisters. How they rise arm in arm, out of the ground. I know they are huge and scary. They drip with straight lines of water – icy, sharp, glittery. I know this place already. I've hidden with souls that live in the nooks and crannies. They seep into the air, whisper in the quiet. They make you smell laughter in the grass and betrayal around the boulders. I know this place.

When I lie still in my Hot House, and try to think what I mean about Glencoe, I mean nothing. But back in my Perfect Red Sea, when I breathed that place in, I just *knew*. That's why they went there. It makes you tired, This Living, and they went there to find something they had forgotten, something they couldn't remember how to know. You can feel you've forgotten something but can't remember what. Almost everyone has memories like Glencoe, lurking deep and mysterious. It's just that doing This Living is so hard, no one seems to remember....

"Are you cold?"

"Just thought you deserved a cuddle."

"People might see."

"Only people with binoculars."

"There's a sheep there. Sheep can be very prudish."

"Doesn't stop them from weeing in public. Look at that one."

"You scared it."

"I only looked at it."

"Well then."

She laughed. "Come on baby. He'll just get a double dose tonight," and we started climbing up and up.

I love climbing mountains. Mountains go on and on and things keep getting better and better. There's always something to keep climbing for. Unless you fall. Falling off a mountain is worse than falling off a flat field, which is really only tripping up, isn't it? Some people would rather live on a flat field and only ever trip up. And that's alright because if you're afraid of falling, maybe you shouldn't climb mountains. But fields are boring and mountains are exciting. I'm going to be a mountaineer when I grow up.

"Turquoise and yellow?" We were out of breath.

"Turquoise and yellow! It won't be able to sleep."

"Babies like bright colours."

"Thought yellow made you go mad."

"My office is yellow."

"There you are then. Anyway there's plenty of time. We'll have changed our minds seven times by then."

And so we bounced along. They forgot to tell me what they could see. That's what happens with parents-to-be. They were making plans, silly plans, just an excuse to splash around in the future. And I played at springing myself from one wall to another, drunk on the feelings sloshing through her blood. Yellow and blue, yellow and white, yellow and yellower, it was all the same to me, but if it made them happy, then it made me happy. I did three somersaults in a row. I just couldn't help it. *Um duddle do, um duddle doo dunk dunk dunk.*

She leant against him, breath short, body heavy.

"I told you not to overdo it."

"I'll have to roll all the way down."

"You will not."

She grinned and we slumped down in the snow.

"Cream-crackered."

"We can sit here for a moment. Give the sheep something to blush about."

And when was all that? You need to know because days are important. It was a spring day. April. It wasn't so long ago. It was a week before I was born.

When I Found My Important Place

Crash sha sha shaaa!

Glencoe!

This is it! Of course. They knew it was an Important Place too, that it must mean something, but they couldn't remember what. Something was drawing them to it and memories stirred in their hearts when they came here.

Those memories are mine now. In this place souls have been before and left their mark and all their stories have seeped into the land. I can feel that the Important Story is here somewhere, maybe hiding behind a tree or under a boulder. But no, it's much deeper than that. Maybe it's spread in handfuls inside the earth. Maybe each pebble that rattles in the waterfall has a bit of the story locked inside it.

Oh, I'm going to find it all out, stories, feelings, things that can't be told in words. I'm going to go back and back inside my rememberings, the ones I snaffled from her, and from her mother, and all the mothers going back into time, and it's all going to fit together somehow.

Day 21

And I-I kno-oh-ow, he will never burden be.
He's not heavy, he's my bay-ay-ay-be...

She would sing it soft and mournful, beating the rhythm gently with her fingers on my see-through walls. And often there were alarms ringing somewhere and she would pitch the notes to match with the *pling pling pling!*

Our path is a weary one, and many have lost their way,
Stumbling through every twist and turn.
But we'll not falter, my shoulder strong till we get there.
He's not heavyyyy, he's my bay-ay-ay-be.

The machine went *clunk thud whoosh*. Lots of times a minute. At first I did nearly all the breathing myself. I was a very good boy. Suckpushsuckpush. But the road was long, with many a winding turn.

Mmmmmmmm– mmmmmmmmm,
And I-I kno-oh-ow, he will never burden be.
He's not heavy, he's my bay-ay-ay-be...

I never really liked this one. It was nice because I knew she was there, but it was really dreary. Who wants dreary? Not me. Dreary made me frightened. I mustn't be frightened, Grandpa told me. I must be strong. But it was hard when she was being so sad. Dreary made my chest go tight and when my chest went tight: *pling pling pling!* All my chimes start and important numbers flash red. She stops singing straightaway, face gone white, eyes flicking to the monitor. The numbers are falling quickly with every flash. She looks at me, bites her lip, eyes back to the monitor, falling, falling, She looks around for a nurse, hiding her panic, then back at me to check I'm not going blue, the Terror rising, numbers falling...There are no nurses anywhere near.

I start to feel dizzy, might get some great starry pictures soon. "Come on Saul. Do some nice breathing." She tries to sound calm as she rubs the whizzydizzy smell on her hands. *Click clack ack ack.* She strokes my chest, that's nice. I try to breathe, spoonful of air, got to squeeeeeeze it past the hurting and the gunge in my chest. *Pling pling pling!* Still chiming but getting better. "Good boy, good little boy." Her voice smells of desperate relief. "Just a few more." She strokes my chest. I'm a good boy. The numbers start to climb back up. "That's better." She takes a breath herself. She can breathe deep, it doesn't hurt and her shoulders droop. One day I'll breathe as deep as that, as easy, as smooth, as painless as that.

Today, I was twenty-one days old. I'd had lots more slithers and falls since the Big Fall. And no matter how often it happened, we never got used to it, even though it could happen lots of times a day. Because we never knew for sure whether it was all suddenly going to end. Every day was full of fighting. Oh, but I never gave up. Even though my body was saying, *enough, enough, enough.* When you're climbing mountains you just have to keep pushing onwards, getting up after every fall and carrying on.

"On your own today?"

"Yeah, Tim's had to go back to work. Used up his holiday allowance."

"That's mean. Can't he get his doctor to give him a sick note?"

"Doesn't get sick pay. And he won't have a job to go back to if he stays away any longer. And Daddy needs a job, doesn't he Saul, to keep you in the manner to which you're accustomed...?"

It was a nurse I didn't know. She switched off the bleep and let the numbers flash with no noise.

"He went down to seventy-five but now he's climbing up again...I don't suppose he needs suction, probably not, I just thought...."

She was trying not to be too pushy. She was always friendly. Always. She wanted them to be nice to me when she wasn't here. The nurse hovered, gave me a glance, checked the machines.

"I could hear you singing over there."

"Oh sorry...."

"No, it's lovely. Go on, sing some more."

"Actually I don't think he likes it very much."

"Course he does."

The nurse swam off around the room, switching alarms off as she went.

You are my everything.
You make me want to sing.
You make the sun shi-ine, and the be-ells ring.
And you can't kno-ow, how much joy you bring.
So ple-ease don't go,
Don't go stopping my everything.

She swallowed, carried on. I liked this one so I let myself go floppy, the Terror falling, numbers rising. She gazed in on me, her mouth right up against the see-through wall. Her face was full of smiling. The numbers rose to high and the chiming started again. She glanced to the side and smiled. Bleeps at the top were good. We sang and danced together, my bleeps, her voice, my toes, her hands.

I arched my back and wiggled into a better position. It wasn't easy, I was strapped down so tight with wires and tubes and things. But I shifted enough to feel a bit more comfy and closed my eyes. The machine went hiss, thunk, hiss, thunk. She went hum, and hum. Hiss and hum, hiss and hum, hiss and hum. Hissum hissum hissummmmmmmm....

When She Had to Rush

I can't ever remember a time in my Perfect Red Sea when I didn't know her. From the beginning, she was all around me, my whole world. I never thought of her as special, she was always...just there. Everything she saw, I saw; everything she felt, or thought, I felt and thought. Everything I am now is linked with her.

I remember hot baths, the smell of baby oil, the steam, and her singing to me as the water sloshed. I remember the taste of chocolate, cold feet warming in front of the fire and socks scorching, falling asleep on the sofa. I remember the cold of the window on her cheek as she leaned against it, the sound of the wheels going *clickety-clickety*, the sickness when she opened her eyes, the way her chest sagged when she knew the tunnel was coming to an end and we'd soon be in the station. *Why don't I just stay on all the way to Scarborough*. I remember doors slamming and climbing stairs that went on forever, up and up two at a time. *Hurry, hurry, can't be late again, third flight, fourth flight, fifth, made it! Thank God*, pant, pant, *feeling dizzy, never mind, ignore it,* pant, pant, and the phone ringing. And no matter what time of day, a sea of faces waiting and you had to try to get up the stairs without anyone stopping you or else you never got where you wanted to get...

"Rosie, can you...."

"Ah, Rosie just the person...."

And she didn't want to but sometimes she couldn't help it – she hated it.

"Oh Naomi, is it important, can it wait, I've a meeting in five minutes and I've *got* to eat something." *Otherwise I'll chuck up all over you.* And then she saw the brown eyes look away so sad, and she felt really mean. She was always feeling really mean.

"Okay, but I've got to eat my sandwiches whilst you're talking...."

And she could tell from those brown eyes that this was going to be a shut-the-door talk, so she shut the door.

"So, how can I help?"

She waited. "Is it something to do with college, or is it personal?"

"Someone said you were the right person... I've got ....problems."

Yeah well that's the trouble with sorting out people's problems, word spreads.

"Have you spoken to your own tutor about this?"

"Oh yeah, like when? She's never fucking *around*."

She wanted to say a lot, but instead she held down a sigh.

"Well let's see what I can do for you then." She smiled at the girl and got an angry stare.

She waited. And glanced at the clock.

The brown eyes saw her and the clock.

"Yeah, like you'd be interested."

A black cloud settled around her heart. *God I'm so crap, so crap.*

"I'm sorry we're all rushed off our feet, sometimes we let the important things...anyway, I'll do my best now, eh? So, what's troubling you?"

"I've been coping with a bit of...shit recently, that's all."

"Like what?"

"My Mum's boyfriend. I've had to move out."

"Right, well I'll get you to see a student counselor this afternoon."

"I don't need no counseling. I've got my brother."

"Right. And this is the brother who...I thought he was in prison."

"It's alright, I'm not into drugs or anything, you think I'm stupid?"

"No, I know you're highly intelligent."

The brown eyes looked angry and defiant, but full of tears.

"Oh Naomi." And she sagged inside, feeling helpless. *So crap, so crap.*

"I'm alright now, I can get my shit together."

"I'll call the student counselor now."

"Yeah right. I can get my own appointments, thanks. Sorry I *wasted* your time."

And the girl was gone. The door slammed. She sighed and wanted to cry. *So crap.*

She glanced at her watch. *Shit!* Grabbed a file. *So crap so crap.* She opened the door, a sea of faces. *Oh bloody hell.* "Is it important, can't it wait?" And she wanted to cry but didn't let it happen.

"Aah, we've been waiting for ages."

"We've climbed all this way an' all." *Bang goes any hope of preparing for this afternoon's classes.*

She looked at faces. Bitten lips, sad eyes. "Okay. You've got twenty seconds each. You first."

When She Felt Sick

Early mornings in my Perfect Red Sea. I was warm, but she was cold and her bones would shiver. Iciness spread up from the ground, through her legs and into me, even though she stamped her feet and tried to hide from the wind.

"We apologise to passengers on platform thirteen, awaiting the delayed seven-twenty-three TransPennine Express. This train has now been cancelled. Passengers should proceed to platform one, where the seven-forty-five to Hull is waiting to depart."

And we sighed. *Here we go again*. She picked up her bags and began to walk. Up the steps. Each one an effort. She wanted to stop and rest, to lean against the dirty walls, to slide down and not get up again. But we had to hurry. Over the bridge and down the steps on the other side.

We ran but the train sailed past us and away. She sagged, too weary. And at last we heaved ourselves back up the steps again. And over the bridge and back to where we started.

"We apologise to passengers on Platform thirteen, waiting for the eight-twelve to Scarborough. This train is reported to be running twenty-two minutes late."

We huddled in a corner, and she sighed and tried not to worry.

...Shit that report needs binding...catch the part-timers before lessons, to organise.... And got to ask her for time off, oh God, must do it before she goes into meeting...if I run all the way from the station....

And the train when it came was full of steamy, angry people. We had to stand all the way. That's how it was in the early mornings.

And at the other end, she dragged us up the hill, and up those stairs, to the top of the mountain where she sank into a chair. She stared at the yellow walls and felt sick.

She had to do it. She was dreading it. She knocked, went in, looked at the desk piled high and the woman behind it, sucking on a cigarette. I could smell it. The air was thick. She tried to take short breaths.

"Er, Hi." *Mustn't cry.*

"Hi there!" Long suck, eyes half closed. "How's things?"

"Er...have you got a moment?"

"Mmm" (Long stream of smoke) "Oh anything exciting to report whilst I was away?"

"Yeah, I put a list of everything on your desk."

"Oooer, had a bit of a landslide this morning. Oh too bad. I'm sure you handled everything wonderfully."

Mustn't cry. She gave up with the little breathing and breathed deep. She swallowed because of the lump in her throat.

"My Gran died on Monday and...and the funeral's next week. I've spoken to Janice, who's prepared to swap some lessons so my classes will be covered...."

"Oh God. I'm so sorry to hear that. What a bugger. And you've been having a lot of time off recently, what with all your ante-natals. Officially you're only allowed time off for immediate family, you know. Mean isn't it, but Grandmothers don't count."

"So, what, I can't go?"

"Well I wonder if I could cover your back, depending how long, an hour or two maybe, so people don't suspect."

She tried not to breathe. Her tummy churned.

Smoke shot into the air in a thick tube. "...Look, what time of day is it?"

"Eleven. And it's a two hour drive from here."

"Well, maybe. As long as you're back for the afternoon...."

When She Wanted to Scream

It was another world now: trains, stairs, smoke, slamming doors, and we were the centre of it, very busy every day. It stopped so suddenly. One day she was running up and down those stairs, and then we're in here, in the middle of a different world and all the details of that other place are forgotten, not really important any more.

I suppose it's still going on without us. Are all the people still waiting at her door? And is another person talking to them and sorting them out, working through the pile of papers on her desk, writing messages on little yellow stickers and putting them on the wall, answering the phone, and always, always watching the hands of the clock, squeezing more and more into each minute?

And does someone else rush downstairs like she did, with her arms full of books and folders? And is someone else stopping on the stairs?

"So if you could just put together a module, sorry it's short notice, by the end of the day if you don't mind, but Evelyn's let us down again..."

And a few more steps down...

"Oh, can we have a meeting at lunchtime?"

"I don't get a lunch break today."

"Oh, well, it's about your request to have your contact hours reduced. Head just made some snide remarks about wimps and shirkers, I'm afraid. In fact, you'll be lucky if I manage to hold them as they are."

And she wanted to scream, but she swallowed it down and made her voice as calm as she could "Oh, come *on*. Didn't you explain to him.... I can't keep this pace...this workload.... It's not...sensible...when I've had to take the odd day off, my classes aren't covered and I come back to chaos, and the students are...." Her voice began to rise, so she had to stop.

And sometimes she would fly into the toilets and lock the door, and slither down the walls and let the books and folders fall onto the floor and the tears fall onto her lap.

But it's all over now, all that, and it doesn't matter anymore.

Day 23

Somehow, whenever Dr Magic was in the Big Air, everything was easier to bear. Today, when I was twenty-three days old, the whole of the Big Air was bubbling with laughter and giggles and chatter. And it was all because of Dr Magic.

"I wasn't always this ugly, I'll have you know. I was quite a pretty little boy, when I was five. So my mother said."

Nurse Clean Flowers was here as well today, but she wasn't looking after me, she had other babies, over where Dr Magic was. "Mothers'll tell you anything, if it'll make you behave. Bet you were a right handful."

"Too well behaved for my own good, from what I remember. Wasted childhood. I should have been learning to kick footballs through neighbours' windows."

Everyone laughed. Except Nurse Chirpy, who was fiddling with my wires, pretending. But her fingers got warm every time Dr Magic spoke, and her chirpy bird heart fluttered.

"Might be playing for Liverpool now, instead of wasting my time playing doctors and nurses in the middle of the night."

A great wave of laughter. We loved it.

"Are you trying to say you don't like working with us, Stephen?"

"Wouldn't dare. You're all a joy and a pleasure to work with. But it's not the same as running around with Ryan Giggs, is it? You haven't got the legs for a start."

They roared.

"When did he get to see your legs, Nina, anyway?"

"In his dreams."

"Is that what *Fantasy Football* is, Stephen?"

"Hey, I like to keep my fantasies realistic. They usually include Liverpool winning the cup."

"And you scoring the winning goal, yeah, yeah."

"I know, sad bastard. I can't help it. I blame my hormones, all this testosterone gets the better of me."

It was great to hear all that loud laughing. (I couldn't see a lot today, my eyes were stuck shut with nasty stuff. Nurse Chirpy had to squeeze cream in them to make the nasty stuff go away. "Not nice to have eye infections, is it cherub? Nasty, nasty bugs...")

Then, when Nurse Chirpy was changing the wires on my belly, Dr Magic came over to my Hot House. Through my sticky eyes I could see he was hiding a smile. "So what do you think about the latest head scan results?"

"What head scan...?" He and she froze. Their faces unsmiled, just for a moment.

"It's all right. It's good news. Very good. Apparently the bleed has almost completely resolved. No evident damage..."

"Now, that *is* brilliant. Isn't that brilliant Ginny?"

"Ah, I expected nothing less," and she grinned. Her head was down, looking in at me, but suddenly her eyes flicked up just enough to look at Dr Magic. He was looking back. Nurse Chirpy quickly looked down again, trying not to smile, but her face wasn't doing what she wanted it to. Her eyes were resting on me, but her inside thoughts were playing all over her face.

Dr Magic laid his arm on the top of my house. "And any further bleeds at this stage are extremely unlikely, you know. So really we can rule out brain damage, now."

"You can? Oh that's....Saul did you hear that?"

Dr Magic often leant on my house like that, when he talked and laughed with them.

But today it was as if his arm was making the air all around it buzz. Nurse Chirpy's shoulder was near it and although she never looked away from me, she must have been able to feel it. You could almost see the air trembling around her shoulder.

Dr Magic grinned. "Thought you'd be pleased."

He and she wanted to hug him, I could tell. "Of course...aren't you?"

"Well let's say, it's satisfactory."

"Satisfactory! Don't you mean brilliant?"

They were all smiling at me.

"Afraid 'brilliant' isn't part of our medical vocab."

"So, is 'satisfactory', doctor-speak for 'really good' then?"

"First thing we learn as doctors, that. To play with the nuances of the word: Satisfactory. There's Quite Satisfactory, which is better than Almost Satisfactory. And between those two, Approaching Satisfactory. In Saul's case I suppose I might even get all adventurous and say: Very pleasing."

Dr Magic's hair flopped over his eyes, but he didn't bother to brush it away.

Nurse Chirpy was sort of frozen, as if she didn't know what to do with the trembling, as if she didn't dare move her shoulder.

I'd been without my nappy now for ages, and the cold made me want to squirt. So I arched my back and sprayed the top of my house. It was great fun. I wiggled at the same time and the golden water hit both walls. Nurse Chirpy wasn't frozen any more. She yelled. Her hands were dripping.

"Saul you bugger!"

Everyone was laughing, especially Dr Magic. "Saul! You don't catch me weeing over nurses like that."

Nurse Chirpy gave him a look. "Wouldn't put it past you. Medical students would do anything for a laugh."

"Ah, but I'm not a medical student. I'm a mature and responsible senior house officer, if you don't mind!"

"Mature! Men can't be mature. You're all the same, with or without your nappies."

More laughing. It was brilliant. And Nurse Chirpy was so pleased with herself, she wasn't even mad about the mess I'd made. "Oh well, I needed to change his incubator anyway."

So, she didn't freeze any more. But she listened out for Dr Magic all day and then pretended to ignore him. When he came over to steal blood from the baby next to me, she pushed him out of the way, "Mind! New incubator coming through!"

He had to stand and watch as Nurse Chirpy lifted me safe and quick out of my old house and into the new. *Peeeeeeeek!* "Our vent!" and Nurse Clean Flowers followed behind with all my tubes and wires in her hands. I sank down into a clean-smelling, woolly bed.

Nurse Chirpy chuckled. "You like that sheepskin don't you? Yes, you're saying, thank you Auntie Ginny for snaffling that away for me. Thought you deserved a bit of luxury. And what about some Oil of Olay mm? NHS standard. Keeps you young."

Dr Magic leant over me, close to Nurse Chirpy. "He's young enough, isn't he?"

But Chirpy Bird was still pretending. She ignored him.

"Tickly toes. Yes, you like that don't you, yes."

Through my sticky eyes I could see her face. She was listening to magic feet disappear down the corridor.

Days 25-27

It just crept up on us. There were so many little hurdles and hurtings, so many comings and goings, that I didn't notice how, bit by bit, ever so slowly, in little ways, I was getting better.

It started with a bit of spring in my fingers, and later in my toes, and the springiness was spreading, and little pockets of space opened up inside until I was nearly breathing on my own, until one day, a doctor came to steal my blood and I looked in his eyes and I knew. The Big Moment was here.

"Thought you'd like to know. I've just done a gas and it's quite good really. I can't reduce his breaths any further. So....looks like you'll have to come off the ventilator , Saul...."

"Really! Today? We didn't think..."

"It might not be for long. They tend to go on and off for a while. He'll need to be on a CPAP machine, at first – nasal prongs, which stop his lungs collapsing completely . But we'll be expecting you to do all the breathing yourself, young Saul."

When the tube slithered out, I was big and empty. They stuck something too fat up my nose. It went SSSSHHHHHHHHHH very loud, a cold burning, right down to my throat. My nostrils were stretched open by it. It kept falling out and then the rushing air burst cold against my cheek. You couldn't hear or smell or even think. I moved my head from side to side, trying to escape, but the mask was on tight.

"He doesn't like it, does he?"

"They never do at first. I haven't been able to get a good seal really. The nasal prongs are far too big for him. And his breathing's started to deteriorate a bit... Maybe it's time we put him back. He's done ever so well though. Five hours is a long time for a little one. Isn't it blossom?"

I punched Nurse Scurry's velvet fingers with my fist. Give me my Tube back!

So they did.

The next time I tried harder. I ignored the way it stung my nose and made my eyes water. See me? Watch me! I can do it. I couldn't hear but I saw them smile. No more *clunk thud whoosh* for me! No more sharp knives slicing. Just me, breathing ever so carefully.

She and he were excited. They'd been waiting a long time, and now they could stop pretending at last.

"Look at his hair, Tim. He's been growing a thick head of hair under his hat all this time..."

"And now you can see his face better, I never noticed before, he's got your ears...Oh, Saul, you're *so* beautiful...."

After a while I didn't want the Tube any more. It was nice to feel big and empty. My mouth and throat were big, empty holes. They sucked in tubes of big empty air down into my big empty chest. And although it was hard to do it on my own, I got to like it and I decided: I'm going to keep breathing like this for ages and ages.

"I don't know if the doctors have told you, but really, we consider him past the Critical stage now. He's still got a long way to go, of course, but he's stable, so he won't suddenly collapse and die on us anymore."

"Do you hear that Saul? You can't die on us any more. Now that's an order!"

"The only way now that we might...lose him, is if an overwhelming infection were to take a hold. And he *will* get infections, so you mustn't worry too much when he does, but we'll just have to hope he's strong enough to fight them off by then."

Day 29

I'd been into the Big Air before. But only for tiny moments. This time it was different.

"Saul, you're a little champion. Fancy being four weeks old! Four whole weeks...!" He was on his own today.

"Mummy's got to wait at home, Saul. For your Great Oak Coffer to be delivered. It's a family heirloom and your Great-granny gave it you just before she died. So you can put all your toys in it, or whatever you want...."

Nurse Chirpy was undoing all my wires and things.

"Actually, I've got to weigh him and I was wondering, since he's got to come out anyway, how about giving him his first cuddle?"

And that was the first time he held me.

His voice boomed out here in the Big Air.

"Oh Saul. You're so...he's like a tiny wired-up little kitten, it's like holding a little Action Man...."

"Let's wrap the blanket a bit tighter. There we go. Just hold the CPAP tubes under your arm to keep them steady. And hold the rest of his wires in your right hand, that's it. And just move his head a little so his neck is straight. There we are. Snug as a bug in a rug."

"It's just...it's just...indescribable!"

I sink into his great sweaty hand and we melt together. I can hear a heartbeat thumping deep and low, and I ebb to and fro on his chest. I am safe, really safe at last, covered in a huge, strong-smelling feeling. I want to stay wrapped up in it for ever.

He sings to me, really deep rumbling, so we shake together. And it's so nice, that I start to sleep. He rocks me gently and strokes my chest with his thumb.

From here, I can look into his eyes. Deep brown eyes. My eyes. I'm gushed full of his feelings. It makes me glad I've tried so hard. My aching chest swells, proud that he belongs to me.

And when I see his eyes go wet and feel him hold me tighter, I know that this is the best moment yet, that this is worth waiting for, that here is a Reason. It's all so that I can lie in his hands like this, that he can hold me safe and strong, so I can look in his eyes and think: this is my Daddy.

Part Four

Day 30

Wouldn't it be nice if it was all easy after that? If I just got fatter and bigger and grew up to be a naughty boy like all the other naughty boys. But I knew that I still had a lot of climbing to do. And so I suppose, when things changed all over again, I wasn't so surprised.

It was when Nurse Chirpy took me out of my Hot House again that I realised how funny I felt.

"It's only fair. Since Daddy's had a cuddle."

I was laid on her chest. I could tell she wasn't calm though. She was stiff with worry. We tried to melt together, to make it like it was with Daddy. But my toes were fizzing. The fizziness spread up my legs and flooded through me. It made me feel hot and cold and hot again. When she sang, her breath was draughty on my face and I didn't like it. Everything she did made it worse.

"What is it darling?"

My bottom was stinging, something nasty going jab jab jab. And I was achy and tired all over. She flicked her eyes to the machines.

"He's not very happy. His sats are falling."

"Let's give him a smidgen more oxygen."

I wanted to be good for her. So I gripped her fingers and ignored the hurting. But you couldn't ignore the fizziness. At last I couldn't bear it any more. I looked into her eyes.

Help me, Mummy, help me! I said it over and over. I knew she heard. A tear dripped from her lashes. And she said, so no one else could hear, *Oh Saul. If I could, I would, but I don't know how to. I don't know what to do.*

Not long after, they put me back into my Hot House. And I stopped thinking about breathing any more.

"His gases aren't good, I'm afraid. Better re-intubate...."

The fizziness was everywhere and I couldn't stop it. It made me feel empty and heavy at the same time.

"Leave him on fifty breaths. Maybe his lungs closed down towards the end. I'll order an x-ray..."

I didn't open my eyes after that, didn't want to see the disappointment hidden in their faces, didn't want to think how much I'd let them down. All day and night I lay still and did nothing, even when Mummy tried to do my nappy, even though she sang to me, even when she gasped and put my legs down quickly.

"Ginny, he's got blood in his nappy. And he's got sort of...black...bruises, no blacker than a bruise, look, on both buttocks, the whole buttock...."

"Don't worry, It's probably just...I'll tell Dr Anderson...."

It wasn't my fault. I really did try to be good. But I'd been taken over. It was stronger than me.

Dr Calm was still calm.

"I'm afraid, we're probably looking at a serious infection. Can you do more blood cultures, and samples from the nasopharyngeal tube, bladder, the usual. Meanwhile we'll get him back on general antibiotics. And those buttocks...very unusual. Could be his clotting process isn't up to scratch. Give him some Vitamin K...and some more blood. Might improve his colour if nothing else... And I don't like the way his hernia's going black...mmmm, perhaps we're talking about necrotic embolisms, although I've never seen it on buttocks before. Awkward place to dress and keep clean too. Vaseline for the moment, I think, nurse...."

Oh, Grandpa. They stuck things in me. Sucked things out of me. Poked and scratched all day and all night. Never let up for longer than a few minutes. Always waking me up. Messing. Hurting. I was sick of them. Sick of it all. I didn't care about Mummy, or Daddy. I didn't care about Reasons. I didn't even care about climbing mountains. I just wanted them all to *leave me alone*.

It was then, for the first time, that I really wanted to die.

Day 31

One day in the wilderness. Voices curl out of the mist.

"Right. So. Saul... Well, rather disappointing... identified two separate forms of septicaemia... Bacterial one...started to respond to the antibiotics so I'm less worried about that one... More worrying is the fungal septicaemia...takes much longer to eliminate... if you see what I mean...three to four weeks of anti-fungal treatment...danger of kidney failure...potent drugs... Be positive, babies *have* recovered from colonisations like this...kidney scan which revealed fungal balls...monitor closely...wounds on his bottom...very unusual...possibly necrotic embolisms...mind if we photograph them...useful for my lectures...."

It goes into my arm. Cold and rushing. Shoots through me. Makes me strange. Mixes with the strangeness already there. I am gone to a different place. A place where shapes and sounds balloon and twist. I am empty. My body isn't mine....

"X-Ray!"

Don't move. There is pain....

"Well, if he needs another blood transfusion, then he's going to need another arterial line. I can't fit all these drugs in as it is, and this one on his arm is definitely on its last legs, and that ruddy syringe driver's broken again....."

Don't move. There is pain.

"Are you Mum? I'm here to do a heart scan......"

Don't move.

"I'm just checking those wounds on your buttocks, poppit...Phooo! They're even worse than...deep aren't they? I'm just going to put some of this gel on, poppit. I'm sorry, it must be ever so painful, so sorry poppit...To draw out the nasty...Doesn't like to be handled does he?"

Pictures in my head. Whizzydizzy sounds. I am strange....

"What kind of side effects?"

"Well, diarrhoea, for a start, which won't help those open wounds on his buttocks – diarrhoea's very acid, you know. Adults also report lethargy, dizziness, confusion, hallucinations...."

They put me on my tummy. I don't move. They put me on my side. I don't move. They put me on my back. I scream.

"The bad news is that the heart scan has revealed that there's a vegetation in the aorta, which leads from the heart. The concern is that if this infected debris breaks off, it could block other vital blood vessels to the kidneys, lungs, digestive system or brain. All of which would be...we wouldn't be able to avoid...."

"And the good news."

"The good news is that at least we know it's there so we can monitor it..."

They talk to me. They touch me. My eyes are shut. Here in this world, I am still.

"More blood cultures, I'm afraid....Why don't you take a break. I'll be about twenty minutes...."

Scrape. Scrape. Go away. Oh please. Grandpa! Tell them. Please!

"Are you Mum? I'm a surgeon. Alistair asked me to check your son's hernia...apparently it's....Jesus! Now that's what I call a hernia."

"Is it big then?"

"Listen, I specialise in operating on prem babies' hernias and I can safely say, a hernia down to the knees is pretty spectacular. Well done, son. Still the bigger they are, the easier to manip...ulate...Oh dear, didn't like that, sorry son, got to be done....For the moment I'll just push...all the gut back inside... Yes, thank you, son, very nice, one of the hazards of playing with hernias that – oh, there's more – nurse! I've got shit all over the shop here... Well don't need to operate on that just yet..."

"Surely he's too little to...."

"Precisely. But if an obstruction occurs, we'll have no choice... Anyway, I'll keep an eye on him. And cheer up – he's in good hands...."

My insides are acid. They squirt out from between my buttocks. Acid on my skin. Burning. They wash it off. But it comes again. My insides bubble and churn and explode.

"Oh Saul! Can you believe it! I've just given him a clean sheet as well. Projectile pooh all over the inside of his incubator...."

Swollen. Sore. Let it happen....

"Sorry about this. Got to do another urine sample. Why don't you both grab another coffee or something...."

Pain can pierce through the swirling. I scream and thrash. Please! Oh Grandpa, Let me die. Oh please. Oh please....

Bleep bleep bleep!

"Can I have some help here. Blocked tube... Right. Re-intubate...that's twice today... Poor little boy...."

I am always thirsty. I dream of water. It is swirling. I feel sick. I am sick. It bubbles up and tastes bad in my mouth. Tubes in. Tubes out. Knives inside.

How's he doing today...? Oh no...that's not very fair....

How's Sauly boy...? Oh what a shame....

How's my little hero...? Oh Poor Saul....

Poorly Sauly....

Days 32-53

And that's how it was for twenty-one days.

When I Tried to Escape

Oh, if I could just tiptoe away, just for a moment, just ramble back to my Important Place, where there will be no hurting, if I could just tiptoe away and not let the hurting find me....

There *is* such a place. Buried somewhere. Under all this, under all my rememberings. I found it before. I've been back to it since. I've been wandering through the great-grand memories, and much further back than that, back to where the grass is silky in the breeze and the water tumbles. If I could just follow the water gushing into the glen. If I could run on the soft cold grass and feel the soft cold air on my buttocks. Oh Grandpa if I could just hide where the hurting can't find me. Help me Grandpa. Help me back to my Important Place.

Day 54

"I've just asked a doctor to prescribe some Calpol. It breaks my heart every time I have to dress those wounds. He never stops crying...."

Hurting comes in waves. Now and now and now. Swamping, from my feet to my head, till I'm too tired to feel any more. The waves keep coming. Now and now and now. Stronger than me. Knocking me back into the sheets. The sheets are hard. When will it stop? At first I fought it. But now...now...now....

"Can I ask you something?"

"Of course. Anything."

"It's just that....Nursing all these poorly babies day after day... How can you bear it? Knowing that what you do is hurting them...I mean, some people might not care, but you obviously do."

"Well it's easier for us than for you, but...the only way...is to think that when they're five years old, they'll have forgotten the pain and be happy little children."

"It's just that...oh, it doesn't matter...."

"What?"

"It's just that...sometimes I feel trapped. Saul's still got so much to get through... I don't know. It's like we're seven weeks down the tunnel and we can't get out now... Unless he goes through more...."

"Think about Saul when he's five years old and running around like other healthy children. Does that make it easier?"

"Maybe... So seven weeks of hell and counting...."

The hurtings were melting. Just enough....

"That seems to have settled him a little anyway."

I open my eyes. Everything is bright and white. No pain? I wriggle my feet and bottom on the sheets, just to check. The pain is there but sort of muffled. I see Mummy. Her forehead is full of creases. And I smile at her and wave. Look at me Mummy! I can move and it doesn't hurt. I can point one toe to the roof and one toe to Mummy. I can turn my head and jiggle my elbows. Everything is warm and feels lovely.

She sings to me.

Dance for your daddy,
My little laddie,
Dance for your daddy,
My little lamb.

But sadly. Oh Mummy. Not *sadly*. Do it happily. Like I do when I punch the air with my feet. Because I'm doing This Living, and I'm all springy and it doesn't hurt. I'm still here. Fighting. Like I promised. Then she smiles. She hears me. And I see the thinking in her eyes. *How can you bear all this?*

So I look in her eyes and tell her all about the Reasons and how I'm going to find it all out soon. And she frowns, she doesn't really understand. But she says if I can bear it, then so can she. And I tell her about Grandpa and Inklings. She smiles, even though she doesn't really know what I mean. And it doesn't matter, it's a lovely chat anyway.

And later, when Daddy came, I danced for them both. I danced, oh for ages. And they sang and looked happy. And she let me suck a white fluffy stick dipped in milk. It was sweet. I sucked really hard until it was dry. And then we sang and danced again. It was fun.

And then, I felt it seeping back, the hurting, like water in sand, until it was stronger than me.

He put his arm around her, both of them smiling. "What a day we've had Saul. We've worn you out. We won't forget today in a hurry, will we?"

And I closed my eyes again. The hurting was back. Coming in waves. Now and now and now....

Ghosts

Great-granny started to see ghosts. She saw me when I was very tiny, right at the beginning when my body wasn't even a body. I could float in and out of all things in those days. She saw me out of the corner of her eye and she smiled.

On Christmas day, she came to our house. She saw a dog. Everyone was sitting around the table eating pudding. Great-granny wanted rum custard.

"Did you put any rum in this?"

"I put half the bottle in."

"I can't taste it."

Everyone laughed.

"Gran! We're all reeling from the fumes."

"I don't call that rum custard. Let's put some more in."

Great-granny was eating her rum custard and drinking her sherry when she saw the dog. She went "Humph!"

"What's the matter now?" (That was Wild Granny)

"I can see a dog. Sitting next to me with its paws up on the table. Get Down!"

Everyone looked at each other with worried eyes. Great-granny saw them.

"No, I'm not going gaga. I know there isn't *really* a dog. Probably just my eyes playing tricks. I just thought you'd like to know."

"It's the sherry and rum fumes, Gran."

"No, it's not.... I've been having visitors for a while now."

The others stopped eating.

"What sort of visitors?"

"Oh, various. Three little children came to tea yesterday. They all sat round the table and grinned, messing around, you know, as little children are wont to do."

"When did this start, why didn't you tell us before?"

"You two started it. When you came to see me a few weeks ago. I thought you had a little boy with you at first. But you didn't mention it. And then I realised that he wasn't real. And it was a week or so after that when the woman started sitting on the end of my bed in the middle of the night."

"Are they, I dunno, shadows or something?"

"I've no idea what they are. But I can see their faces and clothes, details, that sort of thing. This dog, for instance has got lovely brown eyes and a cheeky grin. Very nice red collar. Alsatian, I should think. And there's that little boy around here somewhere, playing under the table probably, looking up people's skirts or some such, I'll be bound."

"And are these people...do you recognise them at all?"

"I don't think I do, really."

"And...aren't you frightened when they...?"

"Oh no. They're all very friendly." Great-granny smiled. "I did get a bit annoyed last week with the woman who kept standing in front of my television. *Blind Date* was on and it's hard enough understanding what they're talking about at the best of times. People talk in such a slovenly fashion on these programmes. And some of them are so sordid and nasty, don't you find? Still, it's worth watching for the get-ups they parade in..."

"Yeah...just going back to these...hallucinations. You don't think, I hope it's not because...you know, ghosts or something, and you can see them because...."

"Because I'm about to kick the bucket? Oh, I do hope so."

"Gran, don't say that!"

"Why not? It's about time. I've been waiting long enough."

"Oh, Gran."

"You get fed up with it, Rosie. I don't know why I've kept hanging on for so long really...."

That's how I knew you could see ghost people, if you wanted. The first time I saw Grandpa, I knew it was him, I don't know how. I didn't just hear him talking in my head, I felt him, and somehow I *saw* him. It happened last night when they thought I was sleeping. There was a sort of hole torn in the Big Air. And the hole was really bright. A sort of sweet-smelling, singing-ringing light. The light made everything else in This Living seem dull and ordinary. And somehow, I can't really explain it, (some things just won't be explained in This Living), I knew Grandpa was inside the light.

Suddenly it all comes flooding back. All the knowings that have slipped away are as clear as before. And Grandpa says that now, if I want to, even though there are still things for me to learn, there is a way back and I can choose it and he'll take me back right now. If that's what I want.

And I think about it. About how everything was easier over there. I'd forgotten how easy it is just to *be*. Gliding. Playing with Grandpa....You see it's easy to forget. In This Living, no one really remembers. I suppose there's so much to learn about pretending, about worrying, about walking all stiff and upright in straight lines from the beginning, to the middle, never stopping till the end. And there's all those rules , the cans and can'ts of living, that get in the way of remembering.

But I remember it now. Gliding.

And I think I can do it all over again. Being there with him.

Let Nature help you, Grandpa says, let the wind and the waves and the water do the work, with the tiniest effort I can twist and turn and skip and dive

or I just *gliiide*... and *gliiiiide*... and *gliiiiide*....

No need for muscles or tendons or bones, no straight lines or hard edges. Everything is possible, everything goes everywhere, no beginnings, no endings, we just dip in and out spinning and twirling and *gliding*... *gliding*... *gliding*....

Bleepbleepbleep! Pling pling...!

"Saul, what are you up to in there? I turn my back for five minutes...."

Chirpy fingers were holding Hisser Snake. It went *zuuuuuuuuuugh*.

"...And you set all your alarms off. What a naughty Sauly. Now, you're not telling me you went to sleep and forgot to breathe...Oh no, it's all this nasty stuff to suck up here. Poor Sauly boy. You can't breathe with all that gunge can you? That's more like it."

And I can't glide any more. Now I'm as heavy as a tree trunk, rooted to This Living.

And it's hard, Grandpa, I know I said I wanted to die, but I'm not so sure, now you've offered. Suppose there's some good living to do just round the corner. And there are all the Reasons and Answers to find out about yet. Oh it's so hard to decide but, but.... this *is* an exciting mountain, Grandpa. And I think about leaving all this behind and I know I'm not quite ready. And I say to Grandpa, I don't really want to give up just yet. But thank you for asking.

And when I look up, there's no hole torn in the Big Air any more. No light. Grandpa has gone.

But now that I've seen Grandpa and now that I can remember everything he said and all about Gliding... Or a bit of what he said... Or, well, oh no, the knowing is slipping away again, and now it's only an Inkling of what he said... Hang onto your inklings, he said because....

Peeeeeeeeek! "My vent" *Uuuuummmmmm.*

I've forgotten.

Day 55

I push myself up on my arms with excitement. Listen, everyone!

"Saul, you're doing press-ups!"

"Full of beans today, aren't we?"

Never mind the hurting. (Which doesn't hurt so much today). I push myself up again. Listen! I look round. Who can I tell? Mummy, Daddy, I saw him again last night. Just for a moment and he told me lots of important things and knowings that you've all forgotten, but they make This Living easier, if you know them again....

But they don't hear. They're too busy talking.

"So if they're not so sure that the *Candida Sepsis* has gone, why are they stopping the anti-fungals?"

"The side effects are pretty severe. His acidosis and low electrolytes are causing problems. Plus, if he stays on the ventilator much longer, there's a risk he may never be weaned off...."

I do another push up.

"...So they want to get him on steroids again and they can't do that until he's finished the anti fungals..."

The doctor pulls my leg up. My arms flop and my face pushes into the sheets. Hey! I try to kick him. But I'm the wrong way up.

"He's certainly a strong little thing. Quite a battle doing a gas, nowadays. And we have to be careful, what with his bones being so brittle...."

Listen! I try to push my face sideways to look at them. Grandpa said you could see it as a sort of dream. When you're inside a dream you think it's real, he said, and you don't think there's anywhere else except that dream. And you can't remember what was going on before you went to sleep, even if you've got an Inkling...oh and the important thing, he said, is to hang on to your Inklings....

Somebody turns me over.

"Open wide, baby. There we are. And the other one."

Something cold is squeezed into my eyes. I try to look for Mummy and Daddy. But I can't see. My eyes are full. It makes them sting and see funny colours.

"We have to check his eyes. These drops dilate them so that the eye doctor can get a good look at the retinas. Then if he's got problems, we can sort them out before anything more drastic happens..."

Colours all mixed up. It's all gone strange.

"And those wounds on his buttocks have healed so well! Who wants to have a look at Saul's buttocks?"

I wave my arms around so Mummy and Daddy will start to listen. The nurse picks up my legs and squashes them up to my face. I can't move. Lots of people jostle my Hot House.

"That's brilliant. Last time I looked...."

"Weren't they deep though. Well done Saul."

"He'll have huge scars but they're healing better than we could have...."

I wiggle to get my legs free.

"Is he all right? He looks a bit red in the face."

"Wouldn't you be, if you had ten women looking at your bottom?"

I struggle.

"Probably hot. I'll turn his incubator down."

She lets me go. I grip my Tube. Mummy, Daddy, Listen!

"Saul! Stop that! If you extubate yourself... Look, let's put these mittens on. And we'll have you on your tummy. And what happens if we put Eric the panda in the way...."

I can't move. I'm flattened by a panda.

"That's put paid to your little games, eh?"

But I want to tell you what Grandpa said. I'm sure it's important. I'm sure you'd want to know. If I can still remember it... He said, he said, something about being part of everything and without me, it wouldn't be everything. I think that's what he said, (I try to push Eric off,) and then I think he said, There *has* to be everything, so you can tell the story. I don't know what the story is, but it's one of the best, he said, a hard story, but it'll go deep, and a good story isn't over with the telling. It will carry on long after you've finished with it, he said.

"Their eyes get sensitive to the light with the drops in. Better cover his whole incubator with this blanket. Then he can get some sleep without us all messing with him."

My house is covered. I can't move. I can't see. They won't hear.

But that's what he *said*, Mummy, Daddy. And he said, he said – oh I knew if I didn't tell someone straightaway, I'd forget it all again.

Day 56

I don't know whether I meant to do it or not. I suppose I did. I suppose I liked being naughty. Maybe I did it because I was so happy to be feeling a bit better. Maybe I did it to make Nurse Scurry laugh. I weed on Dr Calm.

"Very pleasing...Kidney scan clear at last... Aortic vegetation completely disappeared...Acidosis improving.... And good news about the eye tests. Excellent. Rates still a bit variable... And let's have a look at those buttocks, little chap...."

He undid my nappy and began to lift and prod. His tie was lots of different colours. When he had finished he didn't do up my nappy, and he left the door open.

"...Healing very nicely...he's still not putting on much weight. Two pounds four ounces. I've spoken to the parents and warned them that we might be putting him on formula milk. Suggested fifty-fifty with the breast milk...."

I arched my back. Twisted. And then. *Squirrrrrt!* Straight and golden. Out of the door. It hit his tie right in the middle and dripped onto his jacket. He didn't notice.

"...Don't want to upset Mum too much...."

But Nurse Scurry saw.

"Saul!"

"What's up now?"

"Er...he's just, er relieved himself. On your tie."

"Oh really! You little...."

"And it's gone into your jacket pocket as well."

Everyone around was grinning. I giggled with them. Dr Calm splashed water on his tie.

"Really! Trying to tell us something, Saul?"

"He's trying to say, he doesn't want formula, aren't you Saul?"

"What a little... It's probably a dry-cleaning job this...."

I liked Dr Calm. He was long and thin and grey. Tall, so you could never really see into his eyes. His fingers were like him, long and thin. In Control fingers. Know What to Do fingers. Never Do your Nappy Up fingers. Mummy and Daddy liked him too, I could tell. They listened really carefully to him. They watched his face without blinking, like they wanted to see every bit of thinking in his eyes. And whenever he had been talking to them, they smiled more, didn't want to cry as much.

But Nurse Scurry didn't seem to like him. She didn't *not* like him. It was more...she sort of...*bristled* when he talked to her. Like this morning.

"I really don't think it's a good idea to...."

"Yes thank you, I think I know where you nurses stand on the formula versus breast-milk debate. But I want to know what the parents think."

Dr Calm turned away from Nurse Scurry. (That was when she bristled.)

And he looked at Mummy and his voice went a nudge softer. "You see we want him to put more weight on more quickly. Because the bigger he is, the more able he is to withstand infection and the quicker his lungs will outgrow the ventilator, if you see what I mean. I'm not saying your milk isn't good for him, on the contrary, and you mustn't take this... You mustn't be offended, but formula does tend to be more fattening...."

"I'll do whatever you say is best for him. If you told me to eat broken glass, I'd go right home and grind up a milk bottle. I'll do whatever you tell me..."

Nurse Scurry had bristled and bristled the whole time, until Dr Calm had gone and then, "Honestly, we're lucky enough that a mother can keep producing milk this long, and he goes and talks about formula! Doctors, really. Take no notice of him. Saul's nearly doubled his weight, even though he's been so poorly. Sometimes I think they expect too much."

Mummy and Daddy were hiding a smile. It was great to see Nurse Scurry so lit up.

"And I tell you this, a baby as poorly as Saul would never have tolerated formula the way he's tolerated your milk. He's never once had his milk stopped has he? I honestly think without it, he may not have made it."

"But if formula helps him now, I don't mind, really."

"It won't help him. Mother's milk is full of antibodies and lots of things formula just can't provide. If we've got it, we use it. It's not just a food it's a medicine. I tell you what Saul, as long as your mother produces it, you're having breast-milk."

Nurse Scurry's eyes were glowing. She pushed a bit of milk down my tube. It was pink today.

"As if there aren't enough additives in already what with the iron, vitamins, potassium, sodium and whatever else he's on today. And another thing..."

The milk went warm and lovely into me.

"...He doesn't throw up like babies on formula do. One whiff of iron and babies usually chuck it all back at us. But not Saul."

"Probably got a tough stomach like his daddy. Tim's always loved his food. He even eats the rubbish I serve up. I think he draws the line at Saul's milk though. I threatened to make a rice pudding with all the excess in the freezer, once."

Daddy made a face and Nurse Scurry grinned.

"Well since you're producing enough, how about just giving Saul the hind milk, the creamiest. Then maybe we can fatten him up before his next weighing. Don't you worry, Sauly boy, you won't be getting any formula milk. We want it pure and natural and full of goodies, don't we?"

I gripped her velvet fingers and grinned up at her and said, You're lovely Nurse Scurry.

Just Before Dawn

Now is a very quiet time in my Hot House. Just before dawn, a time when the souls of babies that are ready, can glide back to where they came from.

Just before dawn is when I do most of my important thinking. And I think of Grandpa and I smile. He's been giving me clues and hinting at Reasons. But he never gives away too much. It's my story, he says, and I've got to live it.

So I've been piling up ideas, opening up mysteries, matching up the pieces. I get it right, and sometimes I get it wrong.

Just before dawn you get to thinking about Time. You see, I know that once there was a time and it rolled out of another time. It had roots that went back and back. And what you thought was a beginning was only a passing, like a mountain pass, from somewhere to somewhere else. And all the other starting points and finishing points are really only when one time turns into another time.

This living, this morning, this moment, they are all just one of those times.

And suddenly dawn has passed. The details of This Living have broken through into my thinking and now I can only think about going suckpush suckpush. Now everyone else is busy with a brand-new day.

Day 57

When I was on my left side, I could see the big double doors. They flapped loudly when people went in and out. Most people who came in, stared at me. I didn't mind if it was one of my favourite nurses. Then I smiled. But if it was someone I didn't know, one of the Sad People with a baby somewhere deep in the Big Air, then I stared back. It shocked them to see me staring. It made them hurry away to their own babies.

Next to the door was the sink and at the bottom of my house were all my machines making spiky pictures. All of them had wires leading inside my house and under the blanket and into me. And then hanging above me, inside the house, was Eric the panda, black and white and grinning, twisting round to make me laugh.

And in the middle of my roof was a fat tube full of milk with a thinner tube curling down into my mouth.

When they put me on my other side, I could see babies, in their own houses, all the way to the window. The Big Air was full of babies. The houses stayed the same. The babies changed. I'd been there the longest on my row.

The first baby to be next to me was Jamie. I didn't notice him for ages. I was too busy fighting. He was very big – he filled up his house – but he was very poorly. He was a twin. He was already eight weeks old when I first came here. To me, back then, when every day made a difference, eight weeks seemed a long time to do This Living.

"Eight weeks! Eight weeks of this!"

"The first six are the worst. Then it gets easier. The days just go by and before you know it... Yours is doing ever so well, though isn't he? Look at that, Ray. He's only on five breaths. The twins was never on that. They was on fifty, sixty. And he's nearly in air! Look Ray. Jamie was in eighty percent oxygen for some time wasn't he? He still needs lots of oxygen, doesn't he Ray?"

Jamie was fast asleep. He wasn't interested in me. He was somewhere else.

"Twenty six weeks I was. And they called it a *normal* delivery. Meaning I didn't have a Caesarean. Hardly *normal* though is it? Born on the floor of a Ford Capri. Not with Ray going through red lights and shouting, Not yet, don't have the buggers yet, we're still ten minutes from the hospital, and me screaming, I can't stop it, I can't. And there he was, suddenly, in my pants. I thought I'd broken him in half, so tiny he was, two pounds, five ounces. How heavy was yours?"

"One pound four ounces"

"Oh...well... But he's doing ever so well. Ours were much worse than that for, oh a long, long time, wasn't they Ray?"

"We thought we'd lost him three times. Terrible poorly he was."

"Jamie had a bad bleed, didn't he Ray? Has yours had a bleed?"

"A slight one, into the ventricles."

"Not into the brain then? Oh that's nothing to worry about then. Jamie's was so bad, they told us three separate times, he was going to die. Said he wasn't going to see morning. Didn't they Ray?"

"We had to have the hospital chaplain. Emergency christening. I tell you, I haven't cried since I was that high, but I cried that night, sobbed my heart out. All of us standing round his incubator and me squarking like a babby. It was piteous, I'm telling you. Three times he nearly bought it. And now look at him. Five pounds and creating enough to manure an allotment."

"You just wait. When he's eight weeks old like these two, you'll be down the corridor and into the Nursery, getting his cot ready for coming home. You can't help thinking about it when you get them this far."

"Got to keep thinking positive, haven't you? And they're magic here you know. Abso-bloody-lutley magic."

And now I was as old as Jamie was then. Eight weeks old today. That's a long time to keep climbing, isn't it? Jamie was taken home ages ago. There have been lots of babies since, small ones like me and big ones, like Baby Edwards, who could touch both sides of his house with his elbows. He liked to wriggle to the edge of his space and push himself against the wall. "Look at him. Thinks he's on a walking tour of the Lakes, this one. There's no escape young man." Baby Edwards just wanted someone to cuddle.

The big ones never stayed long. But the really small ones didn't either, if they were as small as me. Some didn't like doing This Living. Some tried but it was just too hard. Some slipped away when no one was watching, when I was sleeping. Only once, I was there to say good bye. Lizzie was as small as me.

"We've done all we can, but at twenty-three weeks it was always a slim chance...."

She stayed three days. They put screens around her house, to hide the person who was wailing. Then they switched her machines off. One by one. Starting at the top. The flashes and spiky pictures turned to green lines. Until it was lots of green lines piled up to the ceiling.

So now, I was eight weeks old and the house next to me had screens round again. Not because of an ending, but because of a beginning. I was excited. I wanted to hear everything.

"Rampant septicaemia...chest drain...head knocked during delivery...bad bleed...." I tried to peep round the screens. But then Nurse Columbine came to change my sheets. And then Mummy and Daddy came and sang to me. They all wore me out and I fell asleep.

But in my dreams I knew that I must wake up. Because something important was happening. I opened my eyes. The screens had gone. There was a woman sitting by the house next door. She was staring. Like Mummy used to do. Her cheeks were wet. Mummy was cleaning the roof of my Hot House. She glanced at the woman. Bit her lip.

"It gets easier."

The woman looked at us

Mummy tried a tight little smile. "Well...at least...you start to feel normal again after a while...."

"Is this normal?"

"It is when you've been doing it for eight weeks."

"Oh my God, don't say that! Eight weeks!"

"The first six are the worst. After that...the days just go by and...it becomes your life."

"Lami won't last that long."

Tears ran down the woman's face.

Mummy pretended not to cry.

"How many weeks?"

"Twenty six and five days."

"You never know. You've got to keep positive. They're marvelous here, you know...."

They kept talking. But I stopped listening. I was looking into the house next door. At the baby. Lying half dead. Right next to me. My new best friend.

Part Five

Day 57

Lami was beautiful and full of grace. Her skin was very black. Her arms and legs were very thin. She was perfect. She had a fat tube – much fatter than her arms – cut into her side. It filled with yellow all day. She lay flat on her back, arms and legs straight out. She was hardly alive. The mask cut into her face, squashing her cheeks and eyes. She didn't breathe. Not once. The machine went *clunk thud whoosh* all day. But Lami lay still.

She didn't know I was watching. She was too busy fighting, or maybe working out the sounds and smells and hurtings, remembering how she passed from her Perfect Red Sea into the Big Air, trying to go even further back, maybe searching for Reasons, like I did. Or maybe she wasn't even there at all. Maybe she was gone to her own Important Place. Maybe she was even floating. And then I wished I could go floating with her.

But I just had to lie here and look. Not at *her*. At her body. So close but not close enough. Locked behind her see-through walls. It made my eyes go funny, staring so long in the same place. I had to close them sometimes, but then my heart would lurch in case she'd disappeared, and I'd open them again quickly.

I knew what it was like to be wobbling on the edge. It would have been much easier for her to let go. But she didn't. She wanted to stay. And although she was so poorly, she filled me with light. I sent all my strength into the Big Air for her to catch. I tried to make clouds of Getting Better seep into her house. If only she would open her eyes and smile and say, I'm here now, ready, the worst is over. But she was still and quiet. That's what she was, a great stillness.

I just watched. Until they turned me over onto my other side. Then I could only see the door. I didn't want to look at the door. I wiggled and tried to twist my head back round. The Tube held it tight. I looked into Nurse Clean Flowers' eyes and then into Mummy's eyes and said, Turn me over, turn me over! They didn't. I beat my heels on the sheets. I cried. I pushed and pulled.

"He's determined to lie on his back, this morning isn't he?"

"Can't you let him? If that's what he wants."

"We *could*. But we try to put them in the foetal position as much as possible. They've missed out on that stage in the womb which leads to problems with walking later."

Her hands forced me onto my shoulder and hip. She pulled up my knees to my chin. Put my hand to my mouth. I strained against her, I pushed every bit of me against her. She just laughed.

"He's ever so strong you know. Both physically and emotionally. I reckon he'll be a right handful when you get him home."

I had to try something different. I held my chest tight. Stopped my breath. It didn't take long. The alarms started. Nurse Clean Flowers did all the things she had to do. I didn't help her. I kicked her hands and wriggled away from the cold steel she put on my chest to listen. I pressed my lips together against Hisser Snake and wouldn't let it in.

"You're in a right little paddy, aren't you poppit? Maybe it's easier for him to breathe on the other side."

She turned me over again. I breathed as deep as I could straight away. I gripped the Tube and went suckpushsuckpush really fast. The alarms stopped. Mummy started to go from white to beige again. Nurse Clean Flowers pretended to wipe her forehead.

"Phew! Good boy. That's better. Well he certainly knows what he wants. And he knows how to get it!"

They laughed.

They let me lie on my right side all day after that. Nurse Clean Flowers put a little sign in my house telling other nurses that I liked it better that way. I looked and looked at Lami, until the Big Air melted into the background and there was only her. I listened to her stillness. And the more I listened the louder it became. Her stillness spread out of her and stretched across to me, muffling out the noises of the Big Air.

It was nice to let the stillness fill me up. From my toes it went up and up all the way to my head. When the stillness got to hurting bits, it just glided over and onwards. And I didn't have to scrunch up against the hurtings any more. I just let the stillness melt through the hurtings. Like the hurtings were as thin and easy as water. And I was the sea. I was so deep and cool and open that I had no edges. I wasn't inside my skin any more. My skin was *inside me*. I was stretching outside the edges of my house. Seeping out, slow and calm, never stopping, greater and greater, thinner, thinner, until I was as thin and as black as the sky, and I touched everything, every moment of remembering, every moment of hurting, every moment of loving or hating or sobbing or smiling, every moment ever, floating free inside me, floating, floating, floating...!

I'm *floating*! Not by accident but because I want to!

Floating with Lami! It was hard at first. You kept getting sucked back into your body by the noises and smells of the Big Air. But if you got it just right, you could hang there on the ceiling looking down at all the bodies in the boxes. It was great. We raced along behind people who went down corridors. We hovered with her mummy when she was in the lift. We played at sneaking in behind her just as the doors sucked shut.

You could learn about This Living really quickly when you went floating. I showed Lami everything I had worked out already, about velvet fingers that said *You're safe, we're here now and we will carry you to safety*, about bleeps and plings, about how, when her mummy laughed and put her hand on my mummy's arm, it was just pretend. Really, inside, they were crying. We went down the corridor to see my mummy when she was on her own. We watched the way she put little bottles of milk in the fridge, all neatly piled up in the right order, how she poured the oldest milk down the sink, how she leant on the sink and sobbed to herself, and the way she wiped her eyes quickly when she heard footsteps, so she was ready with a smile when someone else came in.

We followed Nurse Scurry and Nurse Clean Flowers into a little room with dirty walls, and laughed when they sank into the chairs, eyes closed, heads lolled back, pretending to be dead. And the way they giggled, real laughing that wasn't trying to hide something else. Real laughing because when they closed the door they could forget what was happening in the rest of the Big Air....

"It's Eric Cantona for me."

"Oh no! I like straight sex me. I couldn't be doing with all that zee-samon-ees-sweeeming-up-zee-pajamas stuff."

The way they threw their heads back to laugh....

"C'mon, you wouldn't kick him out of bed would you?"

"I'd say – Ereec, was zis what you meant when you zaid you wanted zomeone to 'ead zee ball."

And the way they howled....

"Ereec, mon dieu, you don't get many of zeese to zee demi-kilo!"

And roared....

And Lami and I loved to watch them wipe tears from their eyes and spill their coffee.

And we watched the way, when the mugs were empty, they left the little room with the dirty walls, they left their real smiles behind and went back into the Big Air, where they smiled sad smiles and put their arms round mummies and daddies who were smiling sad smiles too.

We tried to fit the pieces of the jigsaw together. One little mystery after another. And maybe, we thought, it's lots of little reasons adding up to a one big Reason. And although Lami was really poorly, there were good bits about living. Although we'd forgotten the reason for *starting* This Living, we knew lots of reasons for carrying on. Because sometimes it was fun. Because we were both here now. Because our mummies and daddies were here. Because *anything* could happen.

And we decided we were going to stay doing This Living together. We decided that today, when I was eight weeks old and she had just begun, that today was going to be just another beginning. Or maybe the best beginning yet.

Day 58

You could only go floating for so long and then there would always be a jolt. It brought you crashing back through the layers of living and back inside your body.

Thump. Stroke. Thump. Stroke. Someone was thumping me! On my chest. It made all the sticky inside lurch and tear.

"Doesn't it hurt?"

"Well we have to do it gently. But physiotherapy is one of the least aggressive ways to loosen a consolidation like this."

I spluttered and tried to cough. It was all moving around inside, slowly, shifting, like rocks on the move, tearing.

"Right let's see what that's done."

Nurse Columbine stopped thumping me and switched on Hisser Snake. I was sick of Hisser Snake today. I was sick of not being able to breathe properly. I was sick of being sick. And most of all I was sick of seeing Lami hurting. She had been jolted back to This Living just now as well. And whilst Nurse Columbine messed with me, someone else was messing with Lami. Behind the screens.

I began to hear a wail. I couldn't tell where it was coming from at first. It was thin and tired, from somewhere deep. Thin and really piercing. It filled everything. It wasn't a Big Air sort of sound. It was hardly a This Living sort of noise at all. It was a noise from the bottom of Lami's soul.

Lami's Mummy was in the corridor. Her face was creased into pieces. Nurse Chirpy was holding her. "It's all right. Don't worry. Don't worry."

"How can they *say* that? Oh Poor Lami."

"Let's find your husband. Is he still in with the consultant?"

"...They said...how can they say it... I know it's another bad bleed, they think I don't know what that means, I do, they think I don't understand how bad the damage is, it's affected her sight and speech and all the other... I *know* how bad it is, but she's still a person, isn't she? She's still alive...."

Nurse Chirpy held her tight and rocked her. "I know, I know, I know...."

"How can they say it, you tell me, how can they even think it...?"

"Think what?"

"They want to give up on her, end treatment, that's what he said, when she's fought so hard, just to give up on her, when she's still... Oh my Lami, I won't let them, how can they do that...."

The Big Air was torn apart with the wailing, hidden wailing, real wailing, wailing in houses, wailing in corridors. And Lami wailing inside herself. Because she knew what the throbbing in her head meant. And I wailed too.

She must have wanted to go, just for a moment. She must have thought about it. Her head was swollen. Everything bulged.

"They won't take her off the ventilator. They'll just...not resuscitate if she collapses. That way she can decide."

"Oh my Lami!"

And I sent all my hope and strong thinking to Lami to help her keep going. The wail went on and on. Long after the screens had gone. Her body was still there, just alive, with even more tubes coming out of it. The wail became a whimper as if she was near to giving up. All her machines bleeped and flashed. The nurse stood close just looking. Lami's body had grown. No, not grown: blown up, puffy, nastily swollen. She was ready to explode. She didn't move.

Try to float Lami! Run away to a better place! But it wasn't so easy. If it was so easy, then all the little bodies would be empty and the ceiling would be full of people playing. Maybe when you were too swamped by the hurting, too busy fighting, you, didn't have time to escape. And maybe, if you were close to dying, you didn't dare float, in case you couldn't come back.

I couldn't bear it when the doctors stood around my house, just talking cheerily about me, as if there was nothing to be done for Lami....

"...Well it's imperative that we get him off the ventilator soon. I don't see how we can avoid another dose of steroids."

"Trouble is, the mother's been reading about steroids. Got wind of the fact that they depress the immune system."

"Bloody women's magazines."

"Think it was *Health Which* actually."

"A parent reading *Health Which*. God help us...!"

Never mind talking! What about the baby next door! They didn't hear.

And Mummy and Daddy were the same. Talk, talk, talk, ask questions, whisper to themselves, talk, talk....

"I'm afraid it's the devil or the deep blue sea." Dr Too Tired sighed. "He's what – eight and a half weeks now, which is a long time to be ventilated...."

"It's just that...won't steroids open the door to terrible infections again..."

"Well, the *Candida Sepsis* has completely gone. I checked with Microbiology... His lungs have taken a battering. He'll need help to be weaned off ventilation. Some babies never get off you know." He stopped, watching them.

"What, you mean...?"

"So you'll just have to trust us on this one. It's going to be a long, hard struggle."

Daddy sighed. "We know all about long hard struggles."

They looked in at me. At last! Never mind about me, I told them, look at Lami! Tell them to stop her from bursting! They looked back at the doctor. His eyes were half closed.

"Nothing lasts forever. When I was a junior doctor, I was on my knees with exhaustion. Seventy-two hour shifts. Two screaming toddlers at home. Didn't last forever, as I say. Sheer hell for six months though." Mummy and Daddy looked at the floor. Dr Too Tired sighed.

They looked so sad, so forlorn, that next time they looked in, I couldn't shout at them. They couldn't hear me anyway, all blanketed up in their clouds of tiredness. And with all the pain swirling and the sadness in their eyes and Lami whimpering, I couldn't help it, I started to cry. It came from deep down. It heaved at my chest and burned my eyes.

"Oh darling, what's the matter?"

"Try singing to him. We've tried everything else..."

"He hates it."

"Go on."

She started. Quietly at first. Then getting stronger.

Hush little baby don't say a word,
Daddy's gonna buy you...

"I can't remember, what is it...?"

"A mocking bird, isn't it?"

...A mocking bird...
And if Mummy doesn't know the words to the song,
She'll make them up as she goes along.

I cried even harder. I wanted them to give Lami her stillness back, her calm, her loveliness. I wanted us to feel better. I was sick of hurting. Sick of sadness.

...And if that mocking bird...falls down
Daddy's gonna buy you London Town....

Lami's wail started to melt, just a little.

And if London Town is much too dear,
Daddy's gonna buy you.....Blackpool Pier.

And beneath the swollen face, where the mask dug in cruelly and disappeared, under the swollen legs and arms and huge swollen rounded belly, there were shadows of Lami's silence again.

And if Blackpool tower is a bit too high,
Daddy's gonna buy you... a clear blue sky!

Lami's Mummy came out of her trance and smiled at Lami. Just a tiny pretend smile. By now, the silence in Lami had started to glow.

But the best thing that we're gonna do,
Is never ever ever stop loving you.

And there was Lami, swollen but filled with stillness again.

When I Found the Important Story again

Ever since Lami arrived, This Living has been even more fun. Somehow she has made the hard edges more blurred, the straight lines more watery. You feel as if you can cut through real things and all the solid little details to find whatever you need. Lami is wiser than me. She has brought all her Inklings with her. She has held onto knowings that I've begun to lose. And although our stories are different, with different things for us to learn, they fit together.

Lami has her own Important People and Places to discover, and I told her all about how I'd been searching through my great-grand memories, how I'd been back and back, looking for Reasons, but didn't really know what to look for. The trouble is, I told her, I keep finding other exciting stories that are such fun to play in, that I get lost.

Lami told me it didn't matter. Every story gives up something. But some are more important than others. You'll know, she said, when you get to one that will sing its meaning really clearly to you. And she was right.

One day, when I'd wondered back to a place where great, great, great, great, great, great, great, great-grand memories were hiding, I suddenly stopped. Here it is! A story that I need to understand. Here is something special. I sink into it. You have to lose yourself deep, to hide so that jolting fingers can't drag you back.

I was in Glencoe, with the sun rising over the loch, like in lots of other stories. But this time I felt a tingling in my soul.

By the water was a house, cut into the turf. Inside it was dark. That's the wind moaning in the chimney and the ash fluttering in the fireplace. The wind can whistle right down from the hole in the roof. But it's warm and snug under the tartans. She's just awake. This must be my great-great-great...oh too many greats – one of my grandmothers, a very, very great one, but small, only a little girl just now.

It smells of old smoke and fish. *Up there near the roof at the top of the chimney there's a fish hanging. Granda put it up there ages ago and forgot.*

She stretches against the blankets *Something sticking into my buttock, a bit of duck feather? Granda says beds shouldn't be too comfy.*

She looks across to Granda's bed. It's empty already. *But he'll be back soon.* There's the sound of cattle and water lapping outside, and further away women's voices.

She gets up and pulls the tartan rug round her. There's a jug of milk on the table. *Granda must have been up ages, but he won't be angry with me, being in bed till now, cos I've been sickly and now I'm getting better.* She scoops milk into a mug and drinks. Then she licks around her lips *or else they get sticky and Granda will spit on a rag and rub my face hard and that's horrid.*

Her eyes are crusty with sleep. She goes outside, it's bright and she squints. The air is cold, though the sun is out. Her feet are bare and she scrapes her heel on the stones by the water. She leans on a big boulder and splashes her face *Haa! It's freezing.* But she loves the way it makes her face tingle, so she does it again. *Haa! Haa! Really freezing!*. She rubs her face with the tartan, then puts her feet in the water. *Quickly so you can bear it, haaaaa!* Blood from her heels drifts into the water. She wiggles her toes and scoops the water with her feet till the bleeding stops. The stones in the water are blue, pink and white, round and smooth. She takes her feet out and rubs them on the tartan.

The sun is making morning mist, hanging over the loch, rising, swirling. The sunshine slides sideways through it. There's snow on the mountains. *Granda's up there somewhere, high in dangerous places, dangerous snow.*

She smells baking and hears someone calling her name. "Izzy!, Izzy!" *Uhoh! That's the woman from below. So it's either telling off or breakfast.* She picks up her tartan and walks down to the other house. There's a woman with a mole on her chin, thick hairs sticking out of it. She smiles at Izzy and there are black holes where some of her teeth should be, and Izzy smiles back. *Granda doesn't like you, but I don't mind if you've got some bannocks and butter...*

"Would you be needing a bannock, Izzy?" And the woman gives her bannocks all dripping hot with butter and some hot milk, "Put some flesh on you, aye, but your mother was the same before you, weak and spindly..." and the woman with a mole chatters to Izzy who watches her with big round eyes, eating bannocks, "....And what are you at – running around with nothing on your wee feet, you rascal, and the weather on the turn? And where's your Granda to be telling you how to behave, and dressing you in a morning...?"

Izzy finishes her bannock. "He's in the mountains, high up where I canna go. It's too dangerous and you fall and crack your head, he says. He's fetching a rabbit for tea." *Up there the eagle hangs looking for wee girls, to peck out their eyes. And the cliffs cry water. Up there is all ice and rocks, down here it's all nice and brown and green.*

And the mole woman smiles, "Och, well, it canna be easy, I suppose."

And soon she hears something, and she looks into the purple shadows made by the Pinnacle of the Peaks, black shaggy rocks as far as you can see, and a man is walking out of the shadows and into the sun. She runs to meet him. He picks her up and swings her onto his shoulders. He shows her what's in his bag. Rabbits, fur turning white for winter. *See, woman with a mole on your chin, rabbits, Granda's got our tea....*

Aha, found it! This feels like a very Important Story. Now I can come back whenever I need to. My story and this story. Now I'm really going to find out some Answers.

Day 59

"But you had him yesterday."

"I know, but it's better for him to have continuity, so I should have him again. You have him tomorrow."

"But Nina wants him tomorrow, don't you?"

"Only because I haven't had him for ages."

"But I'm his named nurse."

"Yes but I know his recent history....."

Nurse Chirpy was grinning. Nurse Columbine was looking wistful.

"Well, I'll be over to keep an eye on you, sweetpea."

Dr Magic laughed. "All these women fighting over you, Saul. I bet you'll have broken many a heart by the time you're eighteen."

"He will not!" Mummy was washing her hands at the sink. "He's not having *girlfriends*! Not until he's twenty-five at least. We haven't gone through all this so he can catch all sorts of things snogging *girlfriends*! And if you're thinking about motorbikes Saul – forget it!" And she grinned. "Better to get all the motherly guilt-tripping structure in place from the word go, eh?"

Today was a day for laughing. All my favourite people were in at once. Nurse Chirpy was looking after me but all the others were leaning on my house, talking, giggling. Someone (probably Mummy) had done my nappy up a bit floppily and I could get my hand down the top. My hand got all hot and sticky in there.

"Look at that!" Nurse Clean Flowers laughed. "Typical man!"

"I suppose it's a bit boring in there for him, nothing else to play with now Eric the panda's gone."

"What happened to him?"

Mummy went red. "I put him in the steriliser so he's still drying off. I'm afraid he's shrunk. He really is a Saul-size panda now."

I told Lami about which nurse was the best at caring and told her why, and it made us smile inside to know that Nurse Chirpy's eyes were flicking from me to Lami all day, never really resting, not even going for her lunch, because she had two poorly babies to love.

And we listened to nurses whispering in corners... "...And they're thinking of letting her loose in here! God help us all. She only has to look at a baby and she sets its alarm off...I'm telling you, last time I was in Room two, I saw her trying to turn the oxygen up for a baby with cannulas on, and I'm not kidding, it was on absolute minimum and she wazzed it up to maximum, with one flick of the wrist. It came out with such a blast, the cannulas flew out of its nose and across the room... Well, all right, made that last bit up, but honestly, I can't be doing with her. She causes havoc wherever she goes...."

And we knew when our mummies and daddies were waiting outside even before they pressed the buzzer, and we'd come rushing in with them, laughing to ourselves because they thought they were looking at us in our boxes and really we'd been with them all along.

"...We've brought another tin of biscuits... Here...."

Mummy put the tin in the middle of the room. It was like a lot of birds. The nurses and doctors chirruped and cooed.

"Ooh white chocolate chip..."

"Oy, hands off the butterscotch finger thingie, that's got my name on..."

Except Nurse Chirpy. She was doing things to my machines

"Not having some biscuits, Ginny?"

"You're joking. I only have to look at one and I go up a dress size! Anyway, Saul and I are too busy. How do you fancy a really good pamper, Sauly boy? A wash from head to toe and a really good cream, mmm?"

She pushed past Dr Magic who had a biscuit in each hand. "Who could resist an offer like that, Saul?" He said it with his mouth full.

Nurse Chirpy stared at me. But her fingers were hot and her tummy was going flip-flop. Dr Magic went back to the box of biscuits.

She began by washing my hands and feet. Then she undid my mask and took my hat off. I liked new hat days. (Except when I was too tired and then I hated anyone messing.) Today she peeled my ears away from my head and washed behind them for the first time. When she'd finished, I tingled. She thought about me all the time but she was also listening to Dr Magic and Daddy chatting by the biscuits.

"I bet Saul fifty pence. He bet England would reach the semis. I bet it'd be Germany. You owe me fifty pee, Saul"

"Dear me, Saul. You've got a Daddy who backs Germany against England. Shame on him!"

"Come on, England were never in a million years...."

"But didn't you have a twinge of patriotic fervour when Gazza made that run?"

"Yeah, but the rest...England just can't hack it."

Mummy was laughing at them both. "It's no use Stephen. He's half Scottish. The nice half. The English half of him is bitter and twisted."

Nurse Chirpy rolled me over and cleaned my back. I was cool and fresh now in all my creases, even in the folds of my hernia, (which pushed my legs apart and lay sweaty on my knees.) She lifted it gently, washed it, dried it, spread it with cream. Slippery cool. Her fingers glided down to my feet. She pressed a thumb into each sole, stroked my toes. Even my sore heels felt better when she did that. She made me melt into her hands, she made me cool, she made me warm, I didn't want her to stop. I stretched my feet against her palm, gripped her finger with both my hands, and pulled it to my mouth, to say thank you.

"My little boy," she whispered, "Oh I do love you, little Sauly."

I looked into her eyes and I knew that just for that moment, she wasn't pretending. She had forgotten about Dr Magic. All her kindness and bubbliness was for me. Just for that moment. And I thought, you're lovely Nurse Chirpy.

And then Dr Magic's voice broke into our thinkings.

"So you'll be betting on Germany in the semis then?"

"Oh no. Saul and I are together on this one. He's convinced me that it's much better to support the underdogs. Haven't you, Saul?"

Nurse Chirpy grinned at Dr Magic as she went out of the door. "Don't you talk about anything else but Football?" She was gone before Dr Magic could answer.

Mummy grinned too. "You can't help it can you, lads? You'd turn into *Men Behaving Badly*, given half a chance."

"I think that's a bit harsh." Dr Magic pretended to look hurt.

"Well what about the way you flirt with all the nurses?"

"I don't."

"You do!"

"It's not me, it's them. I'm just...responding. It's my...duty to keep them happy."

"Honestly, it's like *Carry on Doctor* in here sometimes."

"You can't blame him, Rose. They're pretty amazing, the nurses here. Complete angels in disguise some of them."

"Yeah but," Dr Magic dropped his voice really low, "shame there isn't a pretty one amongst them."

Nurse Chirpy was behind him in the doorway, holding a bottle of milk. She heard what he said. She froze. Mummy saw her first.

"Oh look Saul, Ginny's brought your milk." A horrible feeling sliced out of the Big Air.

Nurse Chirpy put the bottle of milk on my roof. Her face didn't unfreeze. Dr Magic stayed by the biscuits. He didn't say anything. Daddy was looking at Nurse Chirpy. "Hey Ginny, Nina told me you were a *Star Trek* fan."

"Yeah. Why?" Her voice was frozen too.

"Be careful Ginny," Mummy made a funny face, "*Star Trek* is one of Tim's obsessions. He'll bore you to tears, if you're not careful."

"*Star Trek* isn't boring! She's got no sense of popular culture. Hey, Ginny, in this light you could be Captain Janeway, the early years."

"Yeah," Nurse Chirpy's face brightened just a little, "Going at warp-factor ten all bloody day."

Daddy gripped my house with one hand and the machines in the other hand and pretended to shake. "The ship canni' take it C'ptain." And he laughed. You couldn't help laughing when he laughed. It was loud, round laughing and really smiley. It shook your whole body, in a nice way. Nurse Chirpy unfroze a bit.

"Tell you what, Ginny. How about we take Saul to the *Star Trek* exhibition at the Science Museum? He already knows about how to boldly go where no one has gone before. Not afraid of adventure. He's just spent nine weeks in a place that looks like the Starship Enterprise. We could wheel him into the museum in his incubator. Pretend he's from the delta quadrant or something...."

Daddy talked and laughed and bit by bit he unfroze Nurse Chirpy and made her smile and then grin and then laugh. She joined in the talking. "Should get them in a Vulcan grip – *Resistance is Futile*!"

They made jokes in funny voices. "That's illogical Captain," and they laughed.

"Ooh he can assimilate me any time he likes," and they roared.

"Right up the old Jefferies Tubes," and they nearly choked. Till everyone was joining in the fun.

In the end, Nurse Chirpy was back to normal, all bubbly again. She got two biscuits out of the tin.

"Thought you were on a diet?"

"Ah stuff it!" She looked straight at Dr Magic and pushed both biscuits into her mouth at the same time.

"What's another dress size? I could do with a new wardrobe!"

Day 61

The first time I heard a song of the soul was when I heard the wailing, Lami's. After that I learned to listen to them from the ceiling.

When you listen to a soul song, you have to get underneath the other noises, to touch the *insides* of the Big Air. When you've learned to turn the Big Air noises down, the laughing, shouting, bleeping, banging, right down so they are just a background hum, then you can start to hear the hidden noises, the sound that feelings make.

Lami and I did it together. At first we weren't very good at it. It was so hard. The Big Air is thick, solid with living and you have to peel away the top layers really carefully. At first all we could find were tiny distant noises, very muffled, buried deep. We kept pulling back the layers, straining, trying to push away the surface noise. And then *aaaaaaaaahh!* Lami heard it first. It was like a heart tearing, slowly, quietly, full of hurting. It was Lami's mummy. She was talking and laughing, but underneath, *aaaaaaaaaaaaaahh!* And next to that was an *oh oh oh oh oh!* A heartbeat hurting. That was my mummy. And underneath that a *Howlowwwwwwwwl!* That was my daddy.

And bit by bit we pieced together the soul songs for the whole room, for every mummy and daddy, for every nurse, every doctor. Dr Sun in the Garden went *grgrgrgrgrgr*. Dr Keen (who had a big smile which never stopped even when everything was going wrong) went *whooshooshoosh*. And when you heard all the songs together, you knew why the noises had to be hidden away. Because they were so *loud*. The whole room was throbbing and swirling.

And today was especially noisy. There were more babies than ever, all making wailing, sobbing songs. And it was funny to watch the nurses. On the surface, they were the same, even when more and more babies arrived. They were gliding, smiling, calm. But their insides were jangling, swirling yellow and black. I don't mean blood and wee and stuff, I mean *inside* their insides. And all their feelings and thinkings started to crash together. The busier it got the more the insides crashed, making nasty swirls of bright red and sickly purple.

We weren't scared, not with Nurse Clean Flowers and Nurse Scurry there. You have to have trust, don't you, in This Living? Even when the nurses make all the air spangle with hidden noises, you don't have to be scared, because they probably know what they're doing.

This morning, before the Big Air got so wild, Mummy and Daddy were still here. You could hear their insides singing the sound of hope. Not too much. But it was enough.

"Maybe... I know it's tempting fate but we thought... Maybe we would go to Children's World to look at prams and cots and... if you think Saul's...."

"Of course." Nurse Clean Flowers smiled a big smile, and her insides were all rosy. "You go off and enjoy yourselves."

"Well, since *you're* looking after him today, we thought...."

"You can trust us, you know. He'll be fine."

"Well, be a good boy for Auntie Nina, then...."

And they left, half happy, half worried.

After they'd gone it got busy. All day it got more and more zingly. Just now, Nurse Scurry scurried in and brought a trail of buzzing orange and red in with her. She went *zuzzzzzzzz*.

"Nina, are you up for an emergency trip to Nottingham to pick up some triplets.

"Nottingham?"

"They've tried every other hospital. Just born. Ventilated but they sound in a poor way. Hundred percent oxygen. Eighty breaths per minute."

"Sure. I'll prepare now. Where are you going to put them?"

Nurse Scurry went *zrzrzrzrz*. "I'm doing some clever juggling, got to find some babies in here that can do without intensive care, and put them in room two. Discharge a few from the nursery.... It's not space though. It's staff. I've rung Queen's and the General. You can't get neonatal nurses for love nor money...."

"Who's looking after mine whilst I'm..."

"I'm bringing someone in from Room two."

"Not...!" Nurse Clean Flowers' voice went quiet, but her insides were going *eeeeeeeek!* "Hey look, I've got Lami and Saul today, is she a good idea?"

"Sorry, but Saul's not doing too badly, today and I'll look after Lami myself."

The doors swung open and sucked in more wailing and swirls of desperate colour. Dr Magic wheeled in another baby in a box.

"Right, twenty-six-weeker for you."

"For heaven's sake! I didn't even know about this one."

"That's Delivery for you. I've told them to give it a rest, but these babies just won't listen to reason."

"Oh. Put baby Anstey in the corridor for the moment, then...."

It was brilliant. Nurse Clean Flowers and Dr Sun in the Garden rushed away. Dr Magic and all the other nurses spun and squeaked and wailed. The Big Air was exploding with colour and noise. Exciting. Babies being wheeled around the room, piling up in corners.

"Can someone nip to the canteen and get me some chocolate, I haven't eaten since eight."

"Who's got a spare syringe driver?"

The screech (a real Big Air noise) when they pulled the fat tube out of the wall. "My oxygen!"

Lots of screens up with clumps of doctors. Dr Calm looking calm like always, but underneath going *awwwwwww*! Every machine alarming.

"Can someone see to Baby Ali, he's having a brady and I've got my hands full here."

We loved it.

But then Nurse Nasty came in.

Day 61: Afternoon

We didn't notice Nurse Nasty at first. In all the excitement, her hidden song wasn't anything. I suppose if you really strained, there was a sort of low *dmmmmmmmmm*. She was standing by my house with Nurse Scurry.

"...His breathing is generally good, in oxygen, on five breaths, and his sats have been high all morning but he still needs suction every now and then. He's very good at telling you when he needs it... Just prescribed another blood transfusion... Still on two-hourly feeds, the milk's all ready in the fridge... And then if you could look after little Marty over here as well...."

I hated Nurse Nasty almost straightaway. She put her hands into my house and yanked at my head. It jolted me down from the ceiling and back into my body. She twisted Hisser Snake round and round, scraping, rough, careless. It hurt. (I knew exactly what Hisser Snake should have felt like and it wasn't this.) I pushed her away. Then she did something no one had ever done before. She pushed me back. She jabbed at me. All the others only laughed when I pushed. Even Dr Shaky never *meant* to hurt me. But Nurse Nasty didn't care. She squeezed my wrists between her fingers, held my arms behind my head and then carried on stirring Hisser Snake round my insides. She wasn't even watching what she was doing. She was humming to herself dum dumdy dumm dumm.

I was frightened. I tried not to be. I tried to let her do it. She knew about bleeps and things, didn't she? I tried to think about Mummy and Daddy, they would come back soon, they would tell her.

She wasn't looking at me and so she didn't see how she was pulling at my Tube, lifting my head off the sheets. Then she let go, my head banged down, I saw starry pictures. She lifted my legs, squashed my hernia. I screamed, she didn't notice. She scraped and rubbed, making my sore bits more sore. She did the nappy up too tight. It made my hernia and belly hurt. I couldn't move because even a little bit of moving made it hurt more. She dropped my legs. My hurting heels bounced on the sheets.

And then she was gone. I didn't dare call her back, even though she had left my Tube all twisted. I tried to squeeze the air in past the kink. I wanted to cry but I had to breathe. Breathe really hard. Air dribbled in. There were no alarms, even though I was going whizzy dizzy. Nurse Scurry scurried past and stopped.

"Why is Saul's saturation monitor not alarming. He's down to seventy-five."

"Dunno."

"Does he need suction?"

"Just done it."

Nurse Scurry played with the monitor.

"For heaven's sake! Can't have a faulty monitor, today of all days! I'll get a technician to look at it. Although we haven't got any spare...."

Someone called across the Big Air. "Paula, Delivery are on the phone."

Nurse Scurry hurried away, calling over her shoulder. "You'll have to keep a close eye on him, for the moment. Try more oxygen..."

All afternoon it was like that. I strained, and Nurse Nasty came and twiddled at my machines and made my air sweeter. She never looked at me. I didn't ask her to. I didn't want her hands again. I was scared and lonely.

And it got worse. My left arm, the one with the fat tube of blood going into it, began to throb and swell. It got bigger and bigger, blowing up as big as the rest of me. It felt like it was going to explode. I just didn't know what to do. And at last, (oh thank you, thank you), Mummy and Daddy came back. All smiles and bubbly with hope at first. Until they looked at me. "Saul! What's happened to you! Tim, look at his arm. Oh my God! Look at how he's lying. Why's he all splayed out and twisted. Oh, darling!"

And then, because they were here and I could let go at last, because now I didn't have to do it all on my own, I started to cry.

"Oh, darling! How long's he been left like this? Bloody hell, he's in seventy percent oxygen. He was in air when we left. And look at his sats."

Nurse Nasty came to twiddle with my machine. The air went even sweeter. She didn't look at me. She didn't look at them. Mummy chased after her.

"Excuse me, sorry but...why are you giving him more oxygen?"

"Cos his sats are low."

"But... I don't suppose he needs suction?"

"I give him some before."

"It's just that...where's Nina, his nurse?"

"She had to go. I'm looking after him now."

Mummy and Daddy went pale. That was their faces. Inside they went black, with spots of even blacker.

"Well, how can he...he's been in air for days, why does he suddenly need so much oxygen...isn't too much oxygen bad for them?"

"Well he needs it."

Oh, we definitely hated Nurse Nasty right then. Hate is a bright colour. It was glowing.

"I'll try suction again though. No skin off my nose."

She switched on Hisser Snake again. No, Mummy! Don't let her!

She threw my head back. Scraped and stirred. I looked at Mummy and Daddy. Help me! Their eyes and mouths were wide. They were frightened too. She dropped my head. Thud on the sheets. Starry pictures. Slammed my doors. *CRACK CRACKACKACK!*

"See, there was nothing there."

Daddy was really angry now.

"And what the hell's happened to his arm?"

"Blood transfusion tissued. Line stopped working. Instead of going into a vein it's gone into the tissue. That's all."

"But that's ...doesn't it hurt, his arm's swollen up as big as his body, it looks...."

"It'll go down tomorrow."

She was gone. I had to think only about breathing now. I knew Mummy was trying not to cry, though.

"What's happened to his tube. He looks so...I'm going to try and unkink his tube, he can't breathe properly...make him more comfy or something...."

"Shouldn't we ask a nurse?"

"I'm not letting *her* near him again. She *dropped* him, for God's sake. Bloody bitch... When we get Saul out of here, she's going to be...."

"Well, another nurse, then?"

"Who? Look at them all, it's like... Where did all these babies come from?"

"And look at this, he hasn't been fed since three. Right, I'm calling someone. Stephen, excuse me, sorry to...."

And at last Dr Magic was here. "So how's my favourite little football fan doing today?"

"Terribly. He was fine this morning, and now his sats are all over the place, he's in seventy percent...."

Magic hands. Oh, thank you, thank you Dr Magic. He lifted my head and laid it so that my neck and tube were straight. He waited a while, his fingers stroking my swollen arm. I breathed and breathed and breathed. But I was tired now.

"There we are. Sats at ninety nine. We can bring his oxygen right down now. I'll just have a quick listen, though, he seems to be labouring a bit."

He listened to my chest with the wiggly tubes in his ears and shook his head.

"Sounds like the left lung might have closed down a bit. Have to keep an eye on that."

"And he hasn't been fed since three."

"Who's looking after Saul... Have his feeds been stopped?"

Nurse Nasty called from the Big Air.

"Waiting for it to defrost."

Mummy's hidden noises *really* screamed now. "He doesn't have frozen. Fresh is better for him, Paula said. So I always express plenty for him fresh each day. It's in the fridge."

"Isn't any in the fridge."

"There was plenty this morning"

"Well I've defrosted some now."

"Throw it away. I want him to have fresh. I'll do some more. It'll take me five minutes. Saul's not having frozen milk when I'm producing gallons of it. And Tim, whilst I'm doing it, nest him up nicely, like Nina showed us. Not all splayed out as if nobody cares about him...."

It was nice to see Mummy's hidden noises surge like that. But I was so hungry that when the milk came at last, it made me feel too full straight away. It made me swollen and lumpy.

I was tired of feeling like this. When you know what it feels like to be getting better, it makes you angry to feel bad again.

"Did he have his three-o'clock steroid before the blood transfusion then?"

"He's not on steroids." I wished Nurse Nasty would go away.

But Daddy wouldn't let her. "He's on his fifth day of steroids. The high dose. And they mustn't be stopped suddenly, it's not good for him, Dr Calm explained that to us. He was supposed to have a dose at three. I checked this morning. I check everything he's on."

"Look." Nurse Nasty put some papers on top of my house. "Steroids finished. Line through them."

Daddy was boiling. "Would you mind going and asking a doctor whether Saul's three-week course of steroids that was started five days ago should have finished yet."

She took the papers.

"Bloody hell, Tim. It's a good job we're on the ball."

"God, she must be thick though. It's obvious if you look at the chart that they can't have been stopped. That means they'll be four hours late at least. And they haven't got a line to put them in now that one in his arm...."

"We're not having her again. I know you can't choose your nurses and I know they're busy, but Saul's *not* having her again."

I didn't really stop feeling frightened until I heard Nurse Columbine. "Hello. I've got Saul tonight. How's he been?"

"Oh are we glad to see you, aren't we Saul?"

And they sizzled and muttered to Nurse Columbine, and she listened carefully and nodded. After the panic of the day, she seemed like a great calm river and she flooded us with her smile.

Somehow she promised to pick us all up and carry us to safety. Not in words, of course, but in feelings. Somehow we knew she really loved us. And suddenly it was alright again. My heart went smooth and I beamed up at her and said, Oh you're really lovely Nurse Columbine.

Days 62-64

"The trouble is," Nurse Chirpy was whispering to Nurse Columbine, "you've got to *want* to look after babies like this, haven't you?"

"Well, it was mad yesterday. And when you're short staffed, any nurse is better than no nurse at all...."

Every time the nurses changed over, I was frightened. My heart thumped, like it was trying to swim out of my mouth. I didn't want to have Nurse Nasty again. But I was lucky and Nurse Columbine looked after me three nights in a row and Nurse Chirpy did the days.

So bit by bit, I could feel I was getting better. The fizziness and the fuzziness were now just things to remember, nothing to do with me anymore. I knew my body was growing bigger and stronger. Now, when I pulled at my Tube it seems so small and weak, I knew that if I really tried, I could pull it right out. So they put gloves on my hands.

The delicious feeling of being alive was getting stronger too. You could feel things that you didn't have time to feel before. Like your hair, which tickled your ears and neck, a wispy tickling. And though you could still feel the needle pricks in your heels, there was also the gorgeous tingling of *living* inside my feet.

And it's ever so good that you can't really remember hurting when it's gone. At first everything, my body, my thinkings, me, was inside the hurtings. But now, the hurting was just dots here and there. Easy to bear, easy to forget.

I was nine weeks old today. The beginning of a new way of living that we all knew was going to go on and on: living without the Tube. I saw Dr Calm smiling. He almost bounced up to my house and whispered to Mummy. "Don't tell Saul, but he's doing very well. I think we can be optimistic now, in brackets, cautiously. If you see what I mean."

And she looked at him, her face full of light. She wanted to hug him, you could tell. And when Daddy came in and saw me without the Tube, he wanted to hug everyone. It was the third time they had taken it out. But this time I wanted it gone. I didn't mind the *shhhhhhhing* up my nose. I liked to do all my own breathing. It was easier now. I could breathe deep. I could feel the air going inside me and doing good, making things work, sending life into every bit of me. And the deeper I could breathe, the better it felt. I loved to push all the air out so I could suck it in again. And I was sure now that the Tube would never go back in.

When I breathed before, it was just to stay alive. I *had* to suck the air in. But now it was different. Now I could do lots of new ways of breathing. Sometimes I breathed short and fast. (If I did it like this for too long I could make myself go whizzydizzy). But I liked breathing deep and slow the best. I liked the way it made all my body swell up and I lifted my arms with it. I liked the way, when I pushed it all out again, my body sank back, all soft and melting into the sheets. And sometimes I could just sigh. *Haaaaah.* (You had to be having a good day for that.) Oh, breathing was lots of fun.

And I discovered something else. It happened when Nurse Scurry took me out to weigh me. "There you see. I knew he didn't need formula. That hind milk is obviously doing the trick."

The dish was too cold, it gave me a shock and I began to cry. And when I was in the dish, there was a funny sound. A sort of *eeee-uh, eeee-uh.* Very high and thin, soft but a bit scary, a noise I'd never heard before. I stopped crying to listen better. The noise was gone. Then I remembered the cold, so I cried again. The funny noise came back. I stopped crying, the noise stopped. I cried and there it was again. *Eeee-uh, eeeee-uh.* It was me! I was doing real, noisy crying at last. I wasn't a silent screamer anymore!

"My God, Tim. Is that him? Oh darling what's the matter?"

"He's probably had enough of this dish. Sorry, blossom." And Nurse Scurry flew me back home and snuggled me under a blanket.

Mummy had tears on her cheeks. "He was crying."

Daddy put his arm round her.

"That's good, sweets. It means his vocal chords haven't been damaged. It means he can tell us now if he's unhappy."

"I know, but... I don't want him to cry...and it was so fragile and tiny-sounding...."

"Well, he *is* fragile and tiny," Nurse Scurry tickled me, "he's a baby."

Without the Tube there was another treat as well. I could really *taste* things. My own fingers tasted of me and anyone I'd been clutching that day. It was fun to try and put all my fingers in my mouth at once. Just to see if lots tasted better than one. I tried to taste my blanket and my sheets, until they got cold and wet.

Then the nurse would have to give me new sheets to taste. I could put my toes in my mouth too. They tasted salty and sort of sweet and wheezy.

I liked other people's fingers too. They all tasted of the whizzydizzy smell, but they had lots of other tastes as well. Sometimes sour, often salty, sometimes sharp and nasty. Dr Magic didn't expect it when I did it to him. He had come to steal blood again.

"Well, I think we're going to stop doing the four-hourly heel pricks now. We can afford to extend it to eight."

"Is that good?"

"It's...very pleasing. And it's great for Saul. His heels might get time to recover in between pricks now. And it won't be long before we won't need to check his gases at all."

"Really! Saul, did you hear that?"

"You know that we consider Saul's turned that famous corner, don't you? He's doing fine off the ventilator and there are no signs that he wants to go back. He's been on full milk feeds for ages and hey, look at this. He's saying he's ready to breastfeed."

I clutched his finger and pulled it to my mouth. It was a big finger, as big as Daddy's. I pushed the finger backwards and forwards with my tongue. You had to suck really hard.

"Mr Saul! Your Mummy and Daddy will have to take you home soon if this is what you get up to. Not until he's put on a bit more weight, though, and learnt to feed on his own, but it's really only a matter of time now."

Day 67

I remember when I was only two weeks, old and Mummy and Daddy let Hope fly free.

The doctor (I think it must have been Dr Sun in the Garden), was checking my head, "Well, just don't get your hopes up. It's only a twenty-five percent chance of survival." But when she'd gone, they let their hope soar up, up and away. Mummy lent across my box, whispering. "Yes but that's twenty-five percent of *all* twenty-three-weekers. She didn't say what the chances were for a strong little super-hero. We're talking about *Saul* here. He's a little superfighter."

Hope. Naughty Hope. They really believed it. The next day was The Big Fall. And hope came crashing down. That's why you only dare hope at the right time in the right way when you do This Living. If you hope too much, too soon, you can be disappointed. Disappointment isn't a nice feeling. But you mustn't hope too little, or else you might give up and stop loving. And love is a nice feeling. You have to get it just right.

Doing feelings in This Living is hard. They get all mixed up. You have to learn to smile when you want to cry, laugh when you want to scream, to be sad when you want to hope. Mummy and Daddy learnt how to do it right, after the Big Fall. They kept the tears and screaming hidden and they kept hope tied down. Under control. They had to be full of trust and calm. That's the way to feel when you do This Living.

Like Lami's Mummy had to be today. Lami and her Mummy didn't let hope fly free any more. Their hopes had been smashed. Not tied down, but smashed into pieces. Lami's Mummy picked up a piece and held it to her, thinking of what might have been. Hope didn't waft in clouds for them now. It would always be tiny chunks. But tiny chunks are good, said Grandpa last night when I was sleeping. You have to hold onto the small things as well as the big. That's a good thing to learn.

And Lami could hold onto anything. She knew it was the small things she must hold onto now. And she did. She didn't give up. Even though her mountain was suddenly harder than mine ever was. It was all ice and snow, slippery, almost impossible. And yet

Lami wouldn't give up. Even though her mummy's face was like rock, waiting for the end. Lami had decided. She still had a small piece of hope stuck in her heart. And Lami wouldn't let go of the small things.

When I looked at her, I felt guilty. Because my mummy and daddy had more than small pieces, now. They were filled with hope. Their faces shone with it every time they saw me. You could see their hearts lurch with it. Now, after all the weeks of pushing it down, now that I was nine and a half weeks old, at last they could let hope fly free again. I could see them dreaming about having me at home.

Home was where the cat purred, the phone rang, the bath taps gurgled. I could remember. And they whispered their dreams to me, of playing with me in the sunny garden on the grass. They were dreaming of the middle of the night, when they would watch me sleeping in the quiet, no bleeps and shouting, all peaceful, the fighting all forgotten. No one could stop them from looking ahead now, taking us on dream journeys. And how they smiled at me now, beamed at me, real smiles, real hope. No pretending now.

Day 68

It was lovely to see them bounce and glitter as they came in today. Today was a day for waiting, special waiting, when you knew what was going to happen, when you knew it was going to be something nice. Because yesterday, Mummy had hidden a surprise in my locker for Daddy.

All the nurses were excited. Nurse Clean Flowers couldn't stop grinning.

"Tim, do you mind getting me some cotton buds out of Saul's locker?"

"Sure... This enough?"

"Er...aren't there any more? Get the cotton wool out as well, then."

Daddy rummaged around underneath me. "Here we are."

"Oh Tim," Mummy laughed, "Is that all you can find?"

Now Nurse Columbine was here too. "Can I borrow some of Saul's Vaseline, Tim?"

Daddy bent down again. The nurses and Mummy rolled their eyes and grinned. It was brilliant. I could hardly wait. Come *on* Daddy.

"One tube of Vaseline." Daddy stood up again. Everyone tried not to sigh. They all looked at each other. I clutched the top of my nappy in excitement and wriggled my legs to the roof. Come *on* Daddy.

"I'm sure there's a bigger tube than that."

He bent down again. Then he gasped. This was it! "Who's been keeping Glenmorangie in our little boy's...." We all just *burst*. Laughter, squeals. I tried to clap my hands.

"Isn't Saul clever, Tim? He remembered it's Father's day!"

"Saul! And how did you know it was my favourite?"

"I've got him well trained."

"'Dear Daddy, hope this helps you get some shut-eye. Don't let Mummy have any though, I like my milk as it is. Love you, Saul.'"

"He's learnt to write as well. He's very advanced."

The Big Air was full of smiles and happiness. I squeezed my-self because I loved it all so much.

"P.S. Thanks for being a great da...." Daddy's voice quaked. He wiped his eyes. (That's another thing about This Living. You're allowed to cry when you're happy, but not when you're sad.)

And everyone laughed and everyone cried and everyone was full of hope. Even Lami.

Day 70

It's just another cuddle. But somehow it's different. I suppose it's because all the horrid feelings are starting to melt. And for the very first time, she's calm, really deep-down calm. Everything is going to be all right, and she believes it. It's like we've just been through a terrible storm with thunder and gales and snow and ice, and now it's over and the sun has just come out.

She breathes a big, slow breath. She seems big and safe and sure. She isn't frightened to hold me any more. It feels like she knows what she's doing for the first time. I snuggle into her and I know that she's my *real* mummy. Not pretend, not anyone else's mummy. And I know that at last I'm really, really safe.

I look deep into her eyes and we both remember when I was in my Perfect Red Sea. How we were strong together, one inside the other, how we talked so no one else could hear. And we both feel that thin thread, pulling in my belly, pulling in her chest, pulling us closer together.

Her arms are strong and still.

"You're getting to be a big boy now, aren't you? A strong little superman. But the hard bit's over now. You'll never have to do anything so hard again, Saul. No, you won't, no, I promise."

Nurse Scurry was watching us and she smiled.

"That's what I like to see. Makes this job seem worth the effort!"

And Mummy's big face beamed down at me. "It's like holding...it's like holding a real baby. I feel like a...real mother at last." And I thought I felt her heart bursting. I wished she would hold me this tight forever. She heard my thinkings and I heard hers.

Oh, my baby

I love you, Mummy.

Part Six

Thursday 11 April

Swoolyla lyla lyla

It was a lovely holiday. The whole time there was music: real music in the car, or made up music in our hearts. It was cold, but the sun was always shining. They spent most of the time in Glencoe. They went on visits to other places, to beaches, to castles, but always they were pulled back to the Three Sisters and the waterfalls and the whisper of stories.

They walked across the moor at the top end of the glen, and told me about heather and blue skies. They sat by the loch and Daddy skimmed stones. She forgot about trains and crying in toilets. She just breathed fresh air and had fresh thoughts.

One day we went up in a chair-lift and she slumped in the snow at the top, staring in wonder at the fields of dazzling white.

"I'll just sit here Tim. You climb to the very top and tell me what it's like." While he was gone she whispered to me, "One day baby, you'll climb to the very top too, I promise."

Oh, what a sea of feelings I had to play in. *Crash sha sha sha!* But I was playing with a panic, because I knew that sometime soon, playtime would run out. She didn't know it yet, but my Perfect Red Sea had started to ebb ever so slightly away. I'd felt it for a few weeks now. She thought it was all normal. Hoped it was normal. She didn't want to know that something was looming. Dangerous like a black mountain.

But slowly, even though she loved the mountains and the lochs, she began to understand how deep-down weary she was. She didn't want the holiday to end, but somehow, like me, she sensed something looming. She was clinging to the last pocket of happiness, and she tried to push away hidden feelings. But at last she gave in.

"I *am* enjoying it Tim, I really am, it's been wonderful but it's just that... I'm so tired, I can't really do it any more. And we've still got the wedding party on Saturday to worry about when we get back... I just need to sleep for a long time, to go home, to do nothing...."

So they said goodbye to their favourite place, got in the car and set off on the long journey home.

Saturday 13 April

Remember baby, when we laughed, smiled for the camera, thinking of how happy we would be....

"Oh she looks radiant, doesn't she look...and how far...?"

"Twenty three weeks."

"Ooh, the blooming bride! Let me take a... Smile!"

And what day was that? Because back then every day made a difference. It was a Saturday, a sunny cold day, only two days after the long journey back form Glencoe.

I was washed with so much happiness, my head was swimming with it. She smiled all day, even though she was tired and her legs ached and she felt too heavy and uncomfortable inside, she smiled all day and she meant it.

"...And said, he's not wearing any!" Everyone burst out laughing. I did three spinning wheels just for fun.

Um duddle do, um duddle do, dunk dunk dunk dunk dunk dunk!

"And did you do all this yourself?"

"Well, we couldn't really afford caterers. Trouble is, Tim's far too popular, got too many friends. He should be an old bag like me, then I'd only have had to do a couple of flans and a pasta salad....oh but have you seen the wedding cake? Polly did it, isn't it great?....."

And she cheered with the rest of them when he made the cork pop. *And although I can't drink it, it's nice to see the cork pop and everyone smiling, drinking. And we're drunk on happiness, baby and me.*

"And I'd just like to say thank you to you all for coming to our wedding party and helping to celebrate our marriage. I apologise that you weren't invited to the ceremony. In the circumstances, Rose wanted it small and manageable. So it was as few people as possible. It took me a long time to persuade her that *I'd* have to be there..."

Bubbling laughter.

"...And then we *had* to have a registrar and a couple of witnesses, and in fact, that was the registry office full. She deliberately chose the tiniest registry office in Scotland. We got married in the front room of a council house in a wee Perthshire village. They had to remove the sofa to get us all in...."

And she grinned and squeezed his hand and smiled for the cameras. "Some of you may think we rushed into it. After all it's only taken me thirteen years to get her to say, 'I do'. And she's still not quite sure she's made the right decision."

"Oh I got sick of him asking. Wore me down in the end."

More waves of laughter.

"Oh, yes, don't think this is all because of the baby on the way. I first asked her to marry me a few months after we first met, when she was a mere eighteen, and I've been asking her ever since...."

Murmurs. "Aaaah." "How sweet."

"Actually Tim, it was a few *days* after we met, and I told you not to be so silly, and that I needed more time to think about it."

"And she thought about it for thirteen years. And I reckon she only capitulated because she suddenly realised she'd get to see me in a kilt."

And her heart soared. I twisted and turned and did spinning wheels and falling over headstands.

"...Some people today have been getting a bit personal and have asked me about the *arrangements* under my kilt. Well, I'm only saying this much. On the day of my wedding, I was dressed like a true Scot, and *boy,* was that wind chilly."

And they all laughed loudly.

"I'm sure Rose has got round to you all and told you my best joke. Her favourite part of the ceremony, apart from when I promised to worship and obey her, was when the registrar said, 'And do you know of any just impediment to this marriage', and Rose said, 'No, he's not wearing any."

Everyone hooted.

"...So, consequently our first night together as a married couple was rather unconventional, with Rose five months pregnant, and my wedding tackle frozen solid. We ate peanut butter and banana sandwiches in our little bedroom in the B and B, and crashed out on our single beds...."

Swoolyla lyla lyla.... There were rich waves of love and happiness, and bubbling laughter. It made me quite dizzy.

"...But most of all, I'd like to thank Rose for agreeing to be my girlfriend in the first place, all those years ago, and now, for agreeing to be my wife. It may have been a small ceremony, but as I said on my wedding night, it's not size that counts. And if the length of our courtship is anything to go by, this is the start of a very long and happy family life together...."

Swoooolyla lyla lyla.... And her eyes filled with tears.

"Wait, wait till I've got my camera ready...okey dokey...."

And they held the knife together and smiled for the camera.

We wish for a long and happy life for us both and for the baby.

And they plunged the knife into the cake.

Sunday 14 - Tuesday 16 April

The day after that, the Sunday, she shouted in the garden.

"I *can't*, Tim, I can't do it any more, why don't they all just... Why does she always have to rush into everything, always wanting it done yesterday... I'm supposed to be on bloody holiday, God I need a holiday, I'm so... And we came back from Scotland early, precisely *because* I'm too tired even to...and I find the bloody answering machine crammed with messages from people, all wanting something, with some crisis for me to sort out, people always wanting, wanting... I need to *sleep*... Everyone thinks I'm superwoman and I'm not, I'm not I'm just... And yesterday was nice, and it all went well but parties are tiring, and we should have got in caterers in, and now I've got to clear everything up, on my own, why did they call you into work *today,* couldn't they even leave you alone the day after your wedding party, it's a Sunday for God's sake, and on top of everything else, I've got to find time to rush off to Gran's house and sort out the stupid incompetent estate agent, and tomorrow's going to be mayhem at work. I can't do it all, Tim, there's just too much, I can't do it, I can't do it, I can't, I can't, I can't...."

And he held her and rocked her. "I'll ring her and tell her. And I'll clear up the house when I come back tonight. It'll be alright...."

And she dropped him off at work, and she cleaned the house, and she went to Great-granny's house, and she picked him up again, and she went tippy-tap on the keyboard all night, her eyes sore, her back and neck and head aching, and she went to work the next day. More tired than she had ever been before....

And early the next morning, Tuesday, it was hot, too hot. My Perfect Red Sea was nearly smothering. I tried to hide from the heat but it was everywhere. She moved in her sleep, sweatily, trying to get cool. She was dreaming of a room where women were sobbing and she sobbed with them, beating a soggy wet pillow. The walls, my great billowing, squashy walls, were twitching, just slightly, just gently. I didn't dare move. I didn't want to wake her.

Oh Mummy don't move, with every breath you make the Looming shudder. Oh Daddy, don't leave us this morning, forget about work and all other worryings. It's looming. It's right up against us. It's in Mummy's dreams and makes my walls twitch.

She clutched her belly when she woke and felt me still there.

Thank God, only a dream....

She looked at the clock.

Still early. Still time to rest.

But she didn't rest. She got out of bed. She walked to the bathroom. *Oh Mummy, Mummy. Can't you see it right there in front of you!* But she was too tired to hear and she sat down heavily.

When it happened, it was sudden. My bubble burst and whoosh, I was all dried up. My Perfect Red Sea, my perfect security, it all gushed away.

Tuesday 16 April

We *were* strong together. Her and me. We tried really hard not to let it happen.

She didn't cry. She lay on her side listening for the doctor.

"Well, it sounds as if your waters have broken, I'll send you down for a scan just to check. But there's nothing else we can do. Twenty-three weeks is far too early. You'll have to get to twenty-eight if you want this baby to live. And it's unlikely you'll keep going till then. If you give birth soon, it won't survive, sorry."

She felt like she was being hit in the face. She made herself speak.

"I think I can feel contractions."

"I doubt it. Probably just tense. Anyway, wait here till the porter arrives."

She waited and she didn't cry. Not then. She dug around for something to make us strong, to make it all right. And she talked to me, so no one else could hear:

The doctor said you mustn't be born till twenty-eight weeks. Right. You're staying put for at least five weeks. I'm not letting you go, so don't you go pushing your way out. For at least five weeks. Got that?

Her hand was resting on my roof. I wanted to stretch up and touch her. But I was all dried up. I whispered back, so only she could hear: *I'm staying put*. Not in words, in feelings. I knew she heard. I felt her smile.

And all that day we thought strong thoughts. We thought them together for double strength.

We will last out for five more weeks. We will be strong together. We will, we will be safe together and not let go for five more weeks.

I trusted her. I knew she wouldn't let go. I was staying put.

We stayed in the hospital room and he kept coming and going, sorting out problems, being strong, she told me, buying a sandwich so she could feed me (except she only took a bite and then forgot it.) And when he was gone we wished he'd come back, and when he came back we knew we could keep going for ever.

And sometimes she felt something in her belly and her heart jumped a bit and I felt it too and then she swallowed down the fear and promised me that it was all right and we would be safe together. There was laughing too, even when they didn't feel like it, they couldn't help it.

"Hello, did you call, I'm Avril, always a bit complicated at change over, this door's a bit stiff isn't it, better keep it closed, can do without all those oohs and aahs and happy grannies can't we, did you call then?"

"I think I've been having contractions. I've been timing them. Every twenty minutes"

"Let's have a feel. At least you won't have to go into work tomorrow, that's a blessing, you'll probably have to give it up. Wouldn't mind giving up work myself, it's mad here, you don't have to be mad but it helps. Do you know any good millionaires? Must be sexy, don't like shifty." (And she didn't start to laugh just then, but she wanted to.) "Hey, but wouldn't it be great to win the lottery? I could do with a million or two couldn't you. We'd know how to spend it, my husband and me, well I call him my husband. Are you her husband then, or just a stand-in? Mine's just a stand in, at the moment, at the *moment*, I've told him to marry me but he's too busy working, and him an accountant, you'd think he'd know about tax benefits for married couples, but it's a bad time of year to ask an accountant, terrible time of year for me, he won't be at home when I finish my shift, he'll be working till all hours, new tax year, mountains of tax returns, he'll be fit for nothing and in a foul mood, it'll be effing this and effing that," (and I could feel her pretending not to smile.) "I come in here for a rest, I do, in here it's a doddle compared, they're all stark raving mad, mind. You know that Louisa, the one with the red perm, well she's taking photographs without people knowing, even the doctors, who won't see the funny side and she's going to pin them up in obscure places. I won't let her take any photos of me, why do you think I'm hiding in here, Ooh, don't you like your steak and kidney pud? Don't feel like eating? Don't blame you, waste not want not, bit on the salty side," (and she glanced at him and they were both pretending not to smile,) "I don't have to worry about my weight though, lucky really. Well, I can't feel anything, you're probably just tense, not surprising really, do some deep breathing or something. You're lucky being in here though, well you're not lucky exactly, really you're unlucky, it's damn bad luck when you think about it, but you're lucky being in *here*, if there's anywhere to be, given that what's happened has happened, which is a bugger for you, but this is the best place to be, they're very good here, upstairs I mean, good with prem babies, in fact the best, oh they do such marvelous things, of course they'll have told you that whatever happens now, whichever way it goes, it'll be tough for you, but you know that, I can see from your face. Life's a bitch sometimes, we see a lot of life in here and it's often a bitch. Oooh coast is clear, her camera's run out of battery, see you later."

The door went clunk and he and she laughed out loud. And I giggled on the waves of the laughter, the first laughter of the day.

It was a long day and we were tired in the end, thinking so many strong thoughts. *We won't let go for five more weeks.*

And what day was that, because every day back then made a difference? That was a Tuesday. The day before I was born.

Tuesday 16 and Wednesday 17 April

And all that day, the Tuesday, she watched the clock. Because now, minutes were important.

Just past midnight. That's every ten minutes. Better call the midwife again.

Those walls were strong though. How could something so soft and bouncy suddenly turn so stiff.

"I'm sure I've been feeling them all day but no one can find them."

"Maybe they're looking too high up. With you being so early. I'll just feel down here...."

A cold hand was on my belly and we waited. She watched the clock, I watched the walls. I was tense right through, I tried not to be but I knew something was going to happen and that I had to stop it.

Seven minutes past

My Perfect Red Sea had gone, and now it was just me and those walls, and they were closing in.

And somewhere very far away, a baby was crying.

Eight minutes past

"Ooh, hear that, dear? Cries all night, it's starving but Mum's dead to the world. In a bit I'll have to go and put it to the breast. Not my breast, Mum's breast."

"What, whilst she's asleep?"

"Of course, what else can I do? Don't want to keep all the other mums awake."

Nine minutes past

And here we go again. She gasped and sucked in her breath. I braced my feet against one side and pushed with my back. The walls pressed in like tree trunks. Look, I said, my face all crumpled, I'm staying put. You won't ever squeeze me out! And so they let me go. Oh but Grandpa, that was a long hard squeeze that time, wasn't it?

"Yep, feels like a contraction. Hhm. Nine minutes. Let's wait for another...."

Her heart stumbled but then she dragged up a bit of hope from somewhere and remembered we had made a sort of promise.

"Isn't there a drug that can stop the labour?"

"Well, you don't want to go on that if you can help it, it's pretty nasty. Let's wait again to be sure."

She was trying not to be tense. She closed her eyes, breathed deep, rocked me gently, up, and down, and up, and down. I let myself go floppy and listened to her thoughts, swaying like the sea on her breath. *I will not lose you baby. I will not.* And I believed her.

Deep breathing. *Seven minutes*

Deep breathing. *Eight minutes*

And then I woke. The walls went stiff again. She gasped and sucked in her breath. I went stiff too and pushed with everything, my back, my legs, my arms, even my jaw and my face and the top of my head.

"Right, one more and I'll call a doctor. Won't take kindly to being woken but can't be helped, been in a mood all day."

We waited again.

"Your husband's gone home?"

"They said nothing was going to happen tonight, they didn't believe me. They said he should get some rest."

And she suddenly thought of him alone in the bed, not sleeping, just staring into the dark, worrying, maybe with the TV on but not really watching...

"Have you talked about resuscitating it or not."

Her neck went suddenly tense. She tried to make it go soft again.

"We didn't...we never knew we had a choice... Do I have to choose, do I have...what, now or...."

"Well, no I suppose the doctors will decide...."

"I don't know what...." (and she wished he was here) "...I don't want it to suffer that's all, it's not going to suffer is it?"

And suddenly it came upon us like a great wave: what if it *did* happen? She didn't want to believe it, but there it was looming. And the thought of it happening to me filled her up suddenly with terror. *It won't happen. I won't let it happen.* And another great wave came upon me. *I will not let you suffer baby, I will not.*

"Well, as long as you're prepared. If it's born soon, it could be in intensive care for months. If it's not born, you'll be in here. It's going to be a long haul, whatever."

"I know." (Her voice was hardly there) "Four months in hospital, and that's the best we can hope for."

And she clamped her teeth tight to stop the tears.

We all knew it was coming the next time.

Seven minutes.

I pushed back with my fists. But shapes were changing. Below me something was ....yawning. Those walls at the bottom had opened up. I jammed my fists, feet into the walls, tried to stretch out across the yawning. I'm staying put!

"You were right, my dear, better call the doctor."

It was the same doctor.

"She's probably just tense."

Someone was prodding and shoving at the yawning.

"Okay. Three centimetres. Get her down to Delivery."

"What about Ritodrine...?"

"I don't think so. How pregnant is she?"

"Twenty-three weeks and three days. (Every day makes a difference dear)"

"No point. The baby won't survive. And Ritodrine can't keep her like this for five weeks."

"But the paediatrician said...." *Oh if only he were here.*

"She only had the first steroid nine hours ago. It'd be worth a go, eh, doc? Buy her some time...?"

There was a big sigh. "Well, if that's what you want. I'll have to wake the registrar and it's after midnight...."

They called him back. She thought of his face as he held the phone. She thought of him in the car, racing through red lights. We didn't cry. They put us on a trolley. She looked up at the ceiling going past. She wanted to lie on her side. She was angry. *I'm not going to lose you baby. I'm not.* And I liked her angry, made me feel safe. He met us in a corridor. She saw the look in his eyes. They said nothing. He squeezed her arm.

When they put the needle in her hand, it stung. We didn't mind. The Ugly Drug made our hearts race and hurt her chest. We didn't mind.

"It'll go continuously into the drip. I've put it on the highest dose I dare; we don't want to give you heart failure do we!"

It pumped round and round, *boomdeedee boomdeedee boomdeedee*, made us get hot, made us beat fast.

For a bit it was fun, I suppose, riding on the *boomdeedeeboom* of her heart and mine going *beepdidi beepdidi,* twice as fast, and pushing back the walls and cheering because I was winning. It was a battle, her, me and Ugly Drug against the walls. And he helped too.

"Keep talking so I don't notice the pain."

"Erm... I had to park on a double yellow line, the car park was closed.... Er, I fed the cat. Don't be mad but I rang your mother...."

"Doesn't matter. Nothing matters now."

And the blood went thunder and thunder and thunder away, all around her body, and around mine. It made my head thump. That's it, said Grandpa, never give up, another hour and then another hour and then another....

"It's time for your second steroid, isn't it? Here we go. Sharp prick...Another six hours and it'll reach the baby."

So we jogged along together, never giving up, her, me and Ugly Drug. And for a while the walls began to soften, I could let my arms go floppy, I could rest. She could rest too. She began to drift... *Maybe we've got through the worst of it. Maybe now, with a little bit of fighting, we can do it. We'll all have fun again together. Like before, remember baby? When we laughed, and smiled for the camera, thinking of how happy we would be.... And Daddy wore his kilt with pride, looking lovely....like a true Scot he told them all, even though the wind was chilly. And no-one would believe it. What? Like a true Scot? And we all laughed. Even though the wind's so chilly? And they had some more champagne.*

And although I didn't drink it, it was nice to see the cork pop, and everyone smiling, drinking. I was only drunk on happiness, wasn't I? But maybe there'll be more champagne and corks and laughter popping and we'll all be bubbling and drunk on happiness again....

But the walls went hard again, soon after. Ugly Drug was turned up high. It burnt through our bodies and made us race faster, and the walls got even tighter than before, crushing every bit of me, our blood pumping hard and hurting, her chest burning. I could hear her wheezing and gasping.

Oh, but five weeks of this, I said to her. *Is that a long time? Can less be enough?*

And I heard her saying, in feelings so no one else could hear, *Yes, yes one week we'll make it, one week is enough.*

The walls got even tighter, the squeezing came more often, and every time now she bellowed, I couldn't even push now, my arms and legs were crushed to my sides. I was all jelly, very small, very weak. But I *never* gave up. They made Ugly Drug get stronger, until the pounding made you want to scream, and she started to scream, except she had no breath left to do it. So I screamed for her.

....Six in the morning...that's fifteen hours...he said eighteen... I've just got to keep....

And we had to keep racing. Oh I was so tired, so, so tired. But I didn't give up.

And far away on the other side of the *boomdeedeeboom*, I heard a voice, heavy and dead. "I think we should stop now." I forgot he was there, watching it all.

Oh but, one week of this. Can it be less, can it be days, maybe just one?

....Yes...even a day...makes a difference.

We tried so hard. But she was dying a little with every pounding in her heart and the hurting in her chest.

"...Time is it?"

"It's nearly nine, sweets. Nine in the morning. Have some more gas and air."

"...That's eighteen hours, isn't it? He said eighteen didn't he...? Every two minutes, now...isn't working, is it...?" Her voice was thin and I wanted to cry.

She wheezed and gasped for air, and I knew she was fading. *Oh stop now, we must stop now before... Oh, let me be born, I promise to fight. I can fight on my own, now, I know how to be strong.* And deep in her weariness, hidden in the bellowing and wheezing, I heard what no-one else heard. *Yes...enough is enough...we've done our very best...it's time to stop.*

"...I'm sorry, we've got to stop the Ritodrine now. It's not really working and your system isn't coping any more...but it's bought us some time. We're going to have to let your labour continue normally now, and just hope for the best...."

And together, we didn't want to, but we gave up the race.

Snowdrops

Spring is a good time for things to begin. It's when flowers push themselves into the world. Those little white ones, they're the tiniest, but they're also the bravest, because they come the earliest when winter's not even over. They have soft fairy petals that could tear ever so easily if you pulled them apart.

But even fairy petals have to be strong to squeeze through sharp bits of frozen ground. It must be scary. They don't know what's up there, except some of them might have done the same thing last year.

But it's never *exactly* the same, is it? They still don't know if it's rainy or windy. There might even be snow. Only sometimes, it's sunny and they don't have to suffer. They can dance in the sun till it's time to go back down and they'll wait in the dark for the next Spring to come.

Even flowers must be strong to be born.

Part Seven

Sunday, Monday: Days 75, 76

It's not nice being too hot. When you get too hot, things start to go wrong, and if you keep getting hotter and hotter, then.... Oh, I don't want to remember the next bit. I've forgotten it. Let's just skip to the end....

Except Grandpa says that the next bit is the most important....

It started when I was ten and a half weeks old. It was a Sunday. The hotness had seeped into me when I was sleeping. I woke and I felt a funny feeling, sort of nervous, like this was the beginning of something.

Everything was sweaty and throbbing. My heart went *tacha tacha tacha* so fast it hurt. Little fists punching my chest wall. My head ached badly, it made me feel sick. And mixed up with all the other feelings was one I didn't like. I was frightened.

When Daddy touched me, I wiggled away from him. He frowned.

"Er...sorry to...but we've noticed Saul's heart rate is very high. It's been over a hundred and seventy beats per minute all day, and when he gets upset, it hits two-fifty."

Dr Keen looked at my machines. "Well, a hundred to one-twenty is about right for a baby like Saul. But if he's agitated, it's normal for a heart to race."

"So it's nothing to worry about?"

"No. We'd only do something about it if it was persistently at two-fifty."

"And his temperature...it's okay at thirty-eight degrees?"

"Might well be side effects of the drugs. I'll check to put your mind at rest if you like, but his breathing's fine and all his blood parameters were okay on Friday. So don't get concerned about it."

And Mummy had squeezed Daddy's arm. "There you are. Let's not worry unless the doctors get worried, eh?"

The hotness kept on coming. All night. It just rolled up from somewhere deep inside me in hot, choking waves.

And when all the doctors came in the morning, I tried to look into Dr Magic's eyes to tell him how I felt. But everyone was chatting and laughing

"...And he turned back and said 'Madam, if I were your baby, *I* would be screaming blue murder as well.' And he never had any trouble after that!...Right then. Stephen. Get on with it."

"Okay. Saul. Our little hero. Born twenty-three weeks. Now seventy-six days. Has beaten off a series of nasty infections..."

"Good pair of lungs on him, if all that crying's anything to go by."

"Latest x-ray very pleasing. And a good brain scan."

"Well, excellent progress young man."

"What about this heart rate, Prof. Recorded at two hundred and forty-six last night. And a temp of thirty-eight point six. I... er... Luc thinks it might be side effects."

"So I looked up Imipenem and it does cause fever and tachycardia."

"Well, he doesn't really need Imipenem any more, so let's stop it and see what happens...."

And when I was waiting for Mummy to be allowed in, I cried and a nurse came and looked at me and tutted like a bird and went away again. I cried so hard and loud and long, that the nurse came and opened my doors. "What's all this racket about?" I thought she was going to make me feel better, but she nested me up in a blanket and shut the doors again. I tried to push the blanket away. I arched my back to undo the sweaty stickiness. But the blanket trapped all the hotness in....

It was busy again that day, the Monday. Mummy was allowed in at last and I cried hard for her because I knew she would make it all right again. She saw how hot I was straight away. She opened my doors wide. The cool of the Big Air washed in. She took away the blanket. "Honestly! No wonder you're burning up!" I breathed deep, to pull the cool air inside me. I stretched to feel the cool air on my skin.

"Excuse me, are you Saul's nurse today?"

Even though I was so hot, I shivered inside.

"I am. Nothing wrong with those lungs, eh?"

"I think it's because he's too hot." Mummy's voice was deliciously icy. "Maybe if I tried to cool him down with a wash or something?"

"If you want."

Mummy put cotton wool against my head. It was wet, cool, lovely. She lifted my arm and squeezed the wet so it trickled into my armpit. Oh, thank you Mummy. She slowly washed every bit of me, cool and wet in all my creases, behind my ears, underneath my hernia, in the back of my knees. And the best was when she rested the cotton wool on my forehead. It sucked the hotness right out of my head. Just for a lovely moment. Every bit she touched got hot again straight away, but she kept gliding the cool around my body.

"I don't know Saul. All these drugs. God only knows what else they're doing to you."

We were both pleased when we heard Nurse Columbine's voice.

"And how's my favourite baby boy today?"

"Oh, not very happy, are you darling?"

"Poor sweet pea. I don't feel too good today, either. Must be the weather."

"He's better now Auntie Anthea's here, aren't you? Actually, I'm really glad you've got him today. I've arranged to go to a friend's for lunch. But I didn't want to leave him unless...."

Nurse Columbine laughed and even her laugh made me feel better. "Go on, he'll be fine. You go and have a lovely time."

The Big Air was buzzing, busy and angry and racing. All the nurses rushed. All the alarms rang. Babies cried. Lami wailed. I got hotter. I don't remember seeing Nurse Columbine again. There was too much noise, the same as always but more of it. And above everything else, right inside my house, hammering into my ears and my head, never stopping, was a high squeak. *Eeeh-uh, eeeh-uh.* A horrible screech that came out of my mouth.

I strained to hear Nurse Columbine somewhere in the noise. But I couldn't.

Sometimes a nurse I didn't know came to switch my alarms off. Sometimes someone came to fiddle with my machines or write on charts. But no Nurse Columbine. No Mummy.

It seemed a long time before Mummy and Daddy came in. They stared at me and then at the machines. Then Mummy rushed to wash her hands. "I knew I shouldn't have gone to lunch."

Daddy seemed dazed by all the noise. He looked around for Nurse Columbine. The nurse I didn't know came to us.

"Hi! Are you Saul's Mum and Dad. Anthea's had to go off sick, I'm afraid. So I'm baby-sitting your little boy."

"Oh." Their faces fell. "Poor Anthea...what was wrong...?"

"We do get ill sometimes you know."

"Oh, yes, I didn't mean, but if I'd known he was without a nurse, I'd have come straight back... How's he been?"

"Oh, fine as far as I can tell... Anyway, I'm right in the middle of something, If you need me, you'll have to shout loud, it's mayhem today. I'll be over there with my babies."

The throbbing was very bad now. I clutched my head and scraped at my ears. I wanted to let out the hurting. I opened my mouth wide and let the nasty squeal pour out.

"Oh Saul, this isn't right." Daddy had found his voice at last. "Look, his temperature's thirty-nine point six. And his heart's...I didn't know it was possible...two hundred and seventy-six times a minute...."

Mummy was already opening the doors. "And it's obviously been like that for some time. Look, someone has set the alarms to go off only when he's above two-seventy. So they know. Bloody hell."

They tried to make it better. They washed me cool all over. Daddy put a cool stick in my mouth for me to suck. It was good to have a wet mouth and throat again. But I didn't stop crying.

"Something's wrong, Rose. Call the nurse again."

"I can't ask *again*. They're all too busy. And she's talking to that mother who's baby's just been born. I can't drag her away from someone who's sobbing her heart out. I'll try again in a minute...."

I did try to be a good boy. But when Mummy lifted my legs to do my nappy, it sent knives shooting into my head. A screech, it came from somewhere deep inside, burst out of the front of my face. She put my legs down quickly.

"What did I do...? Did I crush his ankles or something?"

"I don't know but be more careful...."

"I thought I *was*.... You try. You're better at...."

So Daddy lifted my legs. Knives the same. My squeal split the air apart.

"Are his ankles damaged or something...maybe someone's been rough with him or...."

"I don't know." Daddy looked almost dead. His body sagged.

"Oh why won't somebody *come*." Mummy leant her head against my house and screwed up her eyes. "How can they listen to that cry and not *do* something...."

Then she took a deep breath and stood up straight.

"Right. Have a new nappy ready. I won't touch his ankles. I'll lift him at the hips. Ready?"

They did their best and so did I.

"Funny. Have you noticed? His body's burning up, but his hands and feet are cold."

"Yeah. We'll tell a nurse, if we ever see one again....Someone's got to come soon. All his alarms have been ringing for ages...."

"Uh oh...."

I sprayed a burning golden arc into the burning air. It rained down on me.

"Oh Saul. We take our eye off you for a nanosecond.... Right. We can ask someone to help change his bedding, now."

Daddy chewed his inside lip as he waited for Mummy to come back. The noise and the throbbing had squeezed all the thinking out of my head. I gripped both ears and pulled hard. Pull off my ears and let the hurting out. I was frantic now. I pulled harder. And again and again! Yank at the hurting! Go away hurting! Get out! Get out!

"Oh Saul, what's the.... Oh Saul, my little...." Daddy's voice was a jumble. His hot fingers held my hands away from my head until Mummy came back.

"How long are they going to be?"

"She says she's tied up. She said we could do it ourselves."

"What? But he's really upset about something.... I don't think we can...."

"Or we could stand here and wait till someone can find time...."

"We've got to do *something*...we can't just...look at him...he's beside himself...."

Eeeeeeeh-uh, eeeeeeeh-uh.

"It could be because he wants to lie differently. So we've got to turn him. It's as easy to do the sheets as well. Okay?"

"Okay."

"Right, you lift him. And we'll change the tubes over together. We've seen them do it enough times."

It should have been better to be in a cool, clean bed, lying on a different side, with Mummy washing me all over with cool clean water. But everything felt nasty. I couldn't stop crying. A nurse walked by.

"Excuse me...sorry but, we can't seem to calm him down. We've done everything we can think of...."

"Oh they're like that at this age. They do it for attention. A right little attention-grabber, aren't you? See what a state you've got your mum and dad into? He's realised what he's missing out on, that's what it is. He wants a cuddle. Put your hands in and hold him tight. That'll calm him down."

The nurse rushed on. Daddy's hands wrapped sweatily round me. They were plates of fire. Stop it Daddy! I can't...you're making me....

"That's not doing him any good at all, Tim. His heart's going at two-ninety now."

Daddy took his hands away. "Bloody stupid woman. Doing it for attention! Of course he's doing it for bloody attention. That's why babies cry! Because they *need* attention. Because something's *wrong*. Bloody hell, a baby abandoned in the middle of the Sahara desert would get more bloody attention. Does your baby cry too much? Well, stick him in intensive care. Where no one will bother...I mean, if they're not watching him, if they don't record what's...how can they know what's..."

"Oh let's not get angry, Tim. They probably can't help it. We'll make sure we tell the nurse everything at handover."

They looked at me. They looked at the machines, their eyes, welling with terror.

"Hey look, Rose, they've missed his eight o'clock feed. Maybe that's it. We've tried everything else. It's an hour late. Maybe he's hungry."

"Right. I'll go and get it then."

"Are you allowed?"

"No. But if I go into the storeroom and get one of those big syringe things, someone'll stop me and then they'll do it themselves...."

Mummy came back with a fat tube of milk.

"Did they stop you?"

"No. I told them he was desperate for his feed and they told me to do it myself. Warm this in your hands, it's straight out of the fridge, whilst I...what do I do first?"

"Something to do with Litmus. It's in his locker."

"That's it...to check the tube's in the right place...if it goes red, that's alright isn't it...? And then you have to get rid of the bubbles somehow...."

"Don't they pinch the little tube at some point...."

"That's it and then, tip the syringe...."

They spilt milk everywhere. They took much longer than the nurses. It didn't matter. It was something to wait for. I had started playing a game. A waiting game. If I can just bear it till Mummy comes back. Till the milk comes. Till Daddy says something again. Till the alarm stops. Break the nastiness into little pieces. Just do a bit at a time. Like stepping stones. And never look at the long night stretching out ahead of me. Hide from the terror that this might go on forever.

And then suddenly, something sort of went *click* in my head. Nothing changed. It was all still hot and hurting. But all of a sudden it didn't matter any more. I stopped crying. My body was melting. Not nice melting, like when Mummy sang or Daddy stroked my feet. A hot, too hot, melting. I closed my eyes and began to spin....

"Do you think that was it?"

"It couldn't have...what all that because he was hungry?"

"Well, he seems more settled...."

"Oh thank you, thank you God, what a relief...."

I was sinking and swirling into a dark place full of burning, where voices crashed into strange and nasty noises....

"Sorry, bit late doing his nine-o'clock obs. He's fast asleep isn't he?"

"Yes but earlier he was very distressed and screaming and clutching his head as if....and when we lifted his legs it really hurt him."

"And his heart rate went as high as two-ninety and he's burning up, look."

"And his hands and feet are cold, and what else Tim...?"

"You've done a good job quietening him down then. He seems fine now. Don't need us nurses, eh?"

...And I sink deeper into a dangerous pool of fire, where I will burn up, and the burning stretches on and on, but somehow, I must drag myself out of the burning, must swim to the cool and find a way out of the burning....

When We Played Hide

Drag myself away, must go deep, where no one will find me. Too hot, too hot, must find the coldest place, somewhere safe. Back to my Important Place.

It is winter. The snow is thick and the sky is heavy. Izzy looks up. *Orange sky means there'll be more snow, better be getting back.* She is playing Hide along the beck, pretending to be a soldier. The burn tinkles, not very full today. *Too frozen near the top; when the snow melts it'll gush and thunder.* Icicles hang off the snow into the water. Some of them have bits of frozen grass inside.

Then she hears a noise, a man clearing his throat. She turns and sees red through the trees. It's a red jacket, one of the Red Men. He's leaning against a snowy boulder, his uniform soaking up the wet in patches. He's picking his nose with his thumb. She plays Hide, and creeps towards him, dodging from tree to tree. *It's Spiky Hair. He likes it when I play Hide, he'll jump and roar and swear probably, and ruffle my hair and maybe teach me how to be a soldier.*

But his face looks funny, sort of sad and scared and angry all together. He's biting his lip and muttering and then he puts his head in his hands. She creeps nearer. *I'm going to jump out, he won't see me till the very end.* But suddenly he groans and slaps the boulder with both hands. She freezes behind the tree. Suddenly it doesn't feel like a game any more. She strains to hear what he's muttering: "...God Almighty...bastards...itself...I canna.... Och, boulder...you've a right to this glen...knew what's to happen to-night, you wouldna be sitting here, you great fat rock," and he hits the boulder again, "just waiting...."

He's making me frightened. I don't think I'll jump out at him now. I wish Granda was here. I'm going to tell Granda about Spiky Hair.

But she's too scared to move now so she stays hidden till Spiky Hair swallows, adjusts his sword and walks away. Then she runs really fast all the way home until she can see Granda outside, carrying peat into the house, and she runs inside with him. He puts more peat on the fire and it smokes. Izzy runs and hugs him. He is trying to reach up and unhook the smoky fish. "Ach, lassie get off and butter the cakes." He brings down the brown fish, breaks off a piece and offers if to Izzy. She shakes her head. He shrugs and eats it himself. He turns and starts to chop. "Did you find the water kelpies that hide in the burn, Izzy, looking out for wee girls to spirit away to fairy land?"

"No, but I found a Red Man. I was playing Hide and he didn't see me, but I was listening."

"Aye?"

And Izzy told him about the Red Man and what he said and how he made her scared.

"And then I ran all the way home and he didna see me."

Granda looks at her. *Is he angry with me or is he just thinking? Granda likes to do just thinking.* Then he smiles and says "Och, he probably meant nothing by it." But he hugs her tight with his free arm all the same. "They've eaten our broth and slept under our roof. That makes them our friends." And he hugged her again, but just a little too long so she knew it wasn't really all right. "Did I do something wrong, hiding and watching a Red Man?"

"No, Izzy, this is your glen, you play and hide where you want. We've nothing to fear. If they eat at your table, they can be trusted. Even as you trust your own clansmen. That's how it is, that's the way, and everyone knows it. And tonight they'll be eating rabbit broth."

"And brown fish."

"Aye, and an old fish that I forgot was there."

And they laugh, until they hear the boots of the Red Men outside, coming in for tea.

Day 77: Tuesday

I'd climbed a mountain and done really hard things. And even if things did go wrong now, it didn't matter because I was at the top. If I did slither back down a bit, I could climb back up. I could never slither right back down to the bottom, not now. I was a big boy now. I was just waiting to go home. That's what I said to myself. But it didn't help. I was still frightened.

I only saw the Big Air in chinks that day. I would open my eyes for a moment but the light was like needles. It made me even more frightened and I had to close myself in again. Shut out the horridness. I'd rather be locked in with the burning. Being brave on my own. And when was that, because days were still important? That was a Tuesday.

"...Responded since the Imipenem stopped?"

I lifted one eye-lid. I saw lots of doctors, Dr Shaky, Dr Sun in the Garden and Dr Keen, smiling. Dr Keen had big teeth. They weren't scared.

"No change really, Prof. Bit uncooperative. Cries a lot."

"Well, babies do cry. Breathing's still not too bad. Any relevant blood parameters to tell us what's going on?"

"Er, no, yesterday's haven't come back yet."

"That's not very helpful is it? Any tell-tale signs of sepsis, nurse?"

"Well, nothing unusual recorded in the notes for the last day or two."

"Hhm. Well, stick him on some general antibiotics anyway. He's probably just fed up of being in here. Can't say I blame him. Bloody racket, this morning...."

Then they floated away, and I was alone. Except, I felt someone was with me. Grandpa. I didn't see him, but I heard him. Talking about mountains. How looking down from the top of a really high one is a wonderful thing. And he said there are different mountains and ways to climb, and the hardest bit, the most exciting bit, was still to come. And I said I didn't like hard bits any more, I was sick of hurting, and couldn't I have some nice bits to do, please, for a change? And he said the next bit of the climb wasn't about hurting, it was going to be something much harder than that.

And then I was *really* scared.

There were people around but they didn't know what I knew. And I couldn't tell them. I didn't cry all day, even though the hurting and the burning was the same. I just thought and thought about what was looming. And no one noticed how scared I was.

Late in the afternoon, Dr Calm came to see me. I opened one eye a chink. He was angry, I could tell, even though he sounded calm. He looked at my machines and my charts. And then he looked at me.

"I'm not happy about this temperature. How long's it been over 39? Give him some more paracetomol and leave his doors open. He's had quite a few apneas. What are his gases like...? Trying to tell us you want to go back on the ventilator, little chap?"

He glanced at me. I made a big effort and stared into his eyes. Please, Dr Calm, you need to know that there is something worse than hurting on the way. He paused for a tiny moment. "I don't like the look of him. We'll re-intubate immediately. And I want everything cultured again. And I think we'll do an LP."

There was a small gasp of surprise.

"What, you don't think...?"

"But this morning...."

But Dr Calm cut in. "Just to cover ourselves." It was his best Really Knows What to Do voice. Smooth and in control.

"But there's no evidence of Meningitis." Dr Keen tried again. "I've been checking his fontanel and...."

Dr Calm turned to the nurse. "Noticed anything nurse?"

"Apart from the tachycardia and the temperature, which you already know about. There's nothing unusual in the notes."

"And I would have thought," Dr Keen was still smiling, "that with him being so small and very fragile, that a lumbar puncture would be the last...when there's so little evidence...."

All the doctors looked at each other, saying things with their eyes. Dr Calm was looking at me. I looked deep into him. It was only a moment, and then a surge of nastiness washed through me and I had to let my eyelids flop.

"Call it a hunch. But I want an LP done, as soon after the re-intubation as he can handle it."

And it felt now, as if it wasn't just me who smelt the scariness looming.

The next thing I saw was the look on Mummy's face. There are some things that it's better not to see.

"It's just routine really. Just to cover ourselves." It was a nurse I didn't know.

"And what does a lumbar puncture...?"

"We insert a needle into the base of his spine and extract...."

"Yes I know, but it means you're looking for...."

Mummy gripped the top of my house. I saw her heart beating in her throat. Hard ridges stuck out on her neck. Her mouth was a nasty twisted shape. "And er...does it hurt?"

"Not necessarily. Try not to worry. Meningitis is only another infection...."

Mummy swallowed hard. Pretending again.

It was getting dark at the end of the Big Air, when Dr Sun in the Garden wheeled in a silver tray on wheels. It rattled. I knew something horrid was about to happen because Mummy and Daddy left suddenly. They always did that.

The nurse rolled me onto my side and made my back curl. My knees were squashed up to my head. It hurt my hernia. It made the throbbing in my head explode. Oh, it hurts, it hurts. The nurse knew it did but she had to hold me tight.

"Don't let him wriggle. One wrong move and... God I hate these.... I've never done one so small. Right, say a prayer for me. Here goes...."

I didn't scream. It wasn't because it didn't hurt. It wasn't because of the fingers wrapping me up tight and sweaty. I didn't scream because I was too frightened. Hurting didn't matter anymore. So there must be something worse, harder to bear than hurting. And what could be harder than this hurting now?

The needle came out pulling a thread of pain behind it.

"Not getting anything.... Can I have a hand here?"

I let them do it to me over and over. I froze myself against the needle. It was only more pain on top of the rest. I didn't care whether it ended or not. Because when it ended, what then? Something worse.

They stopped when all my alarms began to ring.

"We can't keep this up. We're getting nowhere. Best leave it till tomorrow. Get a registrar to have a go."

I lay still and quiet after that. Frozen, frightened. Sometimes I opened my eyes just enough to check that Mummy and Daddy were still there. Mummy looked like she'd let every feeling drain away, leaving her dead and empty. Daddy spoke quietly.

"It can't be meningitis. They're just covering themselves. He can't.... He's in intensive care. In an incubator, how can he.... Everything they do, everything they've ever done, is supposed to be sterile...."

Mummy's face was a rock. She wasn't listening.

"...I know there was that nurse who was a bit lax when she gave him suction, and that business with the eye infection, but everything else...surely.... No one thinks its meningitis, otherwise, they wouldn't be waiting till tomorrow to do another lumbar.... It's not, everyone knows it's not...."

Mummy was silent, staring at me with flat, dead eyes. Her lips were thin and white. And I thought I saw the looming painted on her face. I didn't want to see it. I closed my eyes and sunk into myself, into the hurtings. If it was going to happen, then I wanted to hide from it for as long as I could.

Red Men Drinking

It goes purple and black in the glen when the sun sets. The white mountains go pink, then red, then the colour of fire. It's really dark now outside and the broth is bubbling and Granda is chopping, and smoke is going straight up the chimney, and outside the Red Men are coming for their tea, scraping the snow off their boots. They have to dip their heads when they come in, very tall like Granda.

They're cold, and they huddle up to the fire. And I chat to them because I like the Red Men. "There's rabbit broth again. Rabbits go brown in the spring, if they're not in the stew. In spring, my linnet will come back. And the blackbirds, and the elderflower. We make elderflower drink which fizzes up your nose and we take the cattle up to the sheilings,. He'll show me the way to the secret cauldrons, one day, when I'm big and strong, when my feet are better and I don't hurt and the snow has melted on top." And I smile at the Red Men because they like me to chatter to them, usually.

When they first came, Granda grasped our two Red Men by the hand and grinned at them and said, "Aye, it's welcome y'are, come in, come in, there's always a fire and a bite to eat for cousins of my Aileen, come in, come in, and this is little Izzy, her daughter, come Izzy, curtsey, for this is one of your mother's cousins, she's a grand wee lassie isn't she? Her mother's gone, God rest her soul, but you'll remember Aileen I've no doubt, married a cousin of yours..." I never heard Granda say so many words all at once. And Spiky Hair laughed and said, "Aye, he married a Macdonald from Glencoe and was never heard of since." And Granda looked stern and said, "He did his duty, mind." and I knew they were talking about my daddy who's gone away to France and can't come back because he's got a price on his head, and the English are going to pay dear, Granda says.

I like the Red Men. The one with spiky hair and shiny eyes is my favourite because he picked me up once and carried me home on his back. He could never let a cousin of his fall, he said. It was when I was jumping over the burn and I slipped. He saw me and ran to catch me. He didn't let me fall down the rocks. He pulled me up and held me in his arms. My knee was bleeding, so he wrapped it in his handkerchief. He sang to me and made me laugh and I forgot about my knee. And when I had to jump over the burn again, he held out his arms and promised to catch me. So I jumped and he caught me and we laughed. He's good at catching. He's safe and strong.

And the other Red Man with the bristles coming out of his nose showed me his musket when he took it to pieces and cleaned it and Granda asked how many English he'd killed with it and Bristle Nose looked embarrassed.

And last night, they ate lots and lots. Granda gave them hot beef and dumplings and cabbage and oatcakes and cheese and pudding and honey and ale. They ate and drank and burped and smiled at me and stroked my hair. I ate till I was full. And when I was in bed, supposed to be asleep (because wee girls can't stay up late, specially when they've been sickly, said Granda), I could hear them softly singing and Granda was wiping his eyes and said, "Haven't heard that since Aileen passed on," and the Red Men nodded and looked sad.

But tonight, the Red Men aren't the same. They don't laugh and sing. They keep their eyes on the fire. And if they catch me watching they look away. Yesterday they tweaked my nose and did magic and found a shiny coin behind my ear, but today, they don't want to play, they just look away. So something's not right. Maybe Granda shouted at them because they're soldiering for the English. Granda thinks a highland man should live off roots and bare earth before wearing an English jacket, and when Granda shouts it's really scary. He's never shouted at me but I've heard him shout at the woman down below with a mole on her chin, and she shouts back and then they don't talk for a few weeks, until she brings us some cake and he gives her an old smoked fish and then they're friends again.

So maybe it's like that. Except it's not, it's something else. There's the way they keep glancing at the door where their muskets are leaning and they're listening out, not to me chattering, or Granda clacking pots, but to something outside. And they hardly touch their food even though it smells really nice.

And at last, Granda looks at them and says, "So gentleman, you canna be billeted here for much longer. How have you enjoyed our highland hospitality?" The Red Men startle, like a rabbit just before Granda shoots it and they don't answer. So Granda looks straight at them, and he's got fierce black eyes sometimes, and the Red Men slide their eyes to the side. So Granda says, "Aye, it was a good day when you accepted Macdonald hospitality...Izzy!" and I run to him. "This wee lass is a product of both our clans, and it's good for her sake, in the name of her poor dead mother, that we're at peace with one another."

The Red Men look at me and then at each other. Spiky Hair drops his eyelids the tiniest bit, like a secret nod. Then Bristle Nose leans forwards and whispers, "We've no quarrel with you, and for certain, not with the bairn," and he looks at me and I look at him, and he looks away in shame. "But listen," and his voice drops as quiet as a wee beastie creeping through the grass, "when we're in these uniforms, we take our orders from the English."

No one says anything for a long time. The fire crackles. Granda holds me tight. I want to wriggle away but I know I mustn't. I can feel his breath hot on my head. His heart is beating too fast. But then he speaks carefully, "And you would follow those orders?" The Red Men don't answer. They stare into the fire, and then Spiky Hair glances up at me and I see a look in his eyes that I will never forget. It makes me want to run into his arms and let him hold me. It's like a hand has squeezed my heart, like he's crying inside but his eyes are dry.

Granda gets up and I want it all to be like yesterday. I want Spiky to ruffle my hair and play five stones with me. But it's all changed.

Granda comes back with four flagons. "I'll wager you'll be wanting to drink more than usual tonight, to help you sleep sound till the morning." Slowly the Red Men begin to smile. "Aye, no' a bad idea." Then they drink up a whole flagon in one go. They start to sing and laugh again and drink another flagon. "Aye, King William didna count on the power of highland hospitality," and Granda laughs out loud, though he doesn't drink. He just keeps filling the mugs and at last the Red Men's eyes are hazy and they droop and they lie down by the fire and begin to snore. He covers them with tartans. Then he puts me to bed. It smells of marshgrass and ducks. It's soft and prickly and musty. He tucks me in tight and kisses me goodnight. Then he goes to sit by the fire. I'm safe and warm.

Somewhere in all these rememberings from long ago, there must be Answers.

Day 78: Wednesday

It was Wednesday. Sad day.

It was like little stars bursting and bubbling. Each star made needles in my head....

"Saul's mum and dad are here, what do we do?"

"Dr Anderson wants to do the gory details, so if they ask difficult questions just do the 'it's hard to tell' line." Dr Keen's voice. "I've got to tell them the bare bones and that's it."

They speared my back again this morning. And my belly. And stole lots of blood. They put jelly on my head and slimed around.

"So have you got any results yet?" Daddy's voice.

"Yes. I'm afraid it's not what we hoped. Microbiology examined the spinal fluid and found white blood cells and a bacteria called *Enterobacter....*"

"So it is meningitis then?" Mummy's voice seemed far away.

"Er...yes. We've changed the antibiotics to ones that will affect the bacteria responsible, and ones that will penetrate the cerebral barrier."

"So what's next? Bubonic plague? Dengue Fever?" It was Mummy's voice but it didn't sound like her.

"Huh... Er... No, we huh...hope not.... Er.... Well. Dr Anderson wants to give you the details...but Saul has recovered from very nasty things before. And the good news is that we've caught it early, so...."

And then a funny thing happened. Even through the throbbing fog and the starbursts in my head, I could feel the force of it: Mummy exploded. All the pretending, all the sizzling mutters, came gushing out of her. It smashed against Dr Keen and Daddy and my house. It tore through the noise and the hurting and made everything go quiet.

"You call that *EARLY*! It's Wednesday evening, for fuck's sake. We noticed his heart rate and temperature weren't right on *Sunday*. Even *I* know that's not...Dear God, I'm not trained, I'm not even an experienced parent and even *I*...I knew, as soon as you said the word meningitis, I knew that's what it was.... That was, bloody hell, that was yesterday, and *even then* you arsed around and waited another twenty-four hours to do another.... We trusted you, you were supposed to be...we handed over our baby, our desperately ill baby, we said, here, we trust you to, we thought you could look after him better than we could, that's why we let you.... Have you any fucking idea how hard that was, handing our baby over to people we didn't even know, because we thought you'd do the very best, we thought at the *very least*, you'd be able to spot the symptoms of...even I know you've got to respond immediately to.... And how the fuck can a baby in intensive care get *meningitis*...and you dare, you dare to pretend you caught it *early*.... *He*'s been suffering for days and none of you.... And I should have, I just believed, I kept hoping you'd, I trusted you to know...."

Nurses swooped in. "It's all right. Come here. It's all right. There we are. That's it, you get angry. Get angry at us, that's what we're here for."

Mummy's voice was muffled now. "It's not fair, not fair, after everything he's been through, I'm sick of it, sick of it, sick of it...."

Heart went *tacha tacha tacha*. Head went burst and burn. Lami was letting nature help her. "We're letting nature take its course. We won't take her off the ventilator, but we won't rush in to resuscitate either...." Another baby on the other side of the Big Air gave up and floated away. Mummies and daddies cried.

Nurses sighed and carried on rushing. My mummy was singing. She knew it was my favourite.

You are my everything.
You make me want to sing.
You make the sun shi-ine, and the be-ells ring.
And you can't kno-ow, how much joy you bring.
So ple-ease don't go,
Don't go stopping my everything.

I watched it all from the little slit of my left eye. Nurse Scurry was standing by another baby. She was sort of frozen, as if she'd forgotten what she was doing. Her eyes were trapped somewhere in the distance. Her mouth half open. Then she remembered she was busy. She snapped her face back to pretending, wiped her eyes and hurried on....

Very busy, noisy. Change of shift. People, nice, friendly, fresh-not-tired, people bounced up to my house. Just come in from the cold. Wanting a chat. Hoping Daddy would make them laugh.

"So how's our little hero then...? What's happened?"

And time stops when they find out. And there is a silence. Until they swim slowly, sadly back into the Big Air and time begins again. And the Big Air gets a bit heavier with every person who comes to see me.

Dr Sun in the Garden tried not to cry. "I just want you to know that we're all rooting for Saul now, even more than before, if that makes it any easier...."

But the saddest bit was with Dr Magic. He'd stolen blood and felt my head lots of times today. Not saying anything. No jokes today. Now he just stood and looked at me.

"So, how are you two coping with it?"

"Oh, you know...."

"Yeah...."

Daddy made his voice light and calm. "So, what's your verdict? Do you think he'll beat this one?"

"Well, it's too early to...better wait to hear it from the horse's mouth, not that I'm comparing your consultant with a horse but, you know...you're seeing him tomorrow aren't you?"

"Yeah"

And then there was a really strange long time when no one said anything.

My heart went *tacha tacha tacha.* My head went sizzle and pop.

I opened my eyes a bit to see if they'd all disappeared. All three of them stood still, silent and staring. Dr Magic took a very long deep breath.

"Right then. I'm off for a few days now. Won't be back on till Sunday."

"Oh... Right...you'll be watching the match on Saturday then?"

"What? Oh yeah.... Yes I will."

I kept the slit open to watch. I couldn't open my eyes any wider, or else my whole head would burst out onto the white sheets. Time had stopped and Daddy was trying to start it again. "I'll probably give it a miss this year. But Saul and I are backing the Czech Republic, aren't we? Supporting the underdogs. Betting together this time. He still hasn't paid me the fifty pence he owes me, from the quarter-finals...."

Dr Magic was watching me. He had his back to Mummy and Daddy. And suddenly his face crumpled into a funny shape. Only I could see. He pretended to write something on a chart. He pushed his chin into his neck and squeezed his eyes shut. Then he swallowed and blinked really hard. He carried on messing with the chart until his face was back to normal.

"Anyway, better get off. So, I probably won't be seeing you...for a while...so...er.... Good luck.... Good luck Mister Saul Kay-Lambert...all the best eh?"

"Yeah. Saul says bye-bye, have a nice break...."

"Thanks...and you, all the best then...."

And he backed away to the door.

All pretending. Then he left. We listened to his footsteps going down the corridor.

And a gap opened up in the Big Air.

Red Men Sleeping

The fire is nearly dead. I hear the breathing of the Red Men, breathing deep and slow, deep in sleep. Granda isn't here. Where has he gone, Granda never goes out in the night? I'm hot inside my tartans. I stick my feet out of the bed, to make them cold. The wind outside is cold, it whistles down the chimney.

The tartans are heavy. I can't breathe. I push them aside and get out of bed. I don't wake the Red Men. I tiptoe carefully to the door.

Outside the air is so cold it burns me when I breathe. It's snowing, very heavy, drifting, a thick, soft fluffy blanket rippled by the wind. It's soft on my feet, but cold. The ground underneath is hard as bones. There's no sound except the wind. And my heart beating. The wind is full of baby icicles. Down the valley there's a sound. People shifting. Boots on snow. And whispers. But then it's hidden in the wind. And snow on snow muffles over everything.

The muskets of the Red Men are still leaning against the wall, wrapped up white. I feel alone suddenly. Someone is coming! Someone sneaking through the blizzard. I go back inside and hide. Someone is coming in here!

It's all right, it's Granda, covered in snow. He is quietly shaking it all off before he comes in. He looks at the Red Men, they're still snoring. He puts his finger to his lips and gathers a tartan around me.

Day 78: Wednesday Night

I only remember it in bits.

I remember the moment I heard Nurse Nasty's voice. And I remember the way my heart, that had been going *tacha tacha tacha* really fast, lurched when I heard her voice, and all the *tachas* crashed into each other and got mixed up.

And I remember when I heard another nurse and felt her fingers and knew she was my nurse for today, I felt really glad. I was glad it wasn't Nurse Nasty's fingers.

And I remember Dr Shaky's hands. And her voice shook too. "I just don't know what else to do...."

And I remember thinking, there's a fire, a great dangerous fire – and I'm too near it. I'm burning. And I tried to wriggle away from the fire, but the fire came with me. And I worked out the fire was in my head all along. How could I forget? I *was* the fire.

And the pain, I'm choking with it now. The pain grips me, twists the knives in my ears and hammers inside my eyes. Going *Slash-Thud.* I am small and easy to hurt and I beg for an ending. I bellow and whimper for the hurting, to make it stop. Please, hurting, stop now, *please*, I will be a good boy, but please, oh please, let the hurting end.

It doesn't end.

I am nothing but hurting, all that is left of me is hurting. I *am* the hurting....

And I remember the moment I tried to open my eyes and I saw that Mummy and Daddy weren't there. A moment of panic. They were here before. I heard them. Where did they go? Why did they leave *now*?

They were here, just moments ago, weren't they? When the nurse was holding something under my arm. "...I've always said we should do axilla temperatures more often, and not rely on the skin probe. Skin monitors aren't as accurate – it's been showing a whole degree lower than when I do it this way...look it's forty-one degrees, dear me, Saul.... Sometimes the old-fashioned ways are the best. Mind you, he wouldn't have got this far, if we'd stuck with the old ways, would he, so there we are. And you've got to remember how prem he was, it's a miracle he's here at all really. So, at least you've had nearly eleven weeks with him, that's something.... Now this will have to be sterilised before we use it on other babies. Got to be extra careful now, specially since I'm looking after Lami as well...if *she* got meningitis – well! And things like that spread like wildfire in here. In the old days, he'd be in isolation by now, and so would you two. Because with the best will in the world, nothing can be one hundred percent sterile, and these little things are so fragile...."

Mummy's voice had been tired and thin. "I think we should go home, Tim."

"You can stay as long as you want, all night, if you want to."

"I know, but I have to express some milk. I've gone way past four hours and it's getting very painful."

They must have sneaked away. I was alone. I tried to clutch at my head, but my hands wouldn't do what I said. They were thrashing and I couldn't stop them. And my legs too. My hands punched into my head. It was like mad dancing. Something was making me dance. Not nice rolling over handstands and bouncing in my Perfect Red Sea sort of dancing. Ugly, cruel, really frantic dancing. Arms jittering and flapping. Nothing to do with me.

The going wrong was going wrong really quickly now. I couldn't stop it. I called out. Dr Magic, come and help me. But Dr Magic was gone. Nurse Scurry! Nurse Clean Flowers! You must know what to do. And Nurse Chirpy, Nurse Columbine, why are you leaving me to do this on my own? I *need* you. I called so loud, so frightened, they *must* have heard me. But they were all gone.

Oh, Mummy, Mummy, Mummy, come now. I need you now. To wash me, to sing to me, to take away the hurting. Doing it on my own is too frightening. Oh Daddy, come now Daddy. Suddenly be here. I can't wait. Oh Daddy, Mummy, why have you left me? Come back Mummy. Come back Daddy. Come back Now! NOW! **NOW!**

When We Ran

Everything was on fire and I was the middle of the fire. But I had icy toes, my icy toes. I just kept thinking and thinking about my icy toes, icy toes, how lovely to have icy toes.....

There are cries in the night and Granda is carrying me. There is fire and smoke behind us. And down the glen, blood on the snow. He puts me down, he's panting. The snow freezes my feet, and he's saying, "Run then. Don't look back." And we run. In tartans. My feet are icy. But I look back and see all the other Red Men down below with swords and guns and fire-sticks and people running away from them, towards us. We're all running away from the Red Men who made the snow go red. Up past the Little Water of the Noisy Sound. Some people fall. I run the fastest and go ahead. Into the snow. Into the wildest parts. I slip. The ice cuts my hands. I get up and run again. Granda is panting behind me. We scramble away from the Red Men down below in the west. They can't catch us, we know where to run.

The snow is deep. Drifting. A strong wind rushing up the valley. Bringing us the sound of screaming. We stumble through the Corrie of the Wet Stones. Many people behind us are falling back. My arm is sore. We head for The Notched Ridge. A monster mountain. A wall. Ice. Glass. Sharp rock. It cuts my feet. My heel bleeds. It hurts. The Notched Ridge can't be climbed. Not in bare feet. Not in the gale. And the snow swirling. The Red Men are behind us to the west. The Notched Ridge to the north. Crazy Pinnacles to the south. Keep going east! Up The Chasm. Away from the Red Men. Some try to climb higher up a ridge of rock. They knock stones down on us. They slip and fall. Some lie down in the snow, not caring now.

There are screams in the night. We scramble faster. Lose our tartans. Past the Peak of the Roaring Water of the Horses. Trying to get to The Devil's Ladder. Others are there already. Climbing. Their cut feet leaving patterns in the snow. I see red. Hidden half-way up the Ladder. Red flashes in the snowflakes. The others climb. They don't see the Red Men hiding above. Waiting. I see them. Granda is urging me up the ladder, but I show him the Red. We shiver for a moment, lost in the snow swirls. There are cries from high up the ladder. Granda pulls me away from the ladder. We move sideways towards the gushing waterfall. Towards the slippery rocks, the freezing spray. We press ourselves against the rock-face, step by step, edging closer and closer to the thunder of the water. Suddenly, there is a split in the rock-face, the secret gully that nobody knows. We squeeze through a gash in the rock. Where the white water bleeds. Where the water roars. We slither down on the wet rock. Down the gully. We slip and slither and squeeze through the night. Slowly, slowly. Out of Glencoe. The only way out. The only safe place. Onto the moor.....

Day 77: Wednesday Night, the last few hours

Dr Shaky shaking...." I've never seen a baby with a temp of forty-two degrees before. He's had his maximum dose of paracetomol and still it's spiralling. And his heart rate's hitting three hundred.... I just don't know what else to do."

The nurse was shaking inside too.

"Well, can't you prescribe some morphine or something."

"I daren't prescribe that, it would kill him."

"Well, phenobarbitone then. At least let's try to control the febrile convulsions."

"I suppose. Phenobarb takes ages to work though. Longer than he's got.... I don't know, have you tried holding him? You know, when babies are distressed they like strong, calm touch...."

"I don't think...."

"What else can we...? Let's try." *Click clack ack ack.* Shaky hands. Burning hands. Wrap me up. My arms and legs thrash against her. Makes the flames burn hotter.

"Well, can we wake the registrar?"

"He hates it when I wake him. He thinks I'm, I'm sure he thinks I'm useless.... Anyway it's three in the morning.... Maybe later...."

"I think I should call the parents back. Maybe they don't realise how serious...."

"They've obviously crashed out. And they don't want to see this."

"Katie, look at him. He's in one hundred percent oxygen, on eighty breaths a minute, his sats are all over the place.... He hasn't got much longer."

"Oh I don't know...."

Pling pling pling.

"Shit, what's happening to Lami...? Can I have some help here please...?

Her hands rush away and leave me to thrash alone.

I think about Grandpa. I listen out for him, strain to feel him. This *is* the hardest Grandpa, like you said. Show me what to do, Grandpa. Tell me what it is I've got to learn so I can do it quickly and then run away from This Living.

There's no answer.

And that's when I knew in my heart, a more terrible knowing than anything I'd known before, that I was totally alone.

When Granda Went to Sleep

The Moor is a dangerous place. The black water looks shallow but it has fingers that will drag you under. There's nowhere to hide. The Moor goes on forever. Behind are the mountains and the glen. The glen is home. But we had to run away from the glen.

Tonight the moor is safer because no one dare follow. Granda knows the moor, from when he was a boy and drove cattle across in secret at night. But tonight the snow is swirling. It whips the black water into froth and makes the pools chop like the sea. Tonight is a very bad night to be out on the moor. And we're lost.

The reeds are sharp. They bite your legs and feet. The wind burns when you breathe and blows cold in your ears, so you can't hear Granda, so you think the inside of your head is burning cold. You have to keep moving to be warm. You have to keep jumping from tussock to tussock.

And Granda is old. His hair is like the snow. His face is like the wind creasing up the water. We stumble onto the Water of the Singing Birds. Suddenly he knows where we are, it's deep into the moor. Too deep. We turn around. The snow swirls and we're lost again. I grip his hand. From tussock to tussock.

We go north, then south, then east. All night. Then he slips and he's hurt, he can't move. He's suddenly very old. He tries to speak to me, he is panting, I have to listen really carefully. He says I have to keep searching. "You must look for the Anvil in the Mist." He is whispering, his breath still heaving. "When you see it, keep it ahead of you, till you come to the Little Water of Blood – the stones around it are red." and he lies back and pants hard, and I say "I'm not going on my own, Granda, I'll stay here and keep you warm." Because his hands are very cold now, and he says very quietly, "Then at the Water of the Blood, you should hear the Etive, the river. We've been there, remember? Follow the river off the Moor," and he lays his head back and closes his eyes.

I won't leave him. We cuddle up together, against a lump of moss. It's wet. My feet are very cold. Granda sleeps.

In the morning, the snow stops. I try to wake him. Granda! I can see the Anvil of the Mist! His lips are blue. That's not right. There is snow frozen in his beard. I stroke his head. You're not going to wake up, are you Granda? I lie with him all day. I don't cry.

And much later, I go the way he told me. On my own.

Day 79: Thursday Morning, just before dawn

I remember Mummy's voice.

"Oh my Dear God!"

Cool water. All over. Still burning. Arms and legs knocking against her. She strokes my forehead. Calming voice

"All right, my darling, all right, poor darling, it's all right, there we are, there we are...."

Can't stop dancing. Can't stop it going wrong. Punch myself in the head. Can't help it.

"Oh Saul.... How long's he been like this?"

"A few hours. We've tried comforting him, cooling him. I know it looks frightening, but it's the temperature. It causes febrile convulsions. Automatic response. It doesn't mean he's in pain."

"Except he *is* in pain. Look at his face. He's screaming. It's all screwed up. You have to be an...if you can't see he's in agony...."

"He's had the maximum dose of paracetomol."

"Paracetomol! Look at him. How can you...there *must* be stronger...how long can he last like this...it's unbearable...."

"That's why I called you. I wouldn't be able to live with myself if...I did wonder about morphine...."

"Well, stop wondering and give him some."

"The doctor wants to wait till the consultants come on duty. At eight."

"Eight o'clock! You're joking. He needs it now. You can't make him wait that long."

"The thing is. He probably wouldn't survive the morphine."

Everything dancing. Ha-ha, said the hurting. Nobody could stop it now.

"Oh Saul...my...little boy...." Her voice is broken. "...it's all right, darling, it's going to be.... Mummy won't let you hurt any more.... Tell the doctor I want him to have some morphine. Now."

And I remember how I hated them all. For not coming when I called. For making me do it all on my own.

I only remember it in bits. Jumbled up. But I remember every moment of it. Each moment going on for ever.

A long time after something cold seeped into my arm. And slowly, the hurting began to pull its fingers out of my head.

"About bloody time. Bloody hell, Tim. It's ten past ten. That's probably eight hours he's had to wait...."

And at last, at last, the going wrong stopped. At last the hurting let me go.

When I'm alone

The snow hides everything. It isn't snowing now, but the whole glen is cuddled up in a thick white blanket. All the little beasties are frozen quiet and heartbeats go slow and slow and slow. Everything is sleeping. The wind has dropped, maybe the wind is sleeping. Sometimes it murmurs in its sleep and makes the trees shiver. Spindly, sticky-arm trees. Their twigs go *click click*! But that's the only sound.

Even the people look asleep, covered in their snowy blankets. Peaceful as if they've forgotten what happened last night. Everything is dead or run away. No screams, no gunshots. Snow muffles over everything, doesn't it Grandpa? Oh but I forgot, you're not here, I've got to do this on my own.

And where is Izzy now? Finding her own Important Place probably. All alone and only a little girl, a wee scrap of a thing, said the woman with a mole. Not such a scrap as me.

The Red Men have all marched away, except the ones who wouldn't shoot, they had to try and escape the muskets too. The houses are all empty and burnt. Most people escaped into the mountains. And that's where they lie today, high in dangerous places, asleep under snowy blankets.

Cold, they must be icy cold, nice to be so cold. I snuggle my feet into the snow, it's so nice and cold. A cold place, not safe – I don't know where *is* safe anymore – but at least it's cold, and empty and quiet, a good place to sit and think.

I'm sitting on Signal Rock. You can see right down the glen from here. It was where the Signal Man sat, Granda told Izzy, waiting to warn about bad men. And where was Signal Man last night? With his family feeding broth and bannocks to Red Men probably. The Red Men pretended to be friends and you shouldn't turn a musket on the man who's fed you bannocks, that's what Granda told Izzy. That's a rule. The Red Men ate the broth and sang songs and cleaned their muskets under the noses of little girls, and no one thought they could stop being friendly. The danger couldn't be seen from Signal Rock, because it was already inside the glen.

I sit on Signal Rock and think. And I think about how This Living is a dangerous place, a cruel, hard-hearted place, where you never know, even if you think you do, who to trust. There are people you love and you think they love you, but they can't be trusted when you need them most. Even though they asked you to fight for them and you did and you never gave up; even though you lay in their hands and let them do whatever they liked to you; even though they *promised* to pick you up and carry you to safety. *We do everything we can to avoid any suffering.* Even the best people can let you down.

I just thought that, when the worst came, I just thought that *one* of them would have been there to help me. But when the worst comes, that's when you are most alone.

We know, creaked the trees. *We've seen it all before. You can't trust anyone, even here, in this place. You give them shelter, you give them food and they still chop you down. But it all means nothing in the end.* And the trees let the snow drip like tears.

And I think, yes, Grandpa was telling the truth when he said the hurting wouldn't be the hardest. You only have to bear the hurting whilst it's happening, you forget it when it's gone. No, Grandpa, worse, much, much worse than that, is Being Alone. I mean really alone. And knowing this terrible aloneness has changed me. My feelings before were soft and warm, nice feelings like love and trust, feelings that make you think you're safe. But now my feelings are thin, hard, mean. I hate everyone.

And never forget, groans the boulder, *because what they did, they can do again. Be strong, be hard, always on your guard. Never need to ask for help. You are always alone. You must learn to do it on your own. Trust no one.*

But you *have* to trust, to do This Living, don't you Grandpa?

Of course, there's no answer. I even have to do the thinking on my own now. So I think: if I want to go back to This Living, I'll have to trust them all, just the same as before. I'll have to love them even, and how can I? I am still small and weak and in their hands. And the horrible thud in my heart when I knew they had forgotten me, how can I ever forgive them for that? I can never forgive Mummy and Daddy for not being there when the hurting made me whimper. I can never forgive Dr Magic for saying goodbye before it was all over. What they've done before, they can do again.

So I can't go back, can I? Trust and love and forgiveness aren't part of me any more. And without them, Living is an ugly place. So, where else can I go? I don't know how to get to Grandpa.

And I suppose, *that* hurts the very, very worst of all. Even Grandpa didn't come to save me. Without him, then I am lost. I am truly and forever alone.

The sun has set. It's dark, it's cold. I'm trapped in an Important Place. It's only a pretend place, a remembering taken from someone else's memory. But I have nowhere else to go.

The trees whisper to me. *It's a nice enough place to be trapped. And maybe there are others who are trapped here with you, hidden amongst the boulders.*

I don't care. I'm not really here. Not really anywhere.

There is a murmur behind me (the wind?). The trees try to whisper to me. I don't listen. I am nothing.

And then I feel her touching me. A hand on mine. I feel her eyes, looking at me in the dark. I think it's Lami. Followed me somehow. Looking for a better place too, maybe. A place to decide what to do. She is calm and clear. She is the moon in a dark sky. Perfect. Shining. Silent. And just *there*. She makes my heart soften a little. We watch the stars get brighter and we think together.

She wants to be strong like me. I want to be calm like her. Let's lean together and think the same thoughts and work out what's best to do.

Day 79: Thursday

Nurse Chirpy was stroking my head.

"Poor little Sauly boy. Who's going to cheer me up now? Who's going to make us all want to come to work. Who's going to make it all worthwhile, eh?"

My body was still in my house, sleeping peacefully as if all the hurtings were forgotten. My arms were above my head. My favourite position. Deep sleep. Just a baby body. Lami and I floated on the ceiling. She had led me back here. What's the harm, we thought. We can watch and see what happens and decide what to do later.

He and she were in a little room. The room where doctors talked to mummies and daddies. Serious talking. Their faces were grey.

"As you know," Dr Calm's face was grey too, "Saul's being treated for meningitis. He is somewhat more stable this morning, which is...good...but what you probably don't know is that yesterday, after the lumbar puncture, we did a head scan...." Dr Calm had deep lines on his face and sad, sad eyes. His heart was thumping in his chest, but only I could hear it. "And the results are...deeply disappointing. Saul has sustained global, severe brain damage.... I'm so sorry."

Dr Calm's words settled on their shoulders. They sagged. The silence was heavy.

"What...er...how does it, the damage, what does it mean?"

"It's hard to tell at this stage. If he survives the meningitis and it's still touch and go, and if he gets off the ventilator again... another big if...then we might be looking at...severe learning difficulties. I can't be exact, it's too early to tell and this sort of...damage can never be accurately predicted."

"You must be able to...."

"Well, the brain scan does tell us that the damage affects several parts of his brain, so we're talking about multiple problems, mental and physical. The frontal lobes, which affect personality, here can you see? And this section here is mobility, so that will affect his ability to walk, and this section here is for speech...."

"So you're saying he'll be...a vegetable."

"Oh no, I'm not saying that at all. I personally think it's much more positive than that. Development depends on lots of things and we can't predict.... It may be that he surprises us again, after all, he's done that so often in the past. He may learn to walk, to talk, maybe his sight and hearing won't be too badly affected. He might be a happy little boy who enjoys life and can learn to do all sorts of thing. On the other hand he may never learn to sit up on his own, or feed without a tube.... So, what I'm saying to you is that, I think it's right that we consider... withdrawing treatment."

He wouldn't look at Dr Calm. He looked at his socks. Dr Calm stared at the black and white blobs in the file he was holding. And she stared at nothing. There was no sound except the thunder of heartbeats and, deep down, the sound of something dying.

"We don't have to decide immediately. It may be that Saul decides for himself. Certainly, if he collapses, I think it's right not to rush in and resuscitate. The question will be, do we continue to ventilate."

"But...if you can't tell us exactly what quality of life he's...how can we make an informed decision?"

"I know. I know.... I have to tell you that if he had sustained such damage at birth, we wouldn't have recommended treatment. Now of course it's far more difficult. Now eleven weeks down the line, everyone's got to know him and...to love him. He's proved he can overcome immense obstacles; who knows what he can do in the future...."

"It's not fair. He's fought so hard, it was obvious he so wanted to live. How can we take life away from him, after everything he's done to get this far...? He's had a bloody shitty life up till now, he deserves a better...it's just *not fair*...."

"I know, I know." His best calm, It'll Be Alright voice. Except it's not going to be all right, is it?

"But from what you're saying, there's a chance that if we decide to continue, then in six months' time we could realise that the quality of his life is wretched, and then it could be too late and he'll be trapped in a life of hell....but if we stop, then we'll never know if he had potential and a happy life ahead of him...."

"There are no easy answers..."

"Oh God, how did we get here…? I always thought these sorts of decisions, when I read about them, I always thought that I'd avoid it somehow...it's like, we thought we were making the right moves, doing the right thing, being responsible parents...and now we've been trapped.... I can't believe we've got to make this decision.... It's impossible...."

"I know, I'm so sorry…."

Silence

Then she looked Dr Calm straight in the eyes.

"If it was your son, what would you do?"

"I don't think that's the right...a fair question, sweets."

"No, it is the right question. I have two children of my own so I do, I'm not.... With that head scan, and Saul's history, if...he were my son, I'd say, I would think it right to...carry on. At least until we have further evidence."

"Right.... Thank you."

"...And maybe, sweets, we should see what Saul wants to do."

"Indeed…. And can I just say.... It's not the news I wanted to give you. It's not what we expected to happen, back in April. After all this time, it's terribly, so terribly...." Dr Calm tried very hard to keep his voice smooth and in control. "Even I'm....and he's not even my baby."

Then she broke. Her head fell, and she sort of choked and howled at the same time. It made him burst as well. Dr Calm leant forward and put an arm round each of them. "*I.... can't... bear... it.*" It was a strangled sort of voice. I think it was her.

I should have cried too. I should have loved them. But I didn't. I was hard. All my feelings were burnt away and I felt nothing.

So I went to watch Nurse Chirpy.

"That's better. Thirty-nine degrees. That's a bit more respectable isn't it?"

She was being kind and gentle. Too late now, I thought.

I stayed there, hovering with Lami, until he and she came to see me. They were almost too frightened to look in my house.

Nurse Chirpy finished the wash. "He's certainly better than last night. Although that's mostly the morphine."

"...Yeah.... He's much more...settled.... Ah, look.... He looks so...peaceful."

I looked down on them. My mummy and daddy.

He leant his head on the see-through roof. "I don't know Saul. Are you even there any more?"

"If you are, darling, tell us what you want us to do. Whatever you decide darling, we'll do it. No matter how hard.... You tell us Saul. Tell Mummy and Daddy if you want to carry on, or if you've had enough. We'll try and listen."

Ah, but it's not so easy. You'll have to wait, like I did. I waited and waited and nobody came. Maybe one day, I'll tell you. Maybe I'll *feel* like telling you, if I ever feel anything ever again. But till then, I'm going to pretend to be asleep. I won't make it easy for you. You made me hard. You let me burn.

They were listening. And they heard me.

Part Eight

Days 80-83

Crash sha sha sha! Doors slamming open.

"You've got to get him *out of here*!" The voice boomed and clanged at the same time. It was Granny.

"Mum! What are you...?"

"I know you didn't want me to know, but Isobel told me. Get him out of this HELL HOLE!"

"Mum, please..."

"It's a filthy place. Hospitals are all filthy places with all these filthy people milling about...."

It made me laugh inside. Granny was so *wild.* She didn't bother pretending. No sizzling mutters with her. Her voice roared across the Big Air. She was angry, *really* angry. And she didn't care who knew it.

He and she tried to calm her. They spoke out of the sides of their mouths, as if they were hoping no one would hear.

"Mum, please, keep your voice...We want him out of here as much as you...but we can't. He's all wired up... You can't wheel a ventilator down the corridor...."

"Well, it's obviously not doing him any good in here, not with all these" (voice suddenly *even* louder) "*awful people* who don't know...."

"Please, Mum, they're doing their best..."

"Well, I don't think it's good enough. Ailsa told me about a couple who insisted on taking their baby home, and *their* baby hasn't got meningitis...."

"That was a completely different case." She made her voice as small as she could. "We still have to...rely on...Mum, please, we can't afford to...."

"Well, it's a disgrace, an absolute scandal...."

I loved it. The anger crashing up against embarrassment, and swilling around with all the shock and sadness. Granny was so big and strong and wild and oh she was *angry*. I laughed inside so hard that all my alarms went off. It made Granny stop. For the first time, she looked at my machines.

"You see, Mum, he can't do without all this."

"Are you sure?"

"This machine breathes for him. He's too ill to breath for himself."

And he and she showed Granny what everything did.

She listened and looked. Before, it felt like she couldn't be bothered with me and my machines, but now she looked closely and asked questions. And as I listened to her, I worked it out. Before, she had been frightened of the noise and the flashing lights and the wires and my sticky-legged bare body. But now she wasn't frightened. Now she was too *angry*.

And it made me think. *I'm* not frightened when I'm angry either. I'm not frightened of being alone any more, as long as I stay angry. I'm not scared of the hurting, as long as I stay angry. I know now that I can get through The Worst, all on my own, but I've got to *stay angry*. I *like* being angry. It makes me feel strong, safe, untouchable.

Maybe that's what made me decide. Alright, I'll carry on doing This Living, I won't give up, but I've got to do it my own way. No more trust. No more loving. Just me, doing it all on my own. That means I've got to learn quickly how to do it without tubes and machines and things. I've got to get away from people who can hurt me. I can't trust them now. I don't want to *have* to trust them. So, I said to myself, I'm going to Escape.

It was like the anger was the wind behind me, holding me up, pushing me forward. It should have been a hard thing to do, to start my escape so soon, because I was so poorly, but it wasn't. You just needed mean feelings, for *everyone*.

Except Lami. I still kept safe a little bit of love for her. I told her what I'd decided, and she was glad. She promised to follow me if I raced away, no wasting time floating or hiding in an Important Place. Every moment, every day from now on was a fight. And I was going to win.

So. That was Friday. On the Monday, no one dared to stop me.

"Well, the latest head scan shows that the damage is resolving in the way we'd expect. That is, the damaged area is draining away to form cysts, which er...as I said, it's not a good scan but....I've got a hunch, that it's not the worst case scenario just yet, if you see what I mean. And his clinical improvement over the weekend is extremely pleasing. He's down to eight breaths already, only in forty percent oxygen, down from...well it was nearly a hundred percent at one point wasn't it? So there's every indication that he'll be off the ventilator sooner rather than later.... I've stopped the morphine.... The infection is obviously on its way, temperature down to thirty-seven degrees. It's all.... It's not what I expected on Thursday. I think we were right to wait and see what his feelings on the matter were. He's clearly telling us that the fight's still on. Eh, little chap?"

Day 83

He and she felt guilty. It oozed out of their eyes and mouths.

"We're going to work hard to get you home and then we'll give you the life you deserve...."

"Mummy and Daddy will never leave you on your own again, sweetheart. One of us will always be here from now on...."

He would sit up till the middle of the night, watching me, stroking my head, talking to me....

Round and round the garden, like a teddy bear,
One step, two steps, tickly under there.
Round and round the haystack, went the little mouse,
One step, two steps, in his little house.

...and when he thought I was asleep, he wrote fast and angry.

And then she would come and he would go away. And she would sing to me, check my charts, let me suck milk from a cotton bud, and when she thought I was asleep, she would write too. Pages and pages. And then he would come back and she would go. So whenever I opened my eyes, one of them was always there, always watching.

When they were in together, they talked in angry mutters.

"...All so fucking complacent – I heard him talking to one of the registrars, this morning, by the x-ray machine. They'd just put a long line in a new baby, and he pointed to the baby's heart, where the end of the long line was and he said, listen to this Tim, he said, 'Let's hope there isn't a lump of *Enterobacter* on the end of it this time.'"

Our corner glowed with it. We all just throbbed with anger. Ugly angry. Clenched teeth and thin mean lips. Sizzling mutters. I loved it. The more we sizzled, the better I got.

"...And she didn't wash her hands all shift, and once, when she came back from the loo, I pointedly put the alcohol rub on top of the incubator, and she pointedly put it back on the shelf, and then she went in with her dirty hands and messed with his I.V. line."

"I know Dr Anderson said they're all rooting for him now, but she's obviously given up. And if she had flu, like she said, she shouldn't have come in at all. It's alright isn't it, she can infect Saul, but he's not allowed out for a cuddle in case he infects anyone else...."

"Yeah. It's alright for children to run around with Chicken Pox...."

"What!"

"Yeah, one of the siblings has got Chicken Pox, and because he's run around all the unit touching other people's babies, including Saul, they've all got to be injected against it."

"For God's sake!"

It was a different place now. It used to be a soft, warm place. But no one dared come over here to laugh now. Dr Keen didn't dare even to smile when he came to steal blood. His big smile had slipped away for ever. And Dr Shaky's hidden noises went *arrrgh!* and her shaking fingers whispered, *oh no, oh no, oh no....*

It was as if they were scared of our hate. Not hidden hate. Red and steaming hate now. He and she weren't friendly with the doctors any more.

"So tell us again. How did he come to catch meningitis?"

"Well, er...really he caught it from himself."

"Oh right, and how does that work then?"

"Well, his immune system was, is, very weak, and bugs which are normally benign, like the one found in his cerebral fluid...."

"*Enterobacter.*"

"Er, yes...well bugs like that can become pathogenic with a weak immune system."

"So, the *Enterobacter* that got into his brain, was already somewhere else in his body?"

"Er, effectively, yes."

"So how did the *Enterobacter* get into his body in the first place?"

"Well, er...it's a normal, common-or-garden.... Everybody has these bugs...."

"Oh, I see. So he had these bugs on him when he was born?"

"Er...possibly...look I think you should ask...."

"And if he's been 'infecting himself', and it's just a benign bug that we all carry around with us, he can't *also* be contagious can he? In which case, why are you suddenly doing LP's on the other babies? Are you expecting an influx of common-or-garden bugs from, well, wherever they come from?"

"It's not as simple as.... Other babies have...I t's become clear that there's a strain that's become resistant to our usual antibiotic treatment and so we've had to change the entire policy of the unit."

"So, is he contagious or not?"

"Well, no, it's not...."

"So, if he's *not* contagious, if it's just because of his weak immune system, then why isn't he allowed out of his incubator...."

And when the doctors huddled round me in the mornings, they didn't talk loudly, all confident as usual.

"...And you know they write a diary. Been making detailed observations since he was born, apparently. Did it for him to read when he grew up...."

"Well just make sure you don't give them anything else to write about."

"Puh! You know what they're like. Always asking the most difficult questions they can think up. And now they're staying downstairs, they're here in shifts. The only time they're *not* here is now, during ward round...."

So, instead of people feeling sorry for me, they crept around. It made me feel strong. It made me forget the horrible hurting in my head. I didn't care about things like hurting now. I screamed, oh yes. Sometimes I screamed all day. Screamed out my anger and hate. Screamed because I *wanted* to. And it was great. Instead of *them* doing things to *me*. *I* was doing things to *them*. I could make them guilty. I could make them cry. I could make them mess with my machines for ages.

And the more I screamed, the quicker I got better.

Days 84-90

After that, no one could stop me. Each day I cheered inside. Escape! Escape! I'm doing it.

On Tuesday, I pulled the Tube out. I breathed on my own, so they took away the *clunk thud whoosh* machine. They put on the hissing mask, but I didn't need it really.

They tried to love me. My favourite nurses, he, she, they tried even harder than before. They cuddled and fussed and were so, so kind. But I was solid with hate. I was a rock. A hard, cold, jagged rock. Like the one in Glencoe that sits in the middle of the loch. It's alone, but it's strong. That's me. No one could hurt me now. They couldn't even reach me. All their nice words and kind cuddles. Too late. Too late.

On Saturday, I escaped from my Hot House into a cot. I just loved and loved it. I stayed awake all night listening and smelling the Big Air. The noises were clearer, closer, but they didn't echo. They didn't hurt my head so much. And for the first time I wore clothes. At last! I was lovely and snug, just the cool air on my hands because Nurse Scurry rolled the sleeves over and over. I felt secure, because I could hide inside my clothes now. It felt as if, for the first time, I didn't belong to everybody else any more. I could wiggle my toes and no one could see. I could squeeze my buttocks and it was my secret.

I didn't need a hat but Nurse Scurry put one on anyway. It was yellow with flaps on. It made him laugh.

"Saul! You look like Buck Rogers!"

It made Nurse Chirpy pretend to be sick. "Urgggg! That's horrible. I'm not looking at that all night." And everyone laughed. I nearly laughed too. And then I remembered, you can't be angry and laugh at the same time, not with really hard, rock-like anger, anyway. So I gave them all a nasty stare instead. And what were he and she doing? Smiling? It didn't take *them* long to forget, did it? You see, I was right, you can't trust anybody. But I didn't care about them. I was too busy escaping.

On the Sunday, I had my first bath. I tried not to like it because I wanted to be hard. But it was *so brilliant!* For a start, there was the fluffy smell of flowers swishing around in the steamy air. And then when I was in the water...oh it was delicious, floating all warm and slippery. I slithered against Nurse Scurry's hands. Nurse Columbine put bubbles on my head and washed my hair. I looked at her smiling down at me. "Oh, I do love you Saul." And I *nearly* smiled back. Luckily I remembered just in time that I was supposed to hate her. So I scowled instead. Then I closed my eyes and pretended I was in my Perfect Red Sea again. *Swoolyla lyla la lala.* Floppy and warm and wafty, back to the time when I didn't even know how nasty This Living could be.

And on Monday, they took the hissing mask away and put a little plastic box over my pillow so that sweet air could waft over my head.

"He isn't even needing much oxygen in his head box. In fact – yes look at that – he's in air. It's amazing. He's supposed to have chronic lung disease. You know at one point the doctors thought he would be on oxygen for as long as two years?"

Dr Calm got a surprise. (I saw a lot of Dr Calm nowadays, he often stopped by to check my charts.) He nodded to her, picked up a chart and then glanced at me. I gave him my nastiest stare. He looked surprised. And then his face broke into a smile.

"What's this? In a head box already, little chap? Well! And a good respiratory drive...eye-tests good...and all the blood parameters good.... You've made your mind up, haven't you?" And he turned to her. "So what's brought about this turnaround, then?"

"Oh he wants to get the hell out of here...."

Day 91

I even hated Grandpa. It wasn't hard to hate him, because he still wasn't there, was he? There was just a silence in the place where he should have been. But it was scary, because it was a bit like hating yourself. It was like hating everything.

I couldn't help it though. He'd left me to do it on my own, hadn't he? He must have known better than anyone that The Worst was coming. And yet even Grandpa had run away. And that hurt more than anything else, ever.

But that morning, I started to get a funny feeling, a scary feeling, a feeling I'd waited so long for, that now it was here, I didn't want it. It was the feeling that Grandpa was coming to find me. My throat was dry. She gave me milk on a cotton bud to suck. My hands were sweaty. Inside my head it went *thud thud thud*. My heart was beating fast and loud.

She was worried. "I'm sorry, but something's not right."

The doctor we didn't know was angry and he wasn't hiding it very well. "Look, we're not testing for infection when his temperature is only thirty-seven point six. It would be pointless."

"It's not just the temperature. I just *know*.... Look at his colour...and something's really agitating him. Has he got a sore throat, maybe, he's always thirsty? Look, Dr Anderson tells us not to look at the charts but to look at the baby. That's what I'm doing. That's why Tim and I spotted symptoms of meningitis and you didn't. Because his charts didn't show it, but his behaviour did. I've been watching Saul very closely, and yes there's not much in his charts, but I'm telling you, there's something wrong."

The doctor looked at the nurse. It was one we didn't know. "Put the parent's concern in your notes, will you?" He turned to go. But she stopped him.

"So?"

He sighed. "Er?"

"So what are you going to do?"

The doctor moved his tongue around his mouth. "All right then. We'll do blood cultures and start him on general antibiotics, if you like. When the SHO gets the time....But please remember, he's the only doctor on and there are twenty-eight other babies for him to look after."

"Yes well I've only got one baby."

It was a sort of fight with words. I'm not sure who won.

Grandpa chose to come when it was just her and me. My nurse was in the milk kitchen. (We hardly ever saw her, she seemed very busy.) Out of the corner of my eyes things were going wibbly. And far away there was a buzzing. Except it wasn't far away, it was in my head. Then *crack*! Bright white humming light! Everything was shining. It filled me up, so strong and gorgeous that it made me go stiff from my head down. And the light was Grandpa.

I wanted to show him how much it hurt when he wasn't there. But I was too scared. And yet, at the same time, I wasn't scared at all. It was like I was feeling all the feelings there were to feel, all at once. And it all added up to a delicious white Calm.

Grandpa knew all about my hate and anger anyway, it was no use hiding it. And he didn't seem to mind. He told me it was alright to be angry. Anger is part of living, he said. And he didn't mind that I hated. It's just another mountain, he told me, making and changing your own feelings, and Grandpa thought what I was doing now was the best mountain of the lot....

I was just going to ask him why he had left me to do The Worst on my own, when I woke up. The Big Air seemed like water. Everything glowed, fresh and new. I felt strange. I blinked lots of times. All my alarms were ringing. She was calling across the room to a nurse.

"...It's stopped now...he's back to normal."

"Oh good. I'll be finished with this baby in two ticks. Who's his nurse?"

"Anya, but she's not here..."

"How long did it last?"

"About two minutes....he screwed his face up and...."

"Oh sounds like he's got wind. He'll give a good fart in a minute and then he'll feel better."

I knew it wasn't over yet. After a while it happened again. The light filled me up, and there was Grandpa again. He told me that doing the Worst was brave and wonderful, and he was proud of me. But doing it all on my own was Even Better. It's the bits of This Living that aren't safe, the dangerous and exciting and scary bits, that are worth doing. The light filled me over and over, in lovely waves.

And I suppose, Grandpa might have been right, (even though I was still too mad with him to let him know). I suppose I *did* feel stronger now that I knew I could do it on my own, and I suppose I *did* feel proud. But I was still angry and full of hate. I was just about to ask him why he had taken so long to come and explain, when I woke up again. The noises were sharp and tinkly. No one was there. But I could hear her voice. "I think it's a fit, but I can't get anyone to...."

She led a nurse to my cot.

The nurse looked in. "Looks alright to me."

"Well he is now, but he was clenching his fists and arms and his heart rate fell to fifty...."

"Probably an apnoea. Shall I suck him out?"

"No, he didn't stop breathing, it wasn't an apnoea."

We were alone again. She watched me all night. Her eyes moving from the machines to me and back again. She watched so closely that every time after that, she knew it was about to happen even before I did. She would stand up.

"It's happening again...anyone!"

And Grandpa told me that it still wasn't finished. It wasn't enough to do the Worst on your own, to be strong, to escape quickly. The bit I'd like the best, he said, would be when I turn anger and hating into something else. I didn't think he got that bit right. I like being angry, I don't want nice feelings, weak and wobbly feelings that let in the hurt, that got you to trust people who couldn't be trusted. He just laughed and said he knew I could do the Nearly Unbelievable. I told him that doing it on my own meant not listening to people telling me to do stupid nice feelings, and then I woke up again.

Nurse Clean Flowers was stroking my face. "Eh, Saul, you like a bit of drama, don't you...? It did look a bit like a fit. I'll get a doctor. Probably prescribe some phenobarbitone to calm him down. And you're going to need another IV line. Poor little poppit."

I thought about what Grandpa said whilst Dr Keen poked needles into my arm. It was nice feeling angry. It was *better* to be angry. And who would want to feel nice feelings for doctors with sharp needles? "Oh, he probably does feel pain when he's having a fit, probably from the pressure on his brain, from the fluid, because he may have hydrocephalus, which means we'll probably have to do ventricle taps, stick a needle into his head to drain off the fluid...." and he kept smiling at her as he went jab, jab, jab in my arm. My heart was like a stone for Dr Keen. I can't unsoften it. No, Grandpa, I'm staying hard and angry and mean.

She was sobbing. Even through the walls I could hear her. She was in the Serious Talking little room with Nurse Clean Flowers. The other nurses could hear it too. They looked at each other, eyes wet with sadness. I wasn't sad. She could sob and sob. I didn't care.

"Oh, Saul, Saul, Saul, Saul, (sob sob). I'd give up everything, it wouldn't matter how damaged he is, I would, I'd sacrifice my whole life, if that's what he wanted. But not for this, not to see him suffer like this, he must never have another night like this...(sob, sob)...oh what have we done to you? It's my fault, I should have *known*. Why didn't I.... I'm well read.... I knew about the symptoms.... I mean meningitis for God's...(sob sob)...I should have kicked up a fuss.... How could we have let him suffer for so long...?" (I still didn't care. I didn't.)

"You can't blame yourself. Even the doctors missed it. It happened right under the noses of three consultants, how could you have...."

"Oh Saul, Saul.... And nothing's changed, has it? If I'm not here...He's had four fits tonight, each lasting, I dunno, twenty minutes, with all the monitors going crazy, and his nurse has missed *all* of them. She still doesn't know, wherever she is."

"We do have to have breaks."

"I know, that's what I'm saying. I know they're all legitimate times when nurses aren't in the room, when you're in the milk kitchen, or the drugs room, or on the phone or in a meeting, I know it's not the nurses fault, but when someone else is baby-sitting him, it's not the same...if I can't even get someone to see him when he's having a fit.... Sometimes at night there's only one nurse in the room with fourteen intensive care babies.... It's not fair on him, after all he's been through.... Oh Saaaaaul!" It was a wail that came straight out of her heart.

And the force of her wailing spiked deep into the Big Air. And deep into me. It spiked even through the hard feelings and touched something.

And later when he and she sat by me, their faces like clouds, puffy and grey, I couldn't help remembering the first days, and the first weeks, and how I used to love them. And here they were now, trying so hard to reach me and I was being mean to them.

"Are you trying to tell us something Saul? We'll do whatever you want, to make up for the terrible start you've had. But we won't keep making you suffer. Tell us darling. Have you had enough?"

And maybe it was the way everything was glowing clean and fresh. Or maybe it was the ache in her voice. Or maybe it was the hurting in their eyes. But I couldn't stop the tiny melting inside.

The icy grip of the hard mean feelings loosened, just a tiny bit. Just enough to feel a soft light flickering in my heart.

I looked up at them and I said to myself, so only I could hear, Oh Mummy, Daddy, I don't know why, and I can't help myself, but I want to forgive you.

Day 92

Dr Calm always made them feel better.

"And he mentioned hydrocephalus did he? Look, hydrocephalus and ventricle taps aren't on the agenda at the moment, and even if there was some pressure on the brain, it doesn't cause pain. The epilepsy isn't so surprising really. Yes it may be a response to the brain damage and be a permanent feature, but it's just as likely to be a response to the stress he's been under. Babies do fit sometimes and it stops once the stress has passed. The phenobarbitone will keep it under control for the moment anyway.... I'm told you feel fairly devastated by last night but...please, it's not as bad as you think. Look at him, he can't be suffering as much as you think, he's coming on in leaps and bounds.... I'm still fairly optimistic...."

She forced a smile. But Dr Calm couldn't make me smile. Oh no, I was too busy escaping again.

I got better and better every day after that. Mummy and Daddy even dared to leave me sometimes, as long as one of the nice nurses was with me. One day, Granny arrived. I was with Nurse Chirpy, she was putting a blue bobble hat on me. We both decided it was a nice hat, though I didn't let her know I liked it, because I still wasn't friends with her.

Then I heard Granny's voice. She was trying to whisper but everyone could hear. I looked out through the bars of my cot and saw her hair shining, all wild and golden. She was in the place where my Hot House used to be. She was talking to a new baby. It was a very poorly baby, all skinny and sticky legged, like I used to be. It was still naked and full of tubes. Not like me, chubby, in a Pooh Bear suit and blue bobble hat, with no tubes at all.

Granny stared in at the sticky-leg baby and frowned. "Don't you think you should get some weight on? Over five pounds, I think your mother told me, that's what you've got to be before they'll even think about a release date.... You seem to have *lost*.... What have you been up to? Anyway, you're going to surprise everyone aren't you? If you're anything like your grandfather, you won't be put off by a few doctors. Don't know what they're talking about, always think the worst, typical of scientists, your grandfather was the same – they only think about facts and figures. And the thing is, you probably had a *marvelous* brain in the first place. The bits you've got left are better than most people have in the first place. Because most people are brainless before they even start. They don't *know* they are, because they haven't had the benefit of a brain scan. So you probably won't be any different from the rest of the population. Except you've had experience of...Well, a friend of mine told me that being in hospital for the first few months of your life is *very* good training. You'll be *very* disciplined when you grow up. Oh yes, and you know, people who sail through life and have it easy, they're *terribly shallow*. So you see you'll be Mature, from a very early age...."

All the nurses were looking at Wild Granny.

"Is she anything to do with that baby?"

Nurse Chirpy grinned and finished tying my ribbons. "Are you looking for Saul? He's moved. Over here."

"Oh, yes.... Thank you.... I thought that baby looked a bit on the manky side.... Oh look!" Wild Granny hadn't seen me in a cot yet. "Oh look, he's like a normal baby!"

"Rosie's just popped downstairs for a bite to eat.... Shall I call her?"

"No, no, what do we need her for? I'll just...."

"Would you like to hold him, whilst you're waiting...?"

"No, I'm not...."

It was exciting. It felt sort of dangerous to be held by someone like Granny. Her voice could bounce across the Big Air and her face could twist into brilliant shapes. But Granny was only wild on the outside. Her hidden noises were all wibbly-wobbly. Other people pretended to be calm outside but were all hot and angry inside. Granny was the other way round. She held me easily and her heart beat long and slow. At first she looked closely at me, touching my face and hands. I squeezed her soft cuddly fingers and looked into her eyes. She wasn't angry any more. She didn't blame me any more. After a few minutes, her eyes drifted off into the distance. We rocked together. An easy emptiness.

We stayed like that for ages. Until Mummy's voice broke into our dreams. "God, I'm so sorry. I keep dropping off in the stupidest places."

Nurse Chirpy was grinning. "Look at him. Granny's obviously got the knack, hasn't she?"

Granny went "Humph! I never get worked up about things, that's the trick of it."

Nurse Chirpy and Mummy grinned. And I couldn't help it. I grinned too.

Day 94

It was because of the laughing.

Nurse Chirpy was trying to make me smile. She tickled my toes. She tickled under my arms. She didn't stop when I pushed her away. She didn't stop smiling at me when I gave her my hard stare. She just kept trying.

"Maybe he's bored. He's at that age when he needs a bit more stimulation, other than people doing horrible things to him."

And she brought me a colourful mirror and a black and white mobile. It's hard to keep crying and doing hard stares when someone is being so nice.

And when she heard Dr Magic coming to steal blood, she hid me under the blankets. "Discharged himself. Got fed up with you and your needles and your weird sense of humour."

Dr Magic started to search everywhere for me. I giggled and gripped my toes in excitement. When I felt his hands on the blankets, I nearly squealed because it was such fun. First he found a foot, then he found an arm. And then he pulled back the blankets and found all of me. Pretend surprise! I forgot to be strong and mean to them. We all laughed and the laughing made something go *crack*! inside me. It was the hard feelings starting to crack open.

"He's not quite so mad at us today, is he?"

"Well, we're working on it."

And then Nurse Scurry took over.

"I don't believe in leaving babies to cry." So she tried swaddling me, cuddling me, stroking, patting, lying me against Mummy's breast where milk dripped into my mouth. (And I had to stop crying then, because it's hard to cry and suck at the same time.)

Nurse Scurry was sorry about the way things had gone wrong. I heard it in her voice. "You two go and eat. I'll sit here and watch him. Don't worry, I won't let him be on his own, I promise."

She sat with me and watched. I only had to do a whimper to get her to love me. I liked to make her fuss me, to know that I was the only one she cared about. And she did care, oh, all the time. You could see it in her eyes when she came in. "I dreamt about you again last night Saul. Yes I did, little one. I dreamt I was giving you a bath and you swam away from me. Would you like another bath today? You love your baths don't you?"

I could see her remembering how I used to be. I could feel it in her velvet fingers when she put a new vest on me. "These prem size vests seem to disappear every time they're sent to laundry. That's why I bought a set especially for him. I was in Mothercare anyway, getting something for my two, and I couldn't resist them. They didn't cost much."

I couldn't keep hating, could I? Not with all that loving. Her love seeped in through the cracks in my hard, mean feelings.

And Nurse Columbine was really excited when she took over. She hadn't seen me for days, and she glowed because it was her turn to look after me. She was so proud of me because I'd done so much escaping.

"I'm taking away his head box, he doesn't need it any more. He's been so amazing, that I thought he deserved a certificate. Here."

"'This is to certify that I, Saul, achieved First-class Honours in the attributes of Determination and Achievement on this day, July 19th 1996.' Oh that's so.... Thank you, that's really lovely. Oh Saul, look what Auntie Anthea's done, isn't that kind?"

You can't stay hard as a rock, when all day you hear people's fingers sighing, *Oh, we're sorry, Saul, we're so, so sorry*. So one day, when all my favourite nurses were in together, (although it was Nurse Chirpy's turn to look after me), I stopped being hard and mean to them.

Nurse Chirpy had found some nice music, especially for me.

Hey, Saul, you, Saul, Pretty Chitty Baby.
Smally Sauly baby, we love you.

It was a friendly, laughing song. Everyone sang along and jigged about as they did their jobs. I watched through the bars of my cot and jiggled my arms. Then I wiggled my toes. And soon, I couldn't stop myself from dancing. I bounced up and down and kicked off the blankets.

Hey, Saul, You, Saul, smally Sauly baby
Smally Sauly baby loves you too!

Nurse Chirpy was so funny. She made my toys dance along my machines. She took Dr Shaky's wiggly worms from around her neck, (before Dr Shaky could stop her) and made the worms dance around the Big Air. She made them kiss everybody:

Oh (kiss), *You* (kiss), *Smally Sauly* (kiss kiss)
Smally Sauly (kiss kiss) *Loves you too!*

She even kissed Dr Magic, who grinned back at her.

Then Nurse Columbine and Nurse Clean Flowers put their arms round each other and skipped from baby to baby. They did all their jobs in time with the music, doing everything in a way to make you laugh. They shut doors with their hips, bounced nappies on their arms, carried charts on their heads.

I giggled and sang and bounced. I couldn't stay stiff and angry. How could I? It was such a lovely day. Maybe the happiest day of my life so far. And at the end of it, my favourite nurses clumped round my cot and Nurse Scurry said, "Well, Saul, we don't want to see you go, but we can't keep you here any longer. It's time you left Intensive Care."

Day 95-104

I wanna – uh – I wanna – uh – I wanna – uh – I wanna – uh – I wanna – wanna – wanna – wanna – wanna – wanna – wanna - uh.... Beeet Eff-Emmmm! Bringing you the best sounds in Meoosic. Through. Out. The. Niiight. Yeah!

Mummy and Daddy weren't allowed in at night. The nurses in this new room put the lights down at night. It was dark and lonely. I could hear the nurses in the middle, laughing, talking loudly.

Dga dga dga thump! thump! thump!
I'm gonna den den den den deaaaance
I wanna get down (thump!) get down, get down (thump!)
get down (thump!)

I didn't like the nights. Except when Mummy sneaked in. Then I knew she would hold me and make it alright. It was nicer in the day when Mummy and Daddy could pick me up whenever I asked. Sometimes I slept all day on Daddy's shoulder.

I started having my milk from a cup. The nurse sat me on her knee and let the milk rest at the edge of the cup. I gulped it down. It was great. The taste, the smell, the feel of it in my throat, all warm right the way to my tummy. It was much better than the milk straight down a tube. I still had to have a tube sometimes because I got so tired, especially if it was Mummy or Daddy holding the cup. Sometimes they held it so the milk was just too far away from my lips. Sometimes they let it splash all over me. They had to learn to hold it just right.

It mattered how fat I got. They weighed me every few days. "Well done, Saul, you've broken the five-pound barrier! Won't Daddy be pleased."

Dr Shaky was pleased too. She was trying to be nice to them. And I suddenly felt sorry for her. And I thought back to The Worst, when her hands shook and she didn't know what to do. And I thought, maybe Dr Shaky had been as frightened as I was. She had been trying to pretend, trying to push down the panic and loneliness. Like me. Panic got in the way. If you didn't push it down you didn't have space in your thinkings to work things out. And Dr Shaky had tried really hard to work things out. And it hadn't been easy with all the noise and the alarms and babies screaming.

"Well, I think we can stop checking his gases now."

"You mean he doesn't have to have those heels pricks any more? Oh Saul, we'll have you out of here soon, darling."

I wished every day that escape could be soon. And I kept on fighting, even though the hurting in my head was getting worse, I had to ignore it. I had to pretend I didn't feel the funny sinking behind my eyes.

We hated it in the hospital now. Mummy was scared in this new room. My favourite nurses came to see me now and then, but usually it was nurses who didn't know me. And then there were the scary people. Like the man with funny eyes, who always drank from a can and swayed above my cot so Mummy had to lean over me to keep him away. He grunted at his baby, who was in the corner, and staggered out of the room.

And then there was the woman with the scratchy voice. "Oh, the only luck I ever have is bad luck. I must be the unluckiest person alive. He can't keep anything down you see. They say, if he doesn't start to feed soon, they'll put a tube down. Can you imagine? Poor little mite. So I'm stuck in here. Just my luck. Yours is looking bonny. You don't know how lucky you are to have one that feeds like that. Nothing goes right for me, he come four weeks early. Can you imagine? I was in the supermarket, when I felt a pain and I thought, never! Oh I have no luck do I? That's why he can't keep anything down. Immature stomach. It'll be days before he's right. And me stuck in here. Hope I'm out of here by Friday, it's my birthday and we've got a right knees-up planned...."

Mummy was too tired even to pretend to be listening.

And then there was the man with muddy boots. He sat in the chair on the other side of my cot. He read a paper out loud.

"Carol, pictured above, before the mid-air disaster, is going to sue British Airways for two thousand pounds. That's one thousand pound for each breast." And the man with muddy boots laughed. He only looked at his baby once, when it had been crying for ages. "Shuddup will ya. Jesus!" Mummy lifted me out of my cot and held me close.

And then there was the family who only ever looked at the floor, even though their baby was wiggling his legs for them in his cot. They had another little boy who ran around the room, shouting, kicking, jumping up and down. Once he grabbed the bars of my cot and started shaking. Mummy took his hands off the bars. "I don't think you should do that. Why don't you go into that little room over there. They've got toys for you to play with." The little boy's family were still staring at the floor. Mummy bit her lip and glanced at them. I could see something beating inside her forehead. She sighed, angry.

And then there was the thin woman who smelt of smoke. She was as stick thin as her baby. She had dark patches under her eyes and black pinpricks up her arms. Mummy pretended not to look. She squeezed me closer.

The thing about this room that made upset me most, was the noise. There weren't so many bleeps and plings but it went:

DuggaDuggaDuggaDuggaDuggaThumpThumpThump BeeeetEfffEmmmm...all day, all night....

It made the sounds of the Big Air seem soft and gentle. The bleeps and plings never made my cot tremble like this. They didn't go jagged into my hurting head.

Eeek! Eeek! Eeek! Eeek! Eeek! Bringing you the newest hip-happening sounds from the heart of the city....

Sometimes you just want to sleep. Sometimes, a lot of the time, you just want peace and quiet. But it was noisy noise. Always thumping. Spiking into my ears. It was push-you-thump-you-make-you-race music. Fast-talking, high-screeching, hard-beating, make-you-scream music.

I believe (bump!) I can fly-ay-y-ay-ay. YeahOwaaaaah!

It wouldn't have mattered so much if my head had felt soft and clear. But inside it was jangling, twisting, humming. All I wanted was nice, sweet, floppy sounds, or just no sound at all. I didn't want get up and jump sounds. I wanted to sleep and sleep and sleep and get better. The music made me scream. Leave me alone! Get out of my head!

One day Mummy went to the black box on the window sill and switched the noise off, and there was space, and quiet thin air and it was lovely, and all the babies breathed the quiet thin air and bit by bit, we all stopped crying and we all went to sleep. Until a nurse switched the noise back on again.

I tried to ignore it, but it was all the time. I couldn't stand it any more. I screamed and didn't stop. Mummy rocked me, whispered to me, laid me down, picked me up, fed me, changed me. But I didn't stop screaming. She tried to turn the noise off. The nurse switched it on again. "It's you Mum, making him cry, you're passing on your anxieties to him. He never cries when you're not here."

And one day when Daddy came in after work, he found her sitting limp, with tears drying on her face. "He's been inconsolable since eight o'clock this morning. I might as well have been at home for all the nursing that's gone on. I can't stand it any more Tim. I've asked to see Dr Anderson."

Dr Calm used his best, soft, calming voice.

"I know, I know...."

"...I mean, how can he thrive in this atmosphere? He cries all day and no one bothers. It's not hygienic. No one seems to care that he's got a history of infection, in fact some of them don't even know he's had meningitis, the hand overs are so poor..."

"I'm sure that...."

"And this bloody racket. It's like Chinese torture. It never bloody stops. Surely, it's common sense that loud music isn't conducive to rest and recovery. I mean if *your* child was desperately ill with a head injury, you wouldn't subject it to Oasis all night would you? No, you'd ask any visitors to creep around as quiet as mice. But not in the 'High Dependency Unit.' Oh no, it's like the Hacienda night club in here...."

"I'll see what I can...."

"And I've got to say Dr Anderson, that *my* nerves can't stand it any more. God knows what it's doing to Saul, after all he's had to cope with so far. So we want to go home. I don't care what it takes, what I have to learn to do. We do most of it ourselves anyway. But I want him home, where he can sleep in peace, where he can start to recover from the awful ordeal he's had so far. And if we can't do it with your blessing and your support, then we'll do it without. I'll bundle him up right now...."

"Well, it might be possible for you to take him home soon, and since you obviously feel so strongly....And I have begun to be concerned about your state of.... Of course there are things that I will have to sort out first, outpatient support and back up oxygen, but if you like I'll start to make the necessary arrangements straightaway...."

Mummy was limp again. Daddy picked me up. "They're going to let us out, Saul. Oh Saul, we're going to take you home...."

When I Start to Work It Out

You can choose anytime, but autumn up here is my favourite. The trees below us and right down the glen are shining all gold and orange. The sky is blue and speckled white. The Crazy Pinnacles behind us are striped purple and silver. Oh it's so beautiful it makes you want to ache.

I need to come back here sometimes, it's a good place to think. I sit on a boulder. I'm not alone. We're in a grassy hollow high up between two pinnacles. It catches the sun. It's a secret place, hidden away so well that you can call out and no one, even if they're in the corrie below, can hear.

Down below, there's a squirrel digging in a panic. Up above there's a cloud of birds flying south. And here in our corrie is a woman making blankets ready for winter. It might be Izzy, all grown up and living in the glen, keeping an eye out for her little girl playing up near the rocks. And in her lap is a baby, gurgling, smiling up at its daddy who is whittling a piece of beechwood into a little ball. But he isn't a Red Man now. His spiky hair is greying a bit and he's wearing the same sort of clothes as Izzy.

Spiky Hair stops whittling, looks at the ball, throws it in the air and catches it. "Maybe it's time we thought of moving down a wee bit."

"Aye, maybe. The sun'll still be hot enough up here though for a few more days."

"They say the winds shifting to the north, could be snow following. Some of them have moved down, back to the loch already."

"Aye."

He looks at her carefully. "I've heard that someone's moved into your old granda's place, what's left of it."

"Aye, I heard that too. Och well, they're welcome to it."

He laughs in relief. "I thought you might be ... that it might get you, in one of your rages."

"One of my rages! Get on with you!" She breathes in the cold air. "I canna be wasting my time getting upset about it any more!"

And we look down the glen. The sun is setting. Everything is golden. The rocks glint yellow. This *is* an important place. No snow, no Red Men, no people at all that you can see. People are too small and the glen is enormous. And it's old, even older than Grandpa (who's very old) and much older than me, and wiser, and somehow even the most terrible things that people do or have done to them, just melt away into the greatness of it all.

"Let the old glen do the brooding for us," she says. "Life's too short to be fighting over a few stones, nursing the past. It was a poor place for a home anyway. I've always fancied one at the other end of the loch...."

He smiles and finishes whittling. "Ah Izzy, it's fine y'are."

She laughs. "And are you giving that to Kirsten or are you playing all day? Get her off those rocks, and then you can be thinking about doing some proper work."

He calls, and the little girl comes running.

The baby begins to whimper, so Izzy wraps it tight in the blanket, with just its face peeping out, and she holds it to her breast. I pretend, for a moment, I am that baby, clutching at her breast. I pretend I am held by her, looking up to my great-great-many-greats-grandmother, my fist touching the soft down on her cheek, and drinking in the smell of her skin, and her feelings, and her love, as smooth and strong as the mountains.

And we breathe in the mountain air and feel a great white Calm. It slides over every boulder and every drop of water and every blade of grass, and through her and then through me. It's lovely. I want to be a part of it for ever. And I know that I'm close to making it all fit together, and that I've worked out one of the most important Reasons of all.

Day 105

Next day Mummy asked Dr Magic to look at me. She couldn't work it out.

"He's obviously in discomfort and wriggling and writhing. I've tried everything I can think of...."

"Well, I can't see anything medically wrong...It's not neurological, if that's what you're.... He's growing out of these nappies though. Perhaps it's too tight and crushing his hernia...."

"Of course...growing out of things, I never thought.... Oh Saul, what a crap mother, I call in the doctor to diagnose 'growing bigger'...."

"It's no problem. It's a pleasure to come and talk to Mr Saul." He stroked my forehead. He wanted to say something and I could see him working out the words.

"I hear you're going home soon?"

"Can't be soon enough, I can tell you."

"Yeah, I can imagine.... You know, when Saul was first born, we all rather hoped he'd escape before we did. Fraid to say we've beaten him to it. You know it's the end of the doctor's six month stint. All the junior doctors are moving on."

"Oh...well...I knew it was coming soon. When are you...?"

"Today's my last day."

Her face fluttered. "Oh."

They both looked at me, but really they were thinking of what to say.

"Well...right, then, thanks for everything...we'll...thanks."

"My pleasure, well not pleasure, it's been...." He looked in my eyes and for a moment he forgot that Mummy was there. He thought only about me. And his eyes and fingers spoke to me so only I could hear. *I wish it had been different. And I wish you could forgive us....*

"...Well, not exactly a pleasure, more a privilege."

I remembered the first time I heard that voice: "This is one of the best units in the country and we like to think we do all we can to avoid suffering." He promised to pick us all up and carry us to safety. And I know now that he meant it. That's what they tried to do, Dr Calm, and my favourite nurses, they all meant to carry me to safety. I couldn't blame them for the bad times. I couldn't hate them. I didn't even hate Dr Keen and Dr Shaky any more. And Nurse Nasty? When I thought of her at that moment, I expected to feel the hate rolling back in. But it didn't. There was no more hate. Instead I started to glow. The mean, hard feelings melted and left a great shaft of happiness, all fresh and clean. And I looked into Dr Magic's eyes and I said, so only he could hear, I don't blame you any more Dr Magic. I love you.

And I love Mummy and Daddy and all my favourite nurses. There's no more hate left.

And he smiled at me, because he knew.

Day 106

I feel as if something has finished. There is a deep calm. But fresh, like a breeze in my heart. And I feel proud. Because I've done the hardest sort of living, but also the best sort. Because loving, this sort of big, stretching, nothing will ever get in the way, sort of loving, is the best bit about being alive. And I feel as if, now that I've done it all on my own, now that I've made this great forgiveness which fills the room and shines out of me and drifts over everyone I've ever loved and hated, now that I've done this, I've done everything there is to do.

And Grandpa and I stand on the top of the mountain, the best, highest, most wonderful mountain. I can see forever, and all the nice, true, real feelings, made by *me*, are all stretched out in front of us. I could throw myself out into those feelings and they would be strong enough to catch me and hold me up. Looking out from the top of this mountain is the best moment I can remember. Ever. And I know that this moment, the moment when I made such a cloud of forgiving, that this is the beginning. And Grandpa glows and the light is a flood.

Grandpa tells me that now is The Moment. Because this is the last time I will see him, or hear him or even know him at all. As I grow up in This Living, I will become like all the other living people, and I will forget where I've come from and where I'm going to and all my knowings will slip away. Now I must choose, for the last time, between going back with Grandpa, or staying here to do This Living all on my own. This is the last chance I will have to make my own choice.

Day 107-110

I need time to think. I have to do the right thing, and I feel a bit muddled nowadays. I have to go away and work this out on my own.

So I close my eyes and go streaming back to a quiet place, to sit on my thinking boulder.

I thought that autumn was my favourite but this is spring and I love it just as much. Everything is new and excited, zinging with life. The leaves all curled up on the branches just itching to unfurl and wave at the world – hello! We're alive! We're here again! And there's the squirrel scrabbling in the old leaves, learning how to live again, and the sky is all bright-eyed and shining, alive with fresh air and bird twitter, and babies everywhere, in trees, in nests, in holes in the ground, are being made and hatched and born. And here am I back in my Important Place, my glen.

It could be any time, anyone's memories, I don't know how great-grand this memory is. It doesn't matter, there are no people in this memory, it's just me and my glen, pulsing with life.

And I think, why has Grandpa asked me whether I want to leave This Living behind, just now, when I've done so much of the hard climb, got to the top of the mountain and everything? It should be an easy choice. Why should I choose to go back with Grandpa? I try to remember it, the place before This Living began, (although now, it's not much more than an Inkling). It was only when I saw Grandpa flooding out like that, that I knew it all over again. It's the best and most brilliant place to be. It's where I want to go in the end. Everybody does. Most of them, says Grandpa, would give up and run off there straightaway, if they could only remember what it's like. But do I want to go there just now?

And I think about Mummy and Daddy, getting ready to take me home. I want to go there and live with them, don't I? And all the lovely things they've planned for me and the promises they've made, because they want me *so* much, (and it's lovely to be wanted like that). And I think about how easy it was to love them again, even after everything. And then I think of Lami, and how she's waiting for me to escape, like I said I would. And it seems that there's still much more living to do yet, how can I even think about running away?

And in the glen I nod my head. I'm a snowdrop today, so I nod my little white head in the fresh breeze and all the other snowdrops nod because they're so glad to have made it back again. There are thousands of us, making the woodland floor dapple with green and white. Every blade of grass is glad to be here too, doing its own bit of living, climbing its own little mountain, trying to be as green and springy as it can be. And all this is living, isn't it, and I'm part of it, I'll always be part of it. (Didn't someone once tell me I was a part of the everything? Grandpa? Izzy? Didn't they tell me it's in my soul now and will be for ever.) It's just so brilliant to be alive.

So no, Grandpa, I'm not ready to go yet.

Something is tugging me back, poking with needles again

"...raised CRP...same infection as the others in this room... that's why I need to give him another IV line, start him on general antibiotics. Fraid it's getting hard to find a suitable vein now, could be some time, why don't you grab a coffee or something, it's not going to be pleasant to watch...."

I'm used to that needle now, and the way they drag their thumb across my skin, but I don't like it and I scream. Yes, there's always some screaming to do in This Living. And I'm screaming and thinking, What will all this be like if there's no Grandpa, if I can hardly remember him, if he just becomes an Inkling? And suppose things go wrong again, suppose it's not all lovely times and going home and cuddles and playing. What if this needle keeps coming back? (Scrape jab, scrape jab). And I'll really be doing it on my own then because there'll be no Grandpa to give me advice, no way back to escape. And my head is hurting.

Ah yes my head. There's been a jumbling up there for a while now and I have to stop pretending that it doesn't matter. If there was no Grandpa, no way back, then maybe the jumbling *would* matter. You can't ignore it for ever when things have been changing in your head. Something shifting. Bubbles sliding together and gently bursting. Sometimes my ideas drain away. Things I want to work out slip into a hole so I can't find them. Sounds and smells and pictures get muddled up. Growing and getting big and strong is much harder when your head is in a muddle...

"...This new head scan result is.... The parents haven't seen it yet have they...? What's the policy on this, it's significantly worse...? Do another one in a few days and then...."

...And I'm the wind and I rush over the Notched Ridge and over the moor and round in little eddies and *weeeeeee*! and back again down to the loch to make it go lap lap lap on the stones. And it's brilliant....

And then Daddy is lifting me onto his shoulder, a lovely place to be, "Oh, Saul, darling, what's the matter, darling," rocking, cuddling because I'm crying (the throbbing in my head? or is it the pain of the needle?) and he coos, warm breath. Snuggle into his warm neck. Oh I do love him.

"Why's he crying like this?"

"Babies do cry, try giving him some milk Mummy."

And Mummy gives me some milk and I gulp it down, looking up at her, and oh, I do love her.

And I think, I could bear all the hurting and I wouldn't mind the muddle in my head, it's still nice doing This Living with them. I could bear it all because they want it so much. That's how much I love them.

And then it's back to the glen. It will always be here, no matter how many times autumn and winter come. The snowdrops and green grass and little leaves will be back and nothing can stop it. The glen will always be alive. I wade through the snowdrops, a sea of white. Perfect, each head gently nodding.

But if you look carefully, some of the little heads have started to droop. Some have faded back into the grass and the ones left behind are not so pretty now, they've started to go brown and wrinkled. And that's what happens to snowdrops. Is that what will happen to me? What happens to people with jumbling in the head? You probably have to be really strong and all the people around you have to be strong too. Is that why Grandpa has given me a choice?

And I think about Mummy and how she has changed. We were so strong together, weren't we? She used to be so full of life, and laughter, even in the bad times, but now she is empty, nearly dead right through. She snaps at people, sits cowed, twisting her hands. Even if *I* can bear it, can they?

"Should his aspirates be yellow? And he's been sick for the last three feeds."

"Your Mummy worries too much, Saul, she should take a day off, go to the seaside or something."

"The seaside?"

"We can look after him. Or why don't you have a lie-in tomorrow morning, read the Sunday papers."

(And Mummy gives the nurse such a look.) "You don't think I go home to *sleep*, do you? I don't sleep. I haven't slept for weeks. Sometimes I fall into a coma and then I sleepwalk because I can hear Saul screaming and I have to find him, and Tim has to wake me up. You think I could lounge around in bed reading glossy magazines whilst Saul's alone in here, crying?" (She shakes her head.) "You've got no bloody idea."

And then I think, maybe they're only doing it for me. Because they think that *I* want it so much. (And I do want it, to explore and grow and learn.) But would it be so good for them? Would Mummy carry on changing, becoming more and more empty and dead.

And secretly, I know that it's going to get worse. I feel the bubbles sliding in my head, the muddling swirling, working it out is getting harder and harder, thinking keeps slipping away from me....Oh it's a horrid choice. I wish I didn't have to make it. But I do. This is my last chance....

And the bubbles slide and collide and I'm still not sure.... Oh, if only I could be in dappled sunshine nodding under the trees forever.... But look, the snowdrops have all died back into the grass. Maybe that's the way it works. Maybe you have to die back down to come again. Some things like the leaves can live the whole summer through, but the tiny white snowdrop can only last a short time. And the finest, most delicate of all flowers might only last a day. And it doesn't matter, because next year it will start all over again. And it has to happen. The snow has to melt to let the flowers grow. You have to give up at the right time to let others come back to life. Nothing ends for ever, it just changes.

And it all has a place and a time, all part of the living and re-living and I'm part of it. Round and round we go, learning each time, getting to know the little things, the easy things, the difficult things, it's all about living, all about life....

"...I'm afraid there's another complication. On the off chance, I asked for a blood-sugar test. And I'm afraid his blood-sugars are seriously out of kilter, if you know what I mean. He's going to need insulin injections, every few hours."

"You mean he's got diabetes?"

"Well, perhaps. It might not be permanent, it might just be a response to current stresses, but it'll mean...about going home...."

And her face nearly crumples, but she takes a breath, and drags on the last trickle of strength somewhere inside her. "I can learn to give him injections, if that's what it takes."

...And suddenly it is clear. The clouds part, and there, shining, blinding, is the answer. I must give up my living. For them. We've done the best bits. The rest, I know now, will just be hard work and crying. I can't do it to them. I don't want to see them crying any more. If this is my last chance to choose, then I must take it.

Grandpa, I am ready.

Day 108

Oh Lami.

She looks at me. Calm. Full of grace. I promised I'd run ahead and wait for you and now....

Jemima knows already. And I know she's sad and her heart lurches a little. My heart lurches a lot. It almost makes me change my mind. But it's the right thing to do. And she agrees.

And we promise not to forget each other in case our stories ever cross again.

Day 111

I'm standing on top of the mountain. On tiptoe. Ready to jump. Scared but excited. Jittery with energy. I am ready.

They promised to listen. But their hearts have been clenched for so long now, they can't hear me. I've been trying for days, I wanted to say goodbye but....

Dadada EEEk!
You just get me going babe (Bumpbump)
Beeeeat Eff Emmmmm....

They're too tired now. The very last bit of them has drained away. Mummy shrinks when anyone comes to us. Daddy's eyes are thin, angry lines. They are lost somewhere I can't reach them.

Today has been a mad, bad day. Everyone really angry. There were too many babies. Mummy couldn't sit down. Nurses shouted.

"I don't bloody believe it. Someone on Surgical's made a complaint, because there's only one nurse in the nursery. But what else can I do? Now I'm going to have to spend my lunch break writing up a.... Aaargh! I've thirty-five babies in here and there should only be twenty-eight, I'm two staff short, off sick, no bank nurses in the whole of the North West, Queen's is closing beds you know, and then Anthea, the only one on today I can trust, faints and has to be sent home. Listen can I ask you mothers to consider staying all day with your babies, because if *I* was a mother with a baby in here, I wouldn't want to...."

"I always stay all day anyway."

A doctor appears: "Excuse me...."

"The answer's *no*! We can't fit any more babies in here, and if anyone asks, I'm handing in my resignation!"

I waited for Daddy to arrive. It got busier. All the Mummies and Daddies and grannies and brothers and sisters of all the babies were in. You could only see bodies.

You got ma body shakin, ooh ooh ooh ooh ah yeah!

It isn't the best time because I haven't said goodbye. But they will never hear me now. I'm ready. I hope they will understand.

I jump off the top of the mountain.

Days 112-114

When you're a baby, it isn't so easy to die. They put me back into the Big Air. Tube down my throat. Machine going *clunk thud whoosh*. I thrashed and tried to pull the Tube out. They put mittens on my hands and tied my arms down.

"I suppose he's got one-to-one care now has he?"

"We wish."

"Lord, how ill do they have to be?"

Everything is locked in. I am trapped. My fists are clenched. I clench everything to make it stop. I wail. I feel my soul wailing a song that only Lami can hear.

Poor Dr Calm, with his nice calm voice. But inside he is screaming. Like me. Poor Mummy and Daddy, they still can't hear me, because they are screaming too.

"I'm afraid we will have to consider a shunt. The neurosurgeon is coming to visit him tomorrow morning, but for the moment anyway, he's too ill to operate on. We'll have to do ventricle taps, I'm afraid, till then. For some reason his whole body seems...out of equilibrium. His digestive system just seems to have gone on strike...There's a surgeon coming to look at his hernia, which is another major worry...."

I don't think Mummy and Daddy could even hear Dr Calm. They looked dazed. Like they were being punched in the face and were too tired to duck.

"Oh and one other thing. As you know, we now have a new batch of fresh junior doctors, some of whom will be understandably...nervous. So could I ask you not to watch them when they have to do procedures on Saul? We're only human and it can sometimes be a little intimidating, if you see what I mean...."

Mummy and Daddy have gone for a walk. The doctor is stealing blood. His hands, his whole body, are shaking. Come back Dr Shaky, I felt safer with you! But it is new doctors now. They hurt more, press too hard, squeeze in the wrong way. He leaves me all crushed up with the Tube twisting round my head. I can't move. Living like this is so hard, Grandpa. I made the right choice didn't I?

Now is a good time to try again. Mummy and Daddy aren't here. No one is watching. Everyone is busy with the new doctors. Grandpa help me, now, when no one is looking! Am I strong enough to do it? To make everything stop, even though the machines are making my body work? It's no use not breathing. I haven't been breathing all day. No, I have to squeeze my heart tight shut. I have to *strain* to stop everything. I have to go slow and slow and slower and slower, until there...is...only a...fizzing...in my head.... No beats....

And it nearly works. Until Mummy and Daddy come back.

"Bloody hell, what's happened to his machines?"

"Nurse – his machines aren't working properly, his heart rate's...and the monitors aren't even flashing...."

Until nurses rush in to drag me back.

"Where's his bag and mask…? Where.... Can someone get me a bag and mask...quickly…?"

"Here, borrow Angie's.... I'll just untangle...."

"Bloody hell, all his machines have.... What's happening…?"

Dr Calm and some new doctors gather round the cot. Mummy and Daddy stand frozen. I stay on the ceiling looking at the baby body with its clenched fists and swollen head. Mummy is raging. White-faced. Breathing fast, and faster and faster until she explodes. She stamps out of the room. She makes the doors slam. *Crash sha sha sha!* Dr Calm turns and sees her with sad eyes. He looks at Nurse Clean Flowers. She sighs and follows Mummy.

Everyone can hear Mummy in the corridor. She is gasping. Not quite screaming. "…And you wonder why we're here all the time. It's because we can't trust you, you can't even, we were only out of the room for forty minutes, you can't even keep an eye on him for, you rely so heavily on machines and then they don't work, you let him, he was in great distress, did you see him, he was dying, all on his own, and no one, not a single doctor or nurse, God knows how long he was like that, could have been half an hour and you wouldn't even have...."

"I'm sorry. I can't explain why the machines weren't working. Honestly I looked in on him a little while ago and the machines were fine then...."

Of course the doctors and nurses get everything back to normal, as usual. Lots of *clunk thud whoosh* and sweet air and rushing around. And I stay on the ceiling.

Still here. Still trapped. Why don't they listen? Grandpa tell them to listen. Grandpa whispers in my head, Give them time. There's no rush. You've got all the time in the world. Just wait....

And so I wait. Hovering all day on the ceiling, looking down on the baby with the clenched fists. And Mummy and Daddy watch my baby body too.

"Oh Tim, this is what it's going to be like his whole life, isn't it? Relying on institutions to.... Machines not working, understaffing. It'll be a constant battle to protect him. And maybe he'll never be able to tell us what's happening to him.... Oh my God, Oh my little boy...."

And I wait....

"Have you noticed his fists? He's furious isn't he? He didn't want to go back on the ventilator...."

It was easy to wait because I knew it was going to be all right....

"I've been thinking, Rose.... Even if he gets better, this time, what's he got to look forward to? Operations for shunts and hernias, all those ventricle taps. I don't know whether.... I don't know.... How can we do it to him?"

And I am patient, because Grandpa is with me, and I have all the time in the world....

"Maybe... Tim, maybe... the machines didn't work because...maybe he waited for us to go out, like Dad did, remember.... As if he was waiting to be on his own when.... Maybe he was trying to slip away...."

And at last the crying is over. They are both calm.

"We have to face it don't we?"

"I think so, sweets. I think it's come to that after all."

Day 115: Friday

"Saul, darling, Mummy and Daddy are just going to make a few phone calls, so if you want to slip away now, you can, you don't have to hang on for us any more."

I didn't choose to slip away just then.

And later, a man came on a motorbike and put water on my head. The motorbike helmet was on top of the Hot House and I was in Daddy's arms. Wild Granny and Auntie Isobel were there. Nurse Chirpy put the screens around us.

"I baptise you in the name of the Father...."

Wild Granny and Auntie Isobel cried. Mummy didn't. Her body was there, but inside she was dead. She put her hand on Daddy's shoulder. Daddy was sobbing very loudly, he could hardly breathe, his shoulders shook up and down, jiggling all my wires till the alarms went off.

And when the man put water on my head it didn't make any difference because it was already wet from Daddy's tears.

Now Granny is with me. She has wrapped her fingers round my clenched fist. We have said goodbye. She lets tears run down her face.

I want to be with her but I must see what Mummy and Daddy are doing in the Serious Talking little room.

Daddy is staring at his socks. His face is already wet. Tears are dripping onto Mummy's blouse. Dr Calm is talking, making them sob. "...Possibly even cruel to keep on...we must think about Saul and his quality of life...and that caring for him would take its toll on you two...Perhaps you are unaware of.... You haven't seen the recent scans have you? The brain damage is now significantly worse than before and I have to say that my earlier optimism...."

Oh, stop, Dr Calm. Don't make them cry any more. They are ready. We are all ready....

"Perhaps if I showed you the scan taken this morning....the black part here, is the damaged tissue and this white, this crescent here, is healthy brain...."

"But there's hardly any brain left at all."

"Well, yes, so that's why we should think about...."

"Yes...it's alright.... We've already thought...."

And what day was that? Because just for a bit longer, days are important. It was a Friday. Three days before I was due to be born.

The *clunk thud whoosh* machine was turned down bit by bit that night. Then, just as it was getting light, everything was switched off. All the wires and tubes were taken away. And at last, I was really doing This Living all on my own.

Day 116: Saturday 10 August

I didn't need to rush. I decided to wait till everyone had said goodbye. Grandpa said I could do the last bit of living as slowly as I liked.

Daddy carries me to a little room. It is very peaceful. No sounds. Just a faraway humming. The air is deliciously calm. Mummy and Daddy aren't crying any more. They make me think of Lami, calm and full of grace. Sometimes they sing songs from the early days.

....And I kno-ow, he will never burden be.
He's not heavy, he's my ba-a-a-by.

....You are my everything...you make me want to sing...

Sometimes they talk, peacefully.

"All over now, sweetheart. You'll never have to bear that awful pain again."

"And we're so proud of you. You've been such a wonderful little boy. Thank you so much, darling, for letting me be your mummy."

"No more hurting ever again, Saul. It's all up to you now. You're free to go when you want. You choose. Whenever you're ready...."

All my relatives have been in. Trying to say goodbye to someone they hardly knew. Auntie Ruth wailed loudly. Uncle Marcos bit his lip. Grandad Bernie's hands wobbled when he touched me. Granny said nothing. She just shook her head and sniffed.

My body feels nothing now. No hurting. No hot or cold. Not even a heaviness in my arms and legs. The air is melting inside me. Everything is melting into the air. I am the air in this room and I float up to the ceiling. *Swoolyla lyla*. It feels so lovely. Close to Grandpa. Secure. Knowing that the way back is open. No more fighting now. From now on it will be easy.

Grandpa and I look down. Two nurses, Mummy, Daddy, and a baby body. Still breathing. Deep and slow. So easy. Nurse Columbine makes tea and toast. Mummy and Daddy don't cry now. They're not angry now. Just gentle and peaceful. Maybe they can feel that Grandpa is here. And I'm proud of the story we've told together.

It's late in the afternoon when Nurse Columbine and Nurse Clean Flowers decide to take a break. They shut the door quietly behind them. Daddy is holding the baby body. They are alone with their baby now for the first time. Now, Grandpa? He is smiling. I drift down into my baby body for the last time. My eyes have been closed all day. But now, I open them wide. I look deep into her eyes. And then into his.

"This is it. Oh Tim! Oh, goodbye Saul, goodbye, darling."

"Goodbye, my little boy."

Goodbye.

Then I do it properly. No going back. The insides of my head go KCHOO THUMP! THUMP! THUMP! The light explodes. CRASH SHA SHA SHAAAAA! And I'm free at last.

KCHoooooooooooooooOOOOOOOOOOOOOOO!!!!!

When I Shine Brightly

In the churchyard is a great, flat tombstone. You have to pull yourself up with your arms to sit on it. It's all green and grey and rough to touch, and the words have nearly rubbed away. Nurse Chirpy is running her fingers over it to work out what it says. She reads out the funny bits: "Beware your.....life hangs by a thread.....In the midst of mine......I woke up dead." And she grins.

It's a good place to sit, near to the church door, so you can see who's going in and out. And it's high, so you can see down the valley to The Hanging Stone and after that The Roaches and after that the blue sky and after that, ah Grandpa, tell us what you see after that....

So that's where we sit, whilst we're waiting. And we look at the hills and listen to the quiet. No one talks, otherwise it would spoil it.

Not everyone likes sitting still. Nurse Chirpy is rubbish at it. She swings her legs and jiggles her toes. She's found an ivy leaf and she's tearing it into tiny pieces, without even looking. The bits flutter to the ground. No one really notices. The ground is full of things already, twigs, grass seeds, little beetles, a line of ants going across the path. The ants are working really hard, like it really matters.

No-one else looks at all the living going on on the ground. They're staring into the air. Nurse Columbine breathes deeply. A puff of wind could blow her right out of the churchyard and into the sky, and she'd float away like a thin pink cloud. Except her legs are so long she rests her toes on the ground, like she's anchored to real life.

Nurse Scurry's legs are much shorter. She is sitting really still. No rushing about for today. Her head rests on her tiny fingers and her eyes are lost in the blue and green distance.

Nurse Clean Flowers is sitting cross-legged on the end of the stone. She tips her face up to catch the sun. She loves the sun. It shines really hot today. It's the sort of sunny day that presses you down and makes all the world go heavy.

Nurse Chirpy jumps down and looks at other graves. She wades through the grass and the white lacy flowers. She's working out which of the dead people are related to which, and when they all died. "Hey look, this guy was ninety-nine! Oh no, it's thirty-nine. '...Mock not, ye....godless...? ...who stand so proud...all men alike must wear a...' ...Dunno....Can't read it. Give up...." The others watch her and sometimes they smile.

Nurse Scurry looks at the others.

"You're not getting sunburnt, are you?"

"Factor thirty." Nurse Columbine pats her cheeks.

"I bet my freckles are going mad, aren't they?" Nurse Chirpy wades back to the big stone. "Maybe they'll join up and I'll have a brilliant tan."

There are lots of other people now. Some are leaning against the wall, and they pull at the ivy. Some go into the church.

"Here we go." Nurse Clean Flowers jumps off the stone.

We look down the hill to the white house. You can't see it properly from here because of the trees, but you can see the chimney and the stream at the back, and the big black wooden gate at the front which is open now.

Because the procession has begun.

A man and a woman are at the front. The others follow behind. She has a red and white dress with a red floaty scarf in her hair. He has a Pooh Bear tie on, and is carrying a white box. On top is a yellow boat with a blue sail, all made from flowers. You can't help feeling excited, can you, Grandpa? I like playing at stories and this is a good one, you said so yourself.

They walk slowly, (especially when they climb up the higgledy-piggledy church steps, all green and slippy), slowly, slowly, under the tunnel of yew branches, and he stumbles once or twice, (he can't see the ground, the box and the boat together fill up his arms and hide his face). They stop, as a man in black and white robes comes out to meet them.

"Put your little burden down a moment." The man in black and white robes pats the tombstone kindly.

"He isn't a burden." Her voice is flat.

"No, no of course not...." The man in black and white wiggles his fingers against his dress, a bit embarrassed.

The white box and the boat are laid on the flat tombstone.

"He was never a burden," she says.

Grandpa and I see everything, the ants, the bits of leaves, the tall grass, the great flat tombstone, the church, the yew trees, the white house, the brook, the field, and all the hills around, everything glistening in the sun. It's a lovely picture, Grandpa.

Some of the people are looking up to the sky, but they're not looking at us, they're trying to tip the tears back into their eyes. The woman in the red and white dress stands up straight. Still. Stiff. Her eyes are dry. The man in the Pooh Bear tie is helping to lower the white box into the ground. He sobs and stumbles. People hold him to stop him from falling. The man in black and white robes is talking. "...sure in the knowledge that nothing is wasted...."

Grandpa and I are shining really brightly today, making the picture less ordinary. Without the shining, the picture is grey and flimsy. The people are so wrapped up in their story that they've forgotten why they're telling it. I suppose if I were doing the living with them all, I'd be sad too. But it isn't sad. Because now I know there are no beginnings and no endings, no dos and don'ts, cans and can'ts. Anything can happen. I might tell another story, when I'm ready for another adventure. But just for the moment, I want to play at being a blossom in Wild Granny's garden in spring, or the breeze in Glencoe in the autumn.

Or maybe Grandpa and I will swoop across the churchyard in winter, cawing loudly, black wing to black wing. And the two people tending our grave will hear us and watch us fly out together, to the valley, to the Hanging Stone and after that the Roaches and after that the blue sky and after that.... And the two people laying the flowers won't be sad any more, because when they see us, they will suddenly remember something. And it will be an Inkling.

To see a World in a grain of Sand
And a Heaven in a Wild Flower
Hold Infinity in the palm of your hand
And Eternity in an Hour

William Blake, 1757-1827

Author's Note

Written on first publication 2000

Saul would be over three years old now, and I look back at his short life with great sadness. But I also feel tremendously lucky.

Of course, I didn't feel lucky at the time of his death. I was filled with rage and despair, and an irrepressible desire to do something constructive with the dreadful experience. That's one reason why I wrote the book. I wanted to give Saul a voice. I wanted to tell his story and illuminate one aspect of neonatal experience.

Tim and I began to raise money for Tommy's, a charity which provides research into prematurity and problem pregnancies. We also discussed Saul's treatment with the hospital: although we acknowledged that, in the main, he received a high standard of care, we still wanted to make suggestions about how the system could be improved so that future families could benefit. To the hospital's credit, they responded positively and changes have been made.

This book is not intended to be a criticism of any of the staff involved in Saul's care. Rather the reverse, it is in part a homage to their dedication; without them his story would not have been so long and interesting. At the time, we were responding to our own tragedy, coping as best we could with our distress. However, we could see how stressful it must be to work in this area of medicine. We remember his carers as extremely kind, hard-working professionals who went way beyond the call of duty to cope with the disaster Saul's birth presented. We are very grateful for what they tried to do, and the consideration, even love, with which they responded. We know this area of medicine is understaffed, partly because of a national shortage of appropriately trained nurses, but also because the nurse/patient ration is less generous than in adult or paediatric intensive care. Staff are regularly expected to perform miracles.

Saul's story isn't necessarily representative of what generally happens in neonatal intensive care. His was an extreme case. He was critically ill (twenty-three weekers rarely survived then, even for a few days), and we hit a period of time when the unit was exceptionally busy. Over five hundred babies pass through this unit every year, and the vast majority have a positive experience and go home to lead healthy lives.

Although the story of Saul's treatment is based upon real events as we recorded them at the time, many of the characters are composites, or have had personal characteristics changed. The character of Lami represents a real baby. She lived for five more months.

After Saul's death, Tim and I decided not to try for any more children, although we had desperately wanted a family for years. We felt we couldn't risk putting another child through what Saul had suffered. However, that's not how it turned out. Two years later, I discovered I was pregnant again. I decided to book into the antenatal clinic at the same hospital; a difficult decision because of the painful memories the place harboured, but a good decision because it is a centre of excellence.

Sadly, despite the superlative attentions of my obstetrician, I delivered prematurely a second time. Saul's sister was nearly born at twenty-three weeks, but they managed to keep me going for another twenty-one days. They were crucial days, and her experience of intensive care was very different. The unit wasn't so busy and the medical advances, since our last visit, made all the difference. She didn't have it easy, and there were many frightening episodes, but she is now at home with us to tell her own story, a lively, alert and completely adorable little girl.

That's why I feel so lucky: lucky to be able to have children at all; lucky to live in a period of history when medicine can turn our tragedy into a successful outcome; lucky to be living in a country where a high standard of healthcare is accessible to everyone; lucky that there are people good enough, clever enough and selfless enough to look after our terribly sick children; and above all, lucky to have been allowed to know and love Saul.

Of course, I wish my children hadn't had to struggle in the way they have. I wish they'd both had a happy, healthy start to life, and that Saul was running around being naughty and pestering his little sister; but I'm glad I've learnt what I have from their difficult experiences. Saul taught me about death; he gave me an understanding that is intangible, inexplicable, a spiritual awareness that is hard to communicate. And my daughter has taught me how to overcome loss, how to look to the future, how to live again.

Update: 2012

Nine years after Saul was born, I went on to have another son, who, despite a tricky pregnancy, was born safely at term. Since then, our second little boy has never given the medical profession anything to worry about and is the perfect addition to a very lucky family.

When I first wrote this book, I had no idea how it would be received. I hoped it would be helpful in some way, and so I've been very moved by the large number of touching letters I've received, from all over the world, and the positive responses I've had on many forums. And over the years it's become obvious that there is a whole community of people, who may have travelled the same journey as us, (and many who have not,) who want to read a book like this.

Many people asked me why it was out of print, and how they could get a copy, so it became clear: at some point I would have to revisit it to republish. It's taken me a long time, because it was painful to write, and just as painful to re-edit to get it ready. But when I read the intensely moving words some people have expressed about their own experiences, and about reading the book, I felt it was something I ought to do.

I have made a few changes, largely to do with formatting, and re-documentation, but also to reflect the passage of time.

I hope that one day, severe premature birth will be so rare that this narrative will seem like a strange historical document. Until then, maybe Saul's story will continue to give people some insight, a little joy, and perhaps even inspiration to climb a few mountains.

Acknowledgements

Thanks to:

Tim, my husband, who is my constant source of strength and support and a wonderful father;

My sister, Isobel, for her advice and encouragement as a writer, and for her invaluable devotion as an auntie;

Dad for his nuggets of wisdom, his inventiveness, and so much more;

Mum for being a continual source of inspiration;

My agent Caradoc at A P Watt, and Linda Shaunessy, who had the courage to believe in this book, and who guided me so gently through the whole process;

Everyone at Hodder-Headline, St Martin's Press and Random House, who championed the book and worked so hard to get it published;

The hospital staff, who cared so selflessly and diligently for us;

Saul's consultant paediatrician, for his kindness, his profound generosity of spirit, and his professionalism;

The nurses who read the unedited manuscript and made me feel that Saul's passing through was important to them;

My obstetrician who gave so much of his time and compassion;

My dear friends, Charlotte, Sue, Gay and William, without whom I couldn't have survived;

Grace and Joel who knew what we were going through;

Joan and Doreen, Peter and Peggy, Janet and Mike, who were always there when we needed them;

Hooley and Watson, Funeral Directors, for their unexpected generosity;

Marlene Richardson who helped us make the hardest choice;

The Reverend Moir, who, with infinite tenderness towards us, baptised our son and then laid him to rest;

And most of all, thank you Saul.

Biography

Rosemary Kay was a lecturer in Performing Arts, when Saul was born, although she had already begun a writing career in radio drama. Her first play *Wilde Belles* won the Alfred Bradley Bursary and a Sony award. After writing *Between Two Eternities*, she moved into film and TV, winning a BAFTA, Prix Europa, Dennis Potter Award, and other accolades. She is currently working on a series for the BBC, and is writing another book: *Anchorage*.

Between Two Eternities was originally published in the UK by Headline; by St Martin's Press in America; and Random House in Canada, where it was called *Saul*. It was translated into several languages, and made into a film (*This Little Life*) by Common Features Film/BBC Film. This revised edition is an amalgamation of the UK and US versions.

Printed in Great Britain
by Amazon